The Short Oxford History of the British Isles

General Editor: Paul Langford

The Fourteenth and Fifteenth Centuries

Edited by Ralph Griffiths

ALSO AVAILABLE

The Roman Era
edited by Peter Salway

From the Vikings to the Normans
edited by Wendy Davies

The Twelfth and Thirteenth Centuries
edited by Barbara Harvey

The Sixteenth Century
edited by Patrick Collinson

The Eighteenth Century
edited by Paul Langford

The Nineteenth Century
edited by Colin Matthew

The British Isles: 1901–1951
edited by Keith Robbins

The British Isles since 1945
edited by Kathleen Burk

IN PREPARATION, VOLUMES COVERING

From the Romans to the Vikings
The Seventeenth Century

Plate 1 Brass rubbing of Margaret, first wife of Thomas Peyton (d. 1484), in St Andrew's church, Isleham, Cambridgeshire. She is shown wearing an elegant, fashionable low-necked gown and an elaborate headdress decorated with the words 'Lady Help Ihesu Mercy'. The Peytons were a prominent local gentry family. Ashmolean Museum, Oxford.

The Short Oxford History of the British Isles

General Editor: Paul Langford

The Fourteenth and Fifteenth Centuries

Edited by Ralph Griffiths

OXFORD
UNIVERSITY PRESS

OXFORD
UNIVERSITY PRESS

Great Clarendon Street, Oxford OX2 6DP

Oxford University Press is a department of the University of Oxford.
It furthers the University's objective of excellence in research, scholarship,
and education by publishing worldwide in

Oxford New York

Auckland Bangkok Buenos Aires Cape Town Chennai
Dar es Salaam Delhi Hong Kong Istanbul Karachi Kolkata
Kuala Lumpur Madrid Melbourne Mexico City Mumbai Nairobi
São Paulo Shanghai Taipei Tokyo Toronto

Oxford is a registered trade mark of Oxford University Press
in the UK and in certain other countries

Published in the United States
by Oxford University Press Inc., New York

British Library Cataloguing in Publication Data
Data available

Library of Congress Cataloging in Publication Data
Data applied for
ISBN 0–19–873141–8 (pbk)
ISBN 0–19–873142–6 (hbk)

1 3 5 7 9 10 8 6 4 2

Typeset in Minion
by RefineCatch Limited, Bungay, Suffolk
Printed in Great Britain by
T.J. International Ltd, Padstow, Cornwall

General Editor's Preface

It is a truism that historical writing is itself culturally determined, reflecting intellectual fashions, political preoccupations, and moral values at the time it is written. In the case of British history this has resulted in a great diversity of perspectives both on the content of what is narrated and on the geopolitical framework in which it is placed. In recent times the process of redefinition has accelerated under the pressure of contemporary change. Some of it has come from within Britain during a period of recurrent racial tension in England and reviving nationalism in Scotland, Wales, and Northern Ireland. But much of it also comes from beyond. There has been a powerful surge of interest in the politics of national identity in response to the break-up of some of the world's great empires, both colonial and continental. The search for new sovereignties, not least in Europe itself, has contributed to a questioning of long-standing political boundaries. Such shifting of the tectonic plates of history is to be expected but for Britain especially, with what is perceived (not very accurately) to be a long period of relative stability lasting from the late seventeenth century to the mid-twentieth century, it has had a particular resonance.

Much controversy and still more confusion arise from the lack of clarity about the subject matter that figures in insular historiography. Historians of England are often accused of ignoring the history of Britain as a whole, while using the terms as if they are synonymous. Historians of Britain are similarly charged with taking Ireland's inclusion for granted without engaging directly with it. And for those who believe they are writing more specifically the history of Ireland, of Wales, or of Scotland, there is the unending tension between so-called metropolis and periphery, and the dilemmas offered by wider contexts, not only British and Irish but European and indeed extra-European. Some of these difficulties arise from the fluctuating fortunes and changing boundaries of the British state as organized from London. But even if the rulers of what is now called England had never taken an interest in dominion beyond its borders, the economic and cultural relationships between the various parts of the British Isles would still have generated many historiographical problems.

This series is based on the premise that whatever the complexities and ambiguities created by this state of affairs, it makes sense to offer an overview, conducted by leading scholars whose research is at the leading edge of their discipline. That overview extends to the whole of the British Isles. The expression is not uncontroversial, especially to many in Ireland, for whom the very word 'British' implies an unacceptable politics of dominion. Yet there is no other formulation that can encapsulate the shared experience of 'these islands', to use another term much employed in Ireland and increasingly heard in Britain, but rather unhelpful to other inhabitants of the planet.

In short we use the words 'British Isles' solely and simply as a geographical expression. No set agenda is implied. It would indeed be difficult to identify one that could stand scrutiny. What constitutes a concept such as 'British history' or 'four nations history' remains the subject of acute disagreement, and varies much depending on the period under discussion. The editors and contributors of this series have been asked only to convey the findings of the most authoritative scholarship, and to flavour them with their own interpretative originality and distinctiveness. In the process we hope to provide not only a stimulating digest of more than two thousand years of history, but also a sense of the intense vitality that continues to mark historical research into the past of all parts of Britain and Ireland.

Lincoln College   PAUL LANGFORD
Oxford

Acknowledgements

The contributors to this book are grateful to the several editors, past and present, at Oxford University Press—and especially Fiona Kinnear, Matthew Cotton and Sarah Barrett—for their expertise and patience in edging the book towards publication. The advice of Paul Langford, the general editor of the *Short Oxford History of the British Isles*, Barbara Harvey, the editor of the book on the twelfth and thirteenth centuries, and several other friends was invaluable in setting the focus of the book. Thanks are also due to Andrea Thomas in respect of chapter 6, and to Keran Williams for figure 3. The editor is especially indebted to the authors of the six chapters for their ready co-operation and tolerance.

Plates, maps, figures and tables are designed both to illustrate and, on occasion within chapters, to supplement the rest.

RALPH GRIFFITHS

Contents

3 The Church
Richard Davies

4 Forms of cultural expression
Michael Bennett

5 Kingdoms and dominions at peace and war
Robin Frame

List of plates

List of maps and figures

Map and table section

Coinages and exchange rates

England's sterling money—a silver coinage—was expressed in pounds (240 pence) and shillings (12 pence). It changed relatively little in value during the fourteenth and fifteenth centuries. The mark was a money of account valued at 13s. 4d. or 160 pence. Half-pennies and quarter-pennies were also minted; groats (valued at 4d.) were introduced in the 1340s. The noble, a gold coin, was introduced in 1344 (worth 6s. 8d.).

Scotland's coinage was also expressed in pounds, shillings and pence, as well as merks (equivalent to English marks). Until 1367 the English currency weighed about the same as the Scottish, but thereafter the latter was devalued at a rapid, if fluctuating, rate. In 1390 the English government fixed the exchange rate at 1:2, in 1452 at 1:3, and in 1485 at 1:6—though the English tended to exaggerate the degree of actual debasement.

List of contributors

MICHAEL BENNETT is Professor of History in the University of Tasmania, Hobart. His books include *Community, Class and Careerism: Cheshire and Lancashire Society in the Age of Sir Gawain and the Green Knight* (1983), *The Battle of Bosworth* (1985), *Lambert Simnel and the Battle of Stoke* (1987), and *Richard II and the Revolution of 1399* (1999).

RICHARD DAVIES is Senior Lecturer in Medieval History in the University of Manchester. With J. H. Denton, he edited *The English Parliament in the Middle Ages* (1981); and his main interests and publications are focused on the Church and society in later medieval England.

ROBIN FRAME is Emeritus Professor of History in the University of Durham. His books include *Colonial Ireland, 1169–1369* (1981), *English Lordship in Ireland, 1318–1361* (1982), *The Political Development of the British Isles, 1100–1400* (1990), and *Ireland and Britain, 1170–1450* (1998).

ANTHONY GOODMAN is Professor Emeritus of Medieval and Renaissance History in the University of Edinburgh. His books include *The Loyal Conspiracy: The Lords Appellant under Richard II* (1971), *The Wars of the Roses: Military Activity and English Society, 1452–97* (1981), *John of Gaunt: The Exercise of Princely Power in Fourteenth-Century Europe* (1992), and *Margery Kempe and Her World* (2002)

RALPH GRIFFITHS is Emeritus Professor of Medieval History in the University of Wales, Swansea. His books include *The Principality of Wales in the Later Middle Ages: South Wales, 1277–1536* (1972), *The Reign of King Henry VI* (1981), (with R. S. Thomas) *The Making of the Tudor Dynasty* (1985), (with J. Cannon) *The Oxford Illustrated History of the British Monarchy* (1988), *King and Country: England and Wales in the Fifteenth Century* (1990), *Sir Rhys ap Thomas and his Family: A Study in the Wars of the Roses and Early Tudor Politics* (1993), and *Conquerors and Conquered in Medieval Wales* (1994).

PHILIP MORGAN is Senior Lecturer in History in the University of Keele. He is the author of *War and Society in Medieval Cheshire*,

1270–1403 (1987), and his interests and publications include studies of later medieval warfare and society, and English gentry culture.

GERVASE ROSSER is Fellow and Tutor in History at St Catherine's College, Oxford. He is the author of *Medieval Westminster, 1200–1540* (1989) and editor (with R. Holt) of *The English Medieval Town: A Reader in English Urban History, 1250–1540* (1990). His interests and publications also extend to Italian Renaissance art and religious history.

Plate 2 The stone bridge at Monmouth was built in the 1270s, and its fortified gate tower added in the early fourteenth century, thereby completing the marcher borough's defences. Crown copyright: RCAHMW.

Introduction

Ralph Griffiths

Several lands and diverse peoples

The peoples of the British Isles in the fourteenth and fifteenth centuries were richly diverse in character and often at odds with one another. Hemmed in by a long coastline and buffeted by boisterous seas, they were organized in two kingdoms, England and a much smaller Scotland, with a third, Denmark, retaining the Orkney and Shetland islands until the mid–1460s. England had two large but reluctant dominions, the lands of Ireland and Wales, as well as the Channel Islands, the surviving remnant of the Anglo-Norman kingdom of the twelfth century, and the Isle of Man. Scotland itself included northern and western isles that maintained a peculiar degree of independence of the Scottish crown and links with the north-east of Ireland, whilst the Highlands and the southern uplands preserved their separate identities too.

The peoples of these lands were a diverse brew of mixed ethnic origins, and they had been added to most recently by immigrants and settlers from western France and the Low Countries in the wake of the Norman conquest of England. Their languages and dialects, customs, fashions and lifestyles also varied, and their relations with one another, though often close, were just as likely to be turbulent. Yet in the fourteenth and fifteenth centuries practically all these peoples were touched by common disasters and confronted by related challenges: plague and other diseases afflicted both man and beast with considerable ferocity, especially in the fourteenth century, and armed conflicts affected many regions of the British Isles, whose two kingdoms and associated dominions were drawn into the great Hundred Years War that was fought principally between England and

France (1337–1453). Above all it was the ambitions, pretensions, and claims of the English and their kings, within the British Isles as well as in France, that determined the attitudes of the other peoples of these islands towards the English. After a century and a half of threats, incursions, and invasions from the south, a Scot declared in 1442 that 'the tyranny and cruelty of the English are notorious throughout the world, as manifestly appears in their usurpations against the French, Scots, Welsh, Irish and neighbouring lands'. The king of Scots, James II, went further in 1456 when he sought to galvanize his continental allies against the English, whom he stigmatized as 'the principal disturbers of the peace of all Christendom'.

The differences and relationships among these several peoples changed the social, cultural, and political complexion of the British Isles in important ways during the fourteenth and fifteenth centuries, fortifying identities into an enduring sense of nationhood, especially in England, Scotland, and Ireland, and preserving everywhere those distinctive characteristics that make the history of these islands in these centuries both formative and fascinating. Only in relation to the Jews had treatment been brutal and decisive. In 1290 a long record of discrimination and persecution culminated in Edward I's expulsion of the only recognized non-Christian community in the British Isles, though individual Jews slipped into England and Ireland at least in the centuries that followed.

In 1300, the territorial frontiers of the English kingdom were widely known and were precisely defined in relation to the kingdom of Scotland and the land of Wales. The only part of the Anglo-Scottish frontier still in dispute was a relatively modest stretch of territory called 'the Debatable Land', presumably to distinguish it from the rest of the frontier; but this did not prevent both the English and the Scots from raiding and campaigning at a number of points across the borderland and from capturing castles and lands from time to time. Toward Wales, by the time of King Edward I's death in 1307, English royal officials had a clear idea of where the English shires ended and the lordships of the March began; but that did not prevent quarrels and conflicts over jurisdiction and property. The territorial configuration of the British Isles had largely stabilized by this date, except in Ireland, where the boundaries between colonial (or Anglo-Irish) and Gaelic lordships, and of the English royal enclaves in the east and south, were much less stable.

It was inevitable that neighbouring peoples in the British Isles should hold distinct, often suspicious, and sometimes hostile opinions of each another. These perceptions differed in their intensity from one group or community to another, depending (for example) on social status or circumstances; they differed too as between one place and another, depending on distance and familiarity. The Scottish historian Walter Bower, who wrote his anglophobic *Scotichronicon* during the 1440s while he was abbot of the monastery on the island of Inchcolm in the Firth of Forth, expressed the hostility felt towards the English by the Scottish political and social élite. He endorsed the tradition that the English were born with tails as a punishment for their ancestors' treatment of St Augustine; this slander of the English was also voiced by other peoples in the later Middle Ages. Moreover, as the political crises in England in the reigns of Edward II (1307–27) and Henry IV (1399–1413) showed, artful declarations of a Celtic unity of purpose could occasionally be made among Welsh, Irish, and Scottish élites against the English and their realm. On another, more regional level, a contrast may be drawn between, on the one hand, the attitude of Bristolians in the fourteenth and fifteenth centuries towards the many Welsh folk who visited, traded, or lived in Bristol, and who could aspire even to become its mayor, and, on the other hand, the attitude of Norfolk folk to whom the Welsh were a quite unfamiliar breed: a correspondent writing in 1457 to John Paston, the Norfolk esquire, about the trial in Hereford of some Welsh border gentry, added in a postscript, 'I send you a bill of the names . . . to see and laugh at their Welsh names descended of old pedigrees.' Comic tales at the expense of the Welsh—their passion for toasted cheese and the material pleasures of life, and their inclination to make the most of other people's misfortunes—were popular in England before the end of the fifteenth century, whose beginning had witnessed the final—and dangerous—outburst of armed rebellion against the English crown under the leadership of Owain Glyn Dŵr.

Changing perceptions

In these centuries, relationships between and within the several lands
of the British Isles were volatile and often tense. By 1300 it seemed
that the wealthy and highly organized kingdom of England, under its
masterful king, Edward I, was poised to impose its authority and
culture decisively on Wales, where the last prince of an autonomous
Gwynedd had been killed in 1283; on Scotland, whose political establishment had recently been forced to acknowledge King Edward's
overlordship as the price of solving the question of the succession to
the Scottish throne; and even on Ireland, where English lordship was
still aggressive and extended to the banks of the River Shannon. In his
latter years, King Edward took to referring to Scotland as 'a land'
rather than as the kingdom it was. The Isle of Man was transferred
finally from Scotland's sovereignty to England's in 1333, and the
Channel Islands, stepping stones to France, were reasonably secure in
their English allegiance. It was a mighty ambition which Edward I
bequeathed to his successors. Even before the Hundred Years War
with France began in 1337, the enormity of the challenge faced by the
English realm was appreciated by its Parliament when it advised
the young Edward III in 1332.

It was announced by Sir Geoffrey le Scrope, in the presence of the King and
all the lords, in full Parliament, how the immediately previous Parliament
had been summoned to Westminster because of affairs concerning the land
of Ireland, the King having arranged a passage there in order to rein in the
malice of the rebels against him there; and how the prelates, earls, barons and
other lords of the Parliament and Knights of the Shires had been charged to
take counsel on the security of the land of England; and how [they] advised
that it would be best if the King were to stay in England, and, because of news
coming from Scotland, move to the North country, because of the dangers to
his people and his realm which might occur if the Scots were to enter there in
order to do evil.

Edward rose to the challenge spectacularly but briefly: during the
1330s his forces occupied Edinburgh and much of southern Scotland,
while the young Scots king, David II Bruce, was forced into exile in
France for a season (to 1341). In Scotland, Wales, and Ireland, such
experiences sustained a common defensive sense of identity that was

rooted in myth, history, and a deep resentment of the English. They also tested the capacity of the English crown to mobilize its resources and retain the loyalty of its subjects.

By 1500, relationships in the British Isles had changed substantially, though the challenges and resentments remained. Scotland had asserted and maintained its independence as a kingdom, usually in alliance with the French from 1295 (later known as 'the Auld Alliance'), and was determined to resist claims and campaigns from the south. It managed to do so with notable success on a number of occasions after the 1290s, despite the capture and enforced exile of several of its kings. At Arbroath in 1320, the Scottish nobility as a body put their seals to a letter—the famous Declaration—which they sent to the pope, denouncing English efforts to conquer Scotland: 'For so long as one hundred men remain alive, we shall never under any conditions submit to the domination of the English.' They spoke for 'the community of the realm'. Scotland's determination meant that English kings faced a permanent commitment to defend their northern border, relying on northern nobles and the rest of the realm's resources.

Wales and the Welsh, and some of the immigrant families from England, France, and Ireland who had long been settled especially in the towns of Wales, retained their sense of identity in their own and their neighbours' eyes. The half-century following Edward I's conquests was punctuated by periodic Welsh uprisings, and some ethnic violence between natives and immigrants, which together unsettled a colonial regime that discriminated against—even victimized—Welsh people in Church and state. At Caernarfon in 1345, the Welsh were reported to 'have become so proud and cruel and malicious towards the English . . . that [the burgesses] dare not go anywhere for fear of death'. Elsewhere in north Wales, it seemed that 'the Welsh have never since the conquest been so disposed as they are now to rise against their liege lord [Edward, the Black Prince] to conquer the land from him, if they can attain their purpose'. Especially after Glyn Dŵr's failed uprising (1400–10), many in the crown's principality of Wales as well as in the territories of the marcher lords, who were among the greater English aristocracy, learned to turn political subjection to a largely English administrative system into practical power and control over their own lives and fortunes.

By 1500, Ireland too revealed the hollowness of English ambitions

whether a nation be understood, as it should be, as a territory equal to that of the French nation, England is a real nation . . .

In 1414 the English argued their case on all three grounds: on claims to authority, language, and territorial extent. And they went further, adding that Scotland, Wales, and Ireland were part of this English nation.

A supporting myth was popularized at the time by the publicists of the English monarchy. This myth was based on the legends of a British past, in which King Arthur and his predecessors ruled far more than England in these islands. British histories and associated prophecies, stemming especially from the pen of Geoffrey of Monmouth in the twelfth century, also made lively reading in Wales and Scotland in the later Middle Ages, especially when they stigmatized the English as descendants of invading Saxons. Yet Edward I and his grandson, Edward III, had a deep interest in Arthur as king of Britain, and later English kings proclaimed their descent from British rulers and sought to appropriate their supposed rights in the British Isles. On occasion, King Arthur was portrayed as symbolizing the English 'empire', and Arthurian romances and origin legends enlisting Brutus were popular long before Sir Thomas Malory wrote his *Morte D'Arthur* in about 1470 and William Caxton made a profit from printing these tales in 1485. They had been celebrated in Edward I's reign (1272–1307) by a Yorkshire chronicler who, at the same time, commended Edward's military and political achievements:

> Now are the islanders all joined together,
> And Albany [Scotland] reunited to the royalties
> Of which King Edward is proclaimed lord.
> Cornwall and Wales are in his power,
> And Ireland the great at his will.
> Arthur had never the fiefs so fully!

Edward III made Windsor Castle his Arthurian shrine; and in so far as personal nomenclature is significant, the English royal families of Lancaster, York, and Tudor favoured the name Arthur for the first time since the Angevins in the twelfth century. It is true that the Scots were popularizing their own origin myth at the same time in order to counter English pretensions, one that claimed even greater antiquity in Greece and Egypt; and in Wales Arthurian prophecies were reinvigorated to meet the needs of Owain Glyn Dŵr, a rebel against King Henry IV. Then, later, they were used to support the schemes of the part-Welsh Henry Tudor, the eminently successful 'son of prophecy' who appropriated by a master-stroke the Arthurian associations and prophecies to the English 'Britain' and a new dynasty of English, Welsh, and French descent. By 1500 Arthur had become an English and a Welsh talisman.

English and foreign observers alike acknowledged as much when they referred in the later fifteenth century to 'the island of England', even 'the British island of England', and 'Great Britain' appeared for the first time in the official government vocabulary of Edward IV and Richard III—to be adapted a century later as Shakespeare's 'scept'red isle' in his play *King Richard II*, completed in 1597. It was Arthurian myth turned into English propaganda in an age when the realities of power and identities in the British Isles signalled something quite different.

Travel and travellers

It is not surprising that travellers to the British islands in the later Middle Ages thought their peoples to be puzzling yet fascinating breeds. The Hundred Years War between England and France may have deterred French visitors, except at times of truce, but others were not discouraged, and in the second half of the fifteenth century, when the military campaigns were largely over, several shrewd observers from Italy, Spain, the Low Countries, and even central Europe visited what they sometimes called 'Britain'; some of them reported what they saw and heard.

To what extent were these visitors knowledgeable about the British Isles and its geography? The seaways were, of course, no barrier to the ships owned or hired by contemporary merchants; rather, they were avenues of communication. And even Mediterranean vessels from Genoa, Florence, and Venice made regular voyages to southern English and Welsh ports, and to the havens of Wales and Ireland. Scotland's trade with France and the Baltic was growing. The so-called portolan charts of continental mariners, in frequent use before the fifteenth century, depicted the British Isles in detail, especially the

English Channel. These charts in turn were based on earlier French *routiers de la mer*, whose use in often hazardous circumstances meant that they rarely survive today. However, they are known to have provided directions for circumnavigating England, Wales, and Ireland, and for sailings to Scotland, and also information about tides and depths of water. Despite acknowledging the difficulties of sailing from 'the Gulf of Bristol' northwards to Scotland in other than small coastal vessels that hugged the western shore, the Milanese ambassador in Paris felt it worthwhile to send to the duke of Milan a chart used by a French fleet making for Scotland by this western route in 1461.

Once on dry land, the visitor could have had access to maps and direction-finders. From the thirteenth century onwards there were maps of Britain in existence, though the earliest of them showed Scotland as an island and sometimes cut in two by the Forth and the Clyde, and Ireland cut in two by the River Boyne—perhaps not utterly bizarre conclusions in a world of small ships. There were detailed itineraries available too, from Bologna to London, via Calais and Dover, and on to the Welsh border and Hadrian's Wall; whilst Gough's Map of about 1360 depicted a network of roads and bridges, river systems, fords and ferries, and distances for England, Wales, and Scotland. Travel between these lands was relatively easy in peaceful times: a stone bridge spanned the River Dee at Chester (constructed in the thirteenth century); the six-arch bridge over the River Wye at Hereford was rebuilt in the fifteenth century; and at Dumfries the River Nith could be crossed on a bridge that had as many as thirteen arches. Military demands were frequently adapted to meet the needs of travellers and traders, pilgrims and migrants.

Of course, the quality of the travellers' knowledge varied greatly from person to person. The Bristol antiquary William Worcester (d. *c.*1485) described how to get as far as the Arran Islands, off the west coast of Ireland, in the 1470s, though as far as is known he had never been there himself; he also knew about the islands between Scotland and Ireland because a Bristol seaman had told him about them. But his perception of the islanders of the Arrans was based on tradition and was somewhat suspect: 'where men who live there cannot die, but when on account of their great age they wish to do so they are taken at their own wish out of the island and there die.'

Although the Venetian nobleman who filed a report on his visit to

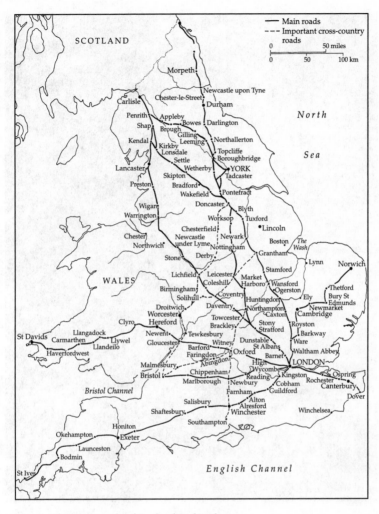

Map 1 The main roads of England and Wales.
Source: K. O. Morgan, *The Oxford Illustrated History of Britain* (Oxford, 1984).

Henry VII's court about 1498 could not say 'what the circumference of this island [of Britain] is, because the Islanders of our day do not care to understand such matters, and I find that writers differ on the subject', the accounts which visitors wrote about England and the English and about Scotland and the Scots were often sharp-eyed and detailed. After all, the kingdoms of England and Scotland, and

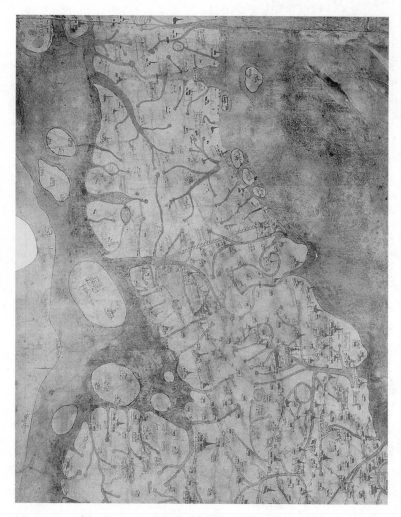

Map 2 Part of the Gough map of England and Wales, c.1360.
Source: MS Gough Gen. Top 16 (Bodleian Library, Oxford).

their kings, were well known in other realms and in diplomatic,
government, and commercial circles. Ireland and the Irish and Wales
and the Welsh attracted fewer comments, perhaps because they had
no independent political identity or were less accessible to continental travellers, or because their countryside and peoples seemed
more distant and less inviting.

Regional characteristics

Regional differences attracted comment from travellers and especially from foreigners. These differences were determined by a variety of factors in a far from uniform combination: by landscape and climate, social mobility and settlement, political and ecclesiastical structures and relationships, languages and dialects, and by the pace of economic change. Some regions had major towns or cities as their focus, and the orbit of London as England's capital and the largest conurbation in these islands in the later Middle Ages was expanding to encompass the Midlands and the north-east and the hinterland of southern Welsh ports. London's population was at least 80,000 in 1300, and perhaps half that in the century following the Black Death (1348–9). Jean Froissart, the Low Countries writer from Hainault, thought it rich and prosperous in the 1360s, and even went so far as to say that without the Londoners 'the rest of the country would neither dare nor be able to do anything'. It was the capital of the English kingdom and, with Westminster up-river, the headquarters of its highly centralized government. A century later, in 1466, travellers from central Europe considered it 'a powerful and busy city'. It was not especially large by European standards, but its overseas trade was extensive; the visitors found its many crafts and businesses to be dominated by the goldsmiths and cloth-workers, who relied on England's 'greatest benefit', its sheep, 'almost as white as snow which graze everywhere and only a few are black'. With perhaps higher urban expectations, even the Venetian visitor to England in 1498 saw London as the 'metropolis of England', with a cosmopolitan population drawn from all parts of the British Isles, as well as from overseas. Whilst acknowledging that London could not compare with some of the great Italian cities, he too was in awe of its goldsmiths: fifty-two of their shops in the Strand alone were 'so rich and full of silver vessels, great and small, that in all the shops of Milan, Rome, Venice and Florence put together, I do not think there would be found so many of the magnificence that are to be seen in London'. Major provincial centres, such as Norwich for East Anglia, York and Newcastle for northern England and the Scottish March, Coventry for the Midlands, and Bristol, the metropolis of the Anglo-Welsh region centred on the Severn vale and estuary, had a similar role, in each case with good communications to London by land and sea. In the mid-fourteenth century, from the perspective of the merchants of Bruges, 'the four great towns of Scotland' were Edinburgh, Aberdeen, Perth, and Dundee; a century later Edinburgh was forging ahead of the others, as Scotland's principal retail and administrative centre.

As for England, the Venetian observer in 1498 judged it 'the most beautiful, the best, and the most fertile part of the whole island'. He may not have ventured far from southern counties, but he had sources of information about other parts of the realm and about Scotland to enable him to reach a broad judgement. A century and a quarter earlier, it had been Froissart's experience that England was a generally peaceful country, 'where every man, whether merchant or farmer, had grown used to living and trading pacifically, and the farmer to living quietly and well off the land, according to the produce of the season'. The disruptions of the early decades of the fourteenth century and the worst of the plague years after 1348 seemed to be things of the past. French raids along the coast had never escalated into invasion; only in the 1390s, in Richard II's last years, did Froissart sense that things were again unsettled. Nevertheless, to all who came to England after the close of the great French war in 1453, the country appeared rich and prosperous, from the king in his elegant court to the country farmer in the provinces. What struck two visitors from Germany in 1466 about the southern counties was the ordered patchwork of 'villages, towns, castles, forests and land under cultivation', where 'the peasants dig ditches round their fields and meadows, and so fence them in that no one can pass on foot or on horseback except by the main road'. Noteworthy, too, were the parks which had been created for recreation and hunting.

To the Venetian a generation later, life's richness was reflected in England's parish churches and monasteries, which impressed him with their beauty and elegance, and those in London with the number of their imposing tombs. Equally noteworthy was the music he heard in England, and the choirs, often up to sixty strong and to be heard in secular surroundings as well as in the parish and greater churches. He was less impressed by the standard of learning of the English he met, even though they seemed to be good practising Christians; apart from the clergy, 'few . . . are addicted to the study of letters', despite having two universities, at Oxford and Cambridge, each of which had a growing number of colleges for poor students but which had fallen into the intellectual doldrums.

Yet other regions, less urbanized or more isolated, seemed distinctive. In 1460 the apprehensive people of southern England learned that a northern force was sweeping south, 'like a whirlwind', 'like so many locusts', committing the 'unutterable crimes' for which those living north of the River Trent were notorious—or so it seemed to southerners in the midst of the Wars of the Roses. An Italian in England in 1506 noted that Cornwall, with its own language and character, was treated as a separate division of the kingdom, 'like Wales'; there 'no human being ever comes, save the few boors who inhabit it'. He was exaggerating, but in part he was echoing the reaction, 180 years earlier, of a new bishop of Exeter, John Grandisson (1327–69), who lamented: 'Here I am not only at the end of the world but even (if I may say so) at the ends of the very end. For this diocese . . . is divided from the rest of England.'

In Scotland, the central and eastern coastlands, increasingly dominated by Edinburgh, itself recognized as 'the principal burgh' or capital city before the end of the fifteenth century, were regularly contrasted by travellers with the Highlands and the southern uplands. John Fordun (d. c.1387), a chronicler who himself came from southern Scotland, delivered a harsh verdict on his fellow Scots of the north and the isles about 1370:

> The people of the coast [Scotland's south-east and eastern coast] are of domestic and civilised habits, trusty, patient and urbane, decent in their attire, affable and peaceful, devout in Divine worship . . . The Highlanders and people of the Islands, on the other hand, are a savage and untamed nation, rude and independent, given to rapine, ease-loving, of a docile and warm disposition, comely in person, but unsightly in dress, hostile to their English people [the southern Scots] and language, and owing to diversity of speech, even to their own nation exceedingly cruel.

Witness, too, John Hardyng, the northern English writer who spent three and a half years as a royal agent in Scotland in Henry V's reign and who came to know its countryside well. The eastern valleys and coasts he thought prosperous and fertile:

> The Carse of Gowrie doth lie, I understand,
> A plentiful country, I you warrant,

> Of corn and cattle, and all commodities,
> You to support in your necessities.

He also knew the south-west, where

> Next from Ayr unto Glasgow go,
> Goodly city and university,
> Where plentiful is the country also,
> Replenished well with all commodities.

These regions he contrasted with the mountains of the Highlands.

As for Scotland's towns, Pedro de Ayala, the Spanish envoy to King James IV's court in the 1490s, admired the stone-built houses he saw, with their fine doors, glass windows, and a great number of chimneys. 'All the furniture that is used in Italy, Spain and France is to be found in their dwellings.' As he confided to the Venetians visiting the English court at the same time, the Scottish nobility have 'excellent houses, built as in Italy of hewn stone or brick, and with magnificent rooms, halls, doors, galleries, chimneys and windows'. The Spaniard was impressed, at least by the living standards of the well-to-do in the towns of the Lowlands.

During the fifteenth century, Scotland's regional, linguistic, and ethnic antagonisms were expressed by the leading Scots poets. Despite their hostility towards the English, they all showed great deference to Chaucer, their acknowledged master. Most startling of all, however, was William Dunbar (d. 1513), who referred to the English tongue ('our English', he declared) as 'flower imperial that raise in Britane evir'. The Highlands' language and customs he decried, and Highlanders he consigned to 'the deepest pot of hell'.

One of the best-informed observers of the regional differences in Wales was the opinionated chronicler Adam of Usk (d. 1430), who was brought up in the anglicized and prosperous south-eastern March, in a lordship whose lord in the later fourteenth century was a Mortimer, earl of March. Adam was widely travelled both within and beyond Wales. He resented the punitive legislation of the English Parliament against the Welsh and their language in 1401–2, during the early phases of Owain Glyn Dŵr's rebellion; yet, like many in his position, he proved equivocal in his loyalties as the rebellion lengthened and Glyn Dŵr descended on southern Wales. To Adam, 'his native country' was the south-east, the English became 'our side', and the fastnesses of Snowdonia, the heartland of the principality of

Gwynedd that Edward I had destroyed, and a major support to Glyn Dŵr and 'his wretches', was the source of all the evil in Wales in Adam's day. Almost a century later the Venetian visitor, who was doubtless able to talk to Welshmen in London, reported on the fertility and productiveness of the island of Anglesey, 'the Mother of Wales' as it was commonly called, yet situated just across the narrow strait from the inhospitable mountains that seemed so threatening to Adam of Usk.

In Ireland, political factors and an unfinished conquest emphasized other contrasts, between the northern and western rim of mountains round the central lowlands, and the towns and lowlands of the east and south with their prospect towards England, Wales, and the continent. There was more than one Ireland: a series of fragmented societies, turbulent in their interrelationships, ranging from native Gaelic to immigrant settler to an English (and Welsh) core of administrators and townsfolk. The British Isles were multi-regional and culturally mixed in the later Middle Ages.

Languages

As the English envoys at Constance in 1414 realized, one of the most powerful expressions of a people's identity was language, and it was one of the most obvious characteristics noted by visitors. In the fourteenth and fifteenth centuries, the traveller in these islands could have encountered at least half a dozen languages, spoken and written, and most of them diversified in several dialects: English, Cornish, Latin, French, Welsh, Irish, and Scots Gaelic. A mid-fourteenth-century chronicler endorsed the view that 'all the language north of the Humber, and especially in York, is so sharp, slitting, grating and unshapen, that we southern men may never understand it'. Despite the march of the English tongue northwards in Scotland and westwards in Wales and Ireland, Welsh, Irish, and Scots Gaelic were still commonly spoken in 1500 by substantial numbers of people, and Welsh certainly was a lively written language in prose and verse, in religious and secular works.

In England, the increased use of the English language and the spread of literacy were twin developments of the fourteenth and fifteenth centuries. They were symptomatic of a greater involvement of the middling ranks of country and town folk in the web of royal administration, their increasing awareness of politics and public affairs, and their growing participation in political, religious, and literary discourse, both centrally and locally. They impinge too on strengthening sentiments of patriotism, xenophobia, and nation-hood, and even help to explain a growing sense among the English of their superiority over other peoples in these islands who spoke lan-guages different from their own. The humanist and statesman Sir Thomas More (1478–1535) estimated that early in the sixteenth cen-tury more than 50 per cent of Englishmen were literate, and this may not have been too wide of the mark. An estimate of their neighbours' literacy is not feasible, although the existence of schools and the penetration of prosperous households by the English language and its literature suggest that literacy was expanding in Scotland and Wales as well. This literate world was increasingly an English world, even in Scotland, Wales, and Ireland.

The ability to understand and speak French (and therefore to read and write it) was in marked decline by the end of the fourteenth century, at least for official and formal business in government and private organizations. Its popularity in more literary circles continued into the fifteenth century, but English became rapidly more common for verse and was widely read in gentle circles. Edward I was self-consciously English, and his antipathy towards France and its mon-archy led him to refer to the latter's detestable intentions to wipe out the English tongue; but his belligerent attitude did not immediately affect the presence of the French language in England. One four-teenth-century poet wrote that 'common men know no French, among a hundred scarcely one'; but it was still learned and taught among the educated classes as the language of chivalry and gentility, and universities sought to halt its declining use during the fourteenth century. In the following century, however, the court and the govern-ment encouraged the use of English, and the resumption of war with France eventually caused the demise of French as a spoken and writ-ten language in England. Both French and Latin remained learned languages, and the latter retained its role in Church and state and the professions as the language of a literate, Christian culture. However, by 1400 grammar schools in England were teaching English grammar, and English was used in all sorts of contexts, official and unofficial.

The reasons for this quiet yet perceptible revolution are complex, but among them may be counted the patriotism and xenophobia generated by the long French war, and the lead given by the crown and the nobility. The triumph of written English was assured in England.

A number of spoken and written English regional dialects were noted by foreign visitors. Despite the spread of a popular form of English, dialects like that of Yorkshire were not easily absorbed into a common spoken idiom, but much headway was made. The spreading tentacles of government helped both in England and in its dominions, and in southern Scotland too, extending the use of written English in official contexts during the first half of the fifteenth century. A further factor was the emergence of London and, rather later, Edinburgh, as the settled capitals of the two kingdoms, with York as a subsidiary administrative centre still in the fourteenth century, and Bristol as England's second commercial metropolis, each speaking a dialect that gradually fused to help form a more standardized English tongue. This tongue was predominantly Midland English, which triumphed at the expense of a London tongue, and perhaps for this reason was the more easily adopted in rural and distant shires. Geoffrey Chaucer (d. 1400) had serious doubts as to whether his writings would be understood across England, and he wrote for a relatively charmed circle:

> And for there is so great diversity
> In English and in writing of our tongue
> So pray I God that none miswrite thee,
> Nor thee mismetre for default of tongue.
> And read whereso thou be, or else sung
> That thou be understood, God I beseech.

In a legal case of 1426, it was stated that words were pronounced differently in different parts of England, 'and one is just as good as the other'. Half a century later William Caxton (d. 1491) could be more confident that his printed editions of several hundreds would, with care, be comprehensible from one shire to another. He realized that 'common English that is spoken in one shire varieth from another', but by using 'English not over rude, nor curious, but in such terms as shall be understood by God's grace', he anticipated little difficulty. The evolution of a standard written and spoken English made great strides in Scotland, Wales, and Ireland, as well as in

England, and by 1500 the English tongue was widely understood and used. It was also promoted by the government and the Church, and by English settlers in the Highlands of Scotland, much of Ireland, and Wales, at the same time conveying a sense of superiority and greater worth in those who used the language, yet in others sharpening cultural differences. By the end of the Middle Ages, the robustness of the English advance had not overwhelmed the Celtic languages, but it had convinced some of the merits of linguistic uniformity.

It is often claimed that England was a trilingual country after 1300, with French in use alongside Latin and English in prose and verse on a variety of subjects, and as much in the north and west and in southern Scotland as in the south and east. Yet in Cornwall a fourth language was still spoken, and possibly written. Cornish, the least resilient of the Celtic tongues in these islands, gradually retreated west of the River Tamar in the later Middle Ages until, by 1500, it was spoken only in the far west and had not produced a written literature for some time. The Truro area was a linguistic borderland, with English advancing relentlessly as the medium of government and trade, especially among the Cornish gentry. It has been estimated that about 60 per cent of Cornish folk spoke Cornish in 1400, less than half that by 1500; the practices of government, commerce, and travel told against it. In the Isle of Man a form of Gaelic was still spoken, but English became the norm.

The use of Gaelic in Scotland was in decline, even in parts of the Highlands. In 1435, Aeneas Silvius Piccolomini (the papal legate who later became Pope Pius II) noted the cultural fault-line in Scotland separating the Gaelic-speaking Highlands and Western Isles from the Lowlands, where Inglis (or Scots English) was spreading northwards along the eastern seaboard—as John Fordun had described about 1370. Yet Gaelic survived in Scotland as more than a spoken dialect: poets, clerks, and noble patrons preserved its literature, too, perhaps through contacts with the Irish literary tradition, which foreign visitors also noticed. It has been estimated that in 1500 half of Scotland's population still spoke Gaelic. The nobility and the court, however, admired the French language and its courtly literature, and for much longer than their counterparts in England. This admiration was sustained by the mutually supportive Franco-Scottish 'Auld Alliance' throughout the later Middle Ages. But it was the English literature of Chaucer and John Gower that was admired most and was developed not only by John Lydgate and Thomas Hoccleve in early fifteenth-century England but also by their near-contemporaries in Scotland, Robert Henryson, William Dunbar, and King James I himself (whose captivity in England from 1406 until 1424, including residence at the Lancastrian court, had been a significant factor).

The Irish form of Gaelic was spoken by a large proportion of Ireland's population, and had a long literary tradition. At the end of the thirteenth century, English and Welsh settlers were most numerous in the east of the island, though even there, beyond castles and towns like Dublin, Waterford, and the like, they and their languages were under growing pressure from the Irish, their culture, and their speech. Alarm bells were sounding by the mid-fourteenth century when (it was claimed) 'Men of the English race in [Ireland] study and speak the Irish language and foster their children among the Irish; . . . our country dwellers of the English stock for the most part are becoming Irish in language.' A traveller at the end of the fourteenth century would have noticed how settler and native were intermarrying and how settler families were prepared to adopt Irish dress and habits, thereby causing anxiety to the governing élite of Dublin. English was then the common idiom in a relatively narrow corridor along the east and south coasts, for all the official efforts made to stem the Irish tide and discourage social integration. The famous and wide-ranging Statute of Kilkenny (1366) even sought to forbid anyone of English descent from conversing with other Englishmen in the Irish language; it tried to force English people in Ireland to use only English surnames, speak English, and maintain English customs. But such heavy-handed measures were bound to fail. A survey in 1513 estimated that two-thirds of the inhabitants of Ireland spoke Irish and practised Irish customs; even outside the walled towns of the six eastern counties, which were probably bilingual, it was noted that many folk spoke Irish. And works of literature from the pens of Irish poets, lawyers, and other writers were patronized by Irish and Anglo-Irish nobles alike.

Wales presents a striking contrast. It too was a multilingual country. In the later Middle Ages, Latin and French were the languages of Church and government, with English rapidly overwhelming French as the fifteenth century wore on. Yet Welsh continued to be spoken by a majority of people, and the Welsh literary tradition skilfully accommodated itself to the collapse of the last independent

Welsh principality and its ruling élite in 1283. More so than in either Scotland or Ireland, the influx of Anglo-French and English conquerors, traders, and settlers, culminating in Edward I's conquests, made English the popular tongue of a growing number of people, creating in the south and east, and especially in the numerous towns, a bilingual society. French was no longer spoken in everyday contexts in Wales; and in the first half of the fifteenth century it was replaced by English in official contexts too. Flemish, which some early colonists in Pembrokeshire had spoken, had long given way to English, according to Ranulf Higden, monk of Chester and chronicler, in the mid-fourteenth century. French literature may once have been as popular in Wales as in Scotland; to take one example, chivalric romances in French had been owned by the Glamorgan rebel leader, Llywelyn Bren (d. 1316). There were strengthened contacts with France during the Hundred Years War and Glyn Dŵr's rebellion; but thereafter even romances in French lost some of their attraction, and the popularity of English grew apace.

At the same time, peace and greater stability encouraged population movements along the channels of communication and trade with England, Ireland, and beyond. Parts of Herefordshire, Shropshire, and Cheshire had Welsh-speaking inhabitants by 1500; Welsh poets visited the houses of bilingual gentry families like the Hanmers of Flintshire, the Herberts of Raglan, and the Vaughans of Tretower, and eastern towns with mixed populations could be admired by Welsh writers, in Oswestry's case as 'the London of Wales', and in Brecon's case (even more extravagantly) as 'the Constantinople of Wales'. Large parts of Wales may have been an increasingly anglicized world, but Welsh writers of poetry, prose, and translations, and those engaged in private record-keeping, kept the native literary and cultural traditions alive and vigorous.

Many folk were monoglot Welsh speakers and required interpreters in official contexts. But bilingualism followed intermarriage, and personal naming practices suggest a mingling of peoples, especially during the fifteenth century, most visibly in well-to-do circles; though the Welsh patronymic style could still amuse distant East Anglians in the middle of the century. The gentry took the lead, and we may imagine some of these families able to read Latin and French and to speak and read English and Welsh as education and literacy spread, not least through schools in the larger towns like

Haverfordwest and Caernarfon and those in the border English shires. By 1500 English was the language of government in Wales and of status, and, of course, it was admired as a literary language of immense richness.

Except in Cornwall and Man, the Celtic languages of the British Isles were in a reasonably healthy state in the later Middle Ages, despite the advances made by English and the efforts of colonial governments in Ireland and Wales to assert its superiority. Yet the English language was undoubtedly growing in popular usage. This was a consequence of military and political conquest, and especially of social and commercial intercourse in a more peaceful environment. The role of government in England and Scotland and in the counties, lordships, and towns in Wales and Ireland, and the seasonal mobility of labour were also influential factors. The gentry and nobility were the first to embrace an English culture, followed by mercantile communities; equally, they were content often to patronize native languages and their practitioners and hence maintain their status, despite a growing prejudice against the use of languages other than English in official, public contexts.

There was thus no linguistic unity within the two kingdoms of Scotland and England, or within the subjugated lands of Wales and Ireland. Rather, many communities were multilingual, and in some a bilingual culture in English and the native tongue was common. This promoted cultural diffusion and sustained a series of regional cultures in the fourteenth and fifteenth centuries. To the continental visitor this was a notable and intriguing feature of these islands.

Fashions and manners

Contacts and relationships with other peoples are among the keys to changing fashions, manners, and customs; wealth and status are others. In these centuries, people moved relatively easily from one region to another and from one country to another, for all the history of tortured relations between the English ruling élite and the other peoples of the British Isles. Numbers of Scots migrated to England and even settled there, not simply in the northern shires but also in East Anglia and the south-east, where they may have encountered less hostility, beyond a natural suspicion. Both governments from time to time sought to discourage such movements but could not halt them. A Scots contemporary of William Dunbar composed in 1501 a ballad in praise of London, 'the flower of Cities all', and its mayor, 'Exemplar, lodestar and guide', that so impressed the citizens that its fifty-six lines were incorporated in popular London chronicles.

Oxford University attracted students from all parts of England, and from Wales, Ireland and Scotland too. They cherished their own regional loyalties, which transcended loyalties to kings and realms: northerners associated with Scots, and their rivalries with the southern English and their friends, the Irish and Welsh students, turned violent in the 1270s and again in the 1380s, though when the Glyn Dŵr rebellion began in 1400 the Welsh were rounded on and forced to flee. Such disturbances did not significantly affect the cosmopolitan character of Oxford's student population in the century that followed. The foundation of universities at St Andrews (1413), Glasgow (1450–1), and Aberdeen (1494) meant that fewer Scots students attended the English universities; but the planned university for Dublin (1320) and Glyn Dŵr's proposals for universities in both north and south Wales (1406) came to nothing, so that Irish and Welsh students made their way to Oxford in particular in even greater numbers.

Unlike the Scots, the Welsh and Irish subjects of the English crown were not generally regarded as aliens in England, despite periodic tensions, as during the Glyn Dŵr rebellion when, as Adam of Usk records from his vantage point in the south-eastern March, loyal Welsh who had been driven across the Severn by the advancing rebels encountered a hostile population in the West Country. The English were suspicious of the Irish and Welsh, and from time to time sought to force them to return to their own country. But they continued to arrive in significant numbers through ports like Chester and Bristol, partly in response to economic hardships at home in Wales or the colonized parts of Ireland. There was little outright or organized hostility towards such migrants after the failure of Glyn Dŵr's rebellion. Bristol had an Irish-born mayor in 1399, and so did Southampton in the 1420s; in 1486 the mayor of Bristol who welcomed Henry Tudor to the city was the Welshman Henry Vaughan, whose family of Bristol merchants may have hailed originally from Cardiganshire. The migrants especially headed for London, which had the largest alien proportion of any town's population in the fifteenth century, for the universities, and for the central and western shires and major towns, with the Scots more common in the north and east.

It was natural that fashion in dress and manners should vary from region to region, from the cosmopolitan culture of London and the courts of kings and nobles in England and Scotland to the well-to-do surroundings of yeomen farmers and gentlemen in prosperous counties and to the harsher environment of scattered and sparsely populated communities in upland northern and western regions. Foreign reporters—albeit exclusively male—were struck by the beauty of the women they met in England, Scotland, and Ireland, and with the exceptionally long gowns they wore. They were especially surprised by the custom of greeting distinguished visitors in their inns, 'for with [English women] to offer a kiss is the same as to hold out the right hand; for they do not shake hands,' the German visitors discovered in 1466. Thirty years earlier, the worldly Italian cleric Aeneas Silvius Piccolomini, later to be pope, discovered in 1435 that the women of Scotland were 'fair, charming and easily won. . . . Women there think less of a kiss than in Italy of a touch of the hand.' Equally (and agreeably) surprised was the Dutch scholar Erasmus, who first visited England in 1499: it seemed to him to be populated by 'goddess girls, divinely fair . . . They come to see you and drink your health in kisses, wherever you go the world is full of kisses.' And whereas the Venetian observer in the 1490s found English men somewhat aloof and phlegmatic, he understood 'that it is quite the contrary with the women, who are very violent in their passions'. Even the Spaniard visiting Scotland found the women there courteous 'in the extreme', and dominant in their homes: 'they are absolute mistresses of their houses, and even of their husbands, in all things concerning the administration of their property, income as well as expenditure.' He also thought them better dressed than the women in England, admiring especially their head-dress as 'the handsomest in the world', though he may not have appreciated that it was a fashion that was changing in English circles.

As for the men, continental fashions had spread to England by the mid-fourteenth century; even soldiers in the royal armies had replaced the cloak with doublet and breeches. The changes were not always welcomed, and to some commentators the tight clothing, pointed shoes, and greater ornamentation favoured by the fashion- and status-conscious seemed to have moral implications. Within decades the changes were influencing the style of peasant clothing, and the greater spending power of the peasantry from the later fourteenth century onwards enabled them to buy the more expensive clothes which the domestic cloth industry could supply. The élites were uneasy, and in England sumptuary legislation from the 1360s sought to curb such tastes and the social pretensions they reflected. Such changes may have been slower to come to parts of Scotland and Ireland: in 1448 a Burgundian knight noted that the Scots, unlike himself, still wore long gowns, and Jean Froissart, when he returned to England in 1396, learned from one of the king's knights, Henry Chrysted, who had lived among the Irish, that even the Gaelic chiefs were, to English eyes, uncouth and poorly dressed. Long after English men had abandoned long cloaks and had adopted breeches, the Gaelic chiefs and their servants 'do not wear breeches. So I had a large quantity of linen drawers made . . . and taught them to wear them'—a custom which the esquire linked with civilizing their 'boorish and unseemly habits, both in dress and other things'. He introduced them to silk and fur-lined clothes, which were common in England. Yet when Froissart heard that the king's uncle, Thomas, duke of Gloucester, had declared that the 'Irish are a poor and nasty people, with a miserable country that is quite uninhabitable', he dismissed the duke's comment as foolish. Quite independently, Raymond, viscount of Perelhos, from the Pyrenees, who visited Gaelic Ulster in 1397, recorded that all the men, regardless of position, went bare-legged and barefoot, and wore little beneath their Irish cloak or mantle.

At the end of the fifteenth century, both the English and the Scots were considered well dressed—the Scots, indeed, somewhat overly concerned with their appearance and their fine clothes. Adam of Usk had reported that the Greek emperor, who came to England in 1400 after touring several European capitals, considered the English to be obsessed with fashionable dress, and that this signified inconstancy and fickleness of heart—though that conclusion may reflect the emperor's disappointment at the response of King Henry IV to his pleas for help in defending Constantinople. The male fashion for short, cropped hair, perhaps a characteristic of generations of armed soldiers, made the English fascinated by the long, beautiful tresses of the central European visitors in 1466; they believed that they had been stuck on with tar.

Two of the most perceptive visitors to these islands in the fourteenth century, Jean le Bel and Jean Froissart, both natives of Hainault, came face to face with the Scots. Le Bel did so when he joined Edward III's first campaign to Scotland in 1327, and Froissart while he was living in England in the 1360s and paid a visit to Scotland. Both writers wrote of the Scots without condescension and with respect. Le Bel found the Scots men he encountered 'extremely bold and tough', their forces given to guerrilla tactics and lightning raids that enabled them to 'well endure the rigours of war' against England. They had 'little fear of the English' in the decades following Edward I's attempts to force the Scots to submit to his superior lordship. Froissart shared this view later in the century, and went further, writing that 'they had little love or respect for the English' following a generation of bitter strife.

Froissart was less forthcoming about the Welsh, though he had travelled to the Welsh March and the West Country with Edward Despenser, one of the major marcher lords, in 1366. Later observers, however, were universally struck by their sense of history and pride in their venerable origins; after the elimination of Welsh princes by the Edwardian conquest, leaving the English king and English marcher lords as an immigrant élite, the Venetian visitor in 1498 perceptively noted that Welshmen 'all consider themselves to be gentlemen'.

Froissart did not visit Ireland, and his reports on the land and its people are tinged with English prejudice, though he was unwilling to believe the more extreme strictures. In the context of Richard II's expedition in 1394–5 (the details of which Froissart very likely acquired on his last visit to England in 1396), he judged Ireland to be 'a strange, wild place consisting of tall forests, great stretches of water, bogs and uninhabitable regions', with no towns to speak of. From Henry Chrysted, the king's knight brought up in Ireland and able to speak Gaelic as well as English and French, he learned that the Irish 'are a very dour people, proud and uncouth, slow-thinking and hard to get to know or make friends with'. Charged by the king with civilizing the four Irish chiefs, the knight confided to Froissart that it was a difficult commission, for even they were 'very uncouth and gross-minded people', presenting the greatest challenge in 'polishing them and moderating their language and characters'.

Reputations

At the end of the fifteenth century, continental observers considered the Scots a poor people, but they detected that during the reign of James IV (1488–1513), the standard of living, prosperity, and trade with the Low Countries and the Baltic were improving. They also thought the Scots more loyal to their kings than the English to theirs, an observation which events during the Wars of the Roses seemed to support.

This fascination with the British Isles and its peoples which foreigners expressed reached its limits when the German visitors in 1466 discussed the English: 'They are treacherous and cunning, plotting against the lives of foreigners, and no matter how they bend the knee they are not to be trusted.' Two centuries of ruthless ambition had made them so. English wars in Scotland, Wales and Ireland, and with France had done most to create that perception within and beyond these islands. In the reign of Edward III (1327–77), Jean Froissart judged that 'the Englishmen were so proud, that they set nothing by any nation but their own'. There may have been a time, in the generation around 1400 (when both Richard II and Henry IV had broader sympathies and continental contacts), and again in the generation around 1500 in the reign of Henry Tudor (whose attitudes to the Welsh, the Scots, and the French were unusual for the age), when perceptions might have been modified; but the consequences of the revolution of 1399, Henry V's great war in France, and Henry VIII's Reformation sharpened rather than dulled the images. A Spanish diarist in 1406, sailing into English waters, well appreciated that the English are 'folk very diverse in character and different from all other nations; they have no fear of any other nation . . . and they have a liking for no other nation.' A Silesian from Breslau who was familiar with western and eastern Europe concluded in 1484 that the English were so self-righteous and self-centred that they thought the world did not exist beyond their shores. The intellectual foundations for such an attitude were provided in England itself by Sir John Fortescue, chief justice of King's Bench and a councillor of kings, when he descanted on the superiority of the laws, customs, and institutions of England over those of other nations, especially the French and the Scots, in his famous treatise, 'In Praise of the Laws of England' (1468–71): England was 'the mightiest and most wealthy realm of the world'. The Venetian visitor in 1498 reported in similar vein from personal experience:

The English are great lovers of themselves, and of everything belonging to them; they think there are no other men than themselves, and no other world but England; and wherever they see a handsome foreigner, they say that 'he looks like an Englishman' and that 'it is a great pity that he should not be an Englishman'; and when they partake of any delicacy with a foreigner, they ask him, 'whether such a thing is made in their country?' They distrust foreigners and imagine that they never come into their island, but to make themselves master of it, and to usurp their goods.

The Spanish envoy contrasted this with the Scots, who positively liked foreigners and 'dispute with one another as to who shall have and treat a foreigner in his house'. And especially was this so for the French, for he noted the number in James IV's reign who spoke French in Scotland, unlike in England, and reported that 'there is a good deal of French education in Scotland'. 'For all the young gentlemen who have no property go to France and are well received there, and therefore the French are liked.' The clash of histories between England and Scotland for two centuries had accentuated their distinctiveness in some ways, and certainly had caused their attitudes to the rest of Europe to diverge, for all the advances made by an anglicizing culture throughout the British Isles.

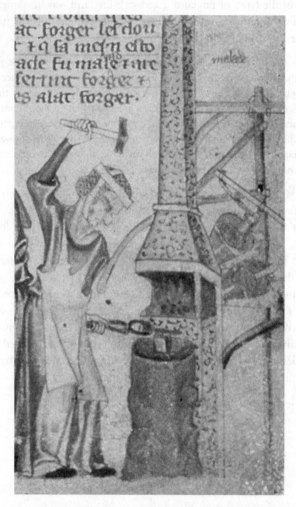

Plate 3 A smith busy at his forge, as illustrated in the Holkham Bible, c.1325–1330. BL Add MS 47682. © The British Library.

The quality of life

Gervase Rosser

On a May morning in the latter part of the fourteenth century, a poet slept on the Malvern hills in south-west Worcestershire and saw in a vision 'a fair field full of folk': the inhabitants of this island. The populous scene which William Langland (c.1325–c.1388) evoked, drawing upon his waking experience, was dynamic and complex. We may be surprised, looking back over 600 years, to encounter such a diversity of crafts and trades, linked together in so intricate a network of economic relations. Two insights into the economy of that time may be learned more directly from the poet of *Piers Plowman* than from more quantifiable but less eloquent data. First, Langland saw production stimulated by patterns of consumption, in a relationship which may strike us as only too familiar in a later age. Toiling ploughmen provide bread, which greedy consumers then squander. The shopper in town is assailed by the blandishments of alewives, butchers, and cooks crying 'Hot pies! hot!' Cloth-workers and tailors feed upon the social ambition of new money. Entertainers tell stories, widening and exploiting a market for leisure. Preachers abound, selling salvation, peddling paradise to the credulous; some of these publicists are virtuous, though fewer than appear so. For the second of Langland's insights is that all of these people inhabit a world of appearances—yet one which is none the less real; and here, too, we may recognize ourselves. Material 'goods'—clothes and money and things—crowd into *Piers Plowman*, yet they have no value in themselves; only in the perception of observers do they acquire significance. Within the first few lines the poet contrasts the ascetic, property-less life chosen by anchoresses and hermits with that of businessmen. Of the latter he remarks, 'they achieve more, as it seems to our eyes that such men prosper'. Since the world judges by superficialities, one's identity depends upon one's trappings: whether those of a fine courtier commanding respect, of a tattered beggar in quest of alms, or of anything between. Possessions are deployed as symbols by which to lay claim to a certain status, to legitimize social distinctions, to justify—and hence to veil—exploitation. The way of the world is epitomized, in the poet's view, by the false pardoner who, equipped with forged papal indulgences, profits from his audience's will to believe him capable of shortening their time in purgatory, so that they 'come up on their knees to kiss his bulls'. Langland's concern is to condemn what he sees as the evil of all 'false seeming'. We do not have to agree with his moral stance (although we might do so), but we can acknowledge that he offers a convincing analysis of how material resources were used in his day to create the divisions and the bonds of society. Wealth, economy, and prosperity have no autonomous existence, but acquire significance as human actors employ them to construct social relationships with one another. This is the sense in which we should understand the saying, then already current, that 'it is always seen nowadays, that money maketh the man'.

A distinctive world

On first encounter, therefore, this fourteenth-century world strikes a chord of recognition in the historian of the third millennium. Yet we—who have, as a general rule, more to learn from the difference than from the similarities between cultures—cannot spend long in study of this world without being impressed, even more, by its remoteness from our own. *This* past, at least, is a foreign country. The point needs to be stressed, as prevailing historical views have tended to assimilate this epoch to more recent times. The continuing strength of those views is exemplified in the common description of the period covered by this book. 'The later Middle Ages' suggest a threshold or transition to 'modernity', and in varying ways during the past century and a half of academic research, the fourteenth and fifteenth centuries have been scrutinized for signs of 'pre-capitalism', 'proto-industrialisation', or 'the economy of the market'. That towns, industry, and commerce are indeed to be encountered in fourteenth- and fifteenth-century Britain is insufficient justification for such teleological readings of the past. This is not only because these economic phenomena existed, as yet, only on a very limited scale, although that is a part of the argument. Towns and markets existed in quantities by 1300, but their distribution was uneven and their fortunes during the following two centuries were highly variable. Complex technologies in both agriculture and industry were understood, but their practical application was fitful and small-scale. Concentrations of wealth abounded, yet the employment of investment capital in economic growth is hardly to be found. Wage labour was widespread, but it was far from being conceived as a proletariat; while production remained, even for long after 1500, concentrated in the household. Beyond these significant points about economic scale, however, lies a profounder point about economic culture. As Langland knew, what counts most in a given society is not the availability of certain material resources or economic structures (although these do delimit a certain range of possibilities) but the way in which human beings decide to use them to enable themselves and others to lead more or less rich and rewarding lives. Some modern economists, rediscovering this truth, have turned from measuring average incomes and gross national products to assessing, in a variety of ways, the quality of life. In the belief that this approach promises both to yield a deeper understanding of other cultures, and to provide a surer basis for their comparison with our own, this chapter will turn to a review, which must necessarily be highly selective, of the quality of life in these islands in the fourteenth and fifteenth centuries.

Population and peasantry

What, then, was the experience of the individual who inhabited, in 1300, a small archipelago of islands more densely populated than at any other time in its history before the eighteenth century? The population had (for reasons which are unclear) been growing, at an increasing rate, since the early Middle Ages, and by the early fourteenth century some seven million people were living in Britain, of whom about five million were in England. Notwithstanding a greater concentration in the south and east than towards the north and west, demographic expansion had helped not only to foster a crowding of settlement in such rich lands as the southern Lincoln-shire fens but, even more vigorously, to drive the colonization of new lands in poorer terrain. On the southern slopes of the Scottish Highlands, on ridges high above the Welsh valleys, on the tops of the Peak and Dartmoor and in low-lying County Meath, heath, bracken, woods, and rock yielded to the advance of human settlement. The period of maximum demographic expansion, in the twelfth and thirteenth centuries, has often been described by historians as one of 'growth'. But the bitter experience of hundreds of thousands of people in the years around 1300 gives the lie to such a shallow reading of economic history. A series of crises striking at this period cruelly exposed the lack of development of the British economy at large, and the consequent vulnerability of most individuals. The most terrible disaster was the Great Famine of 1315–17, when probably a tenth of the population died. All regions—England, Ireland and Wales certainly—experienced 'the bad years'. Meanwhile, on some manors in Hampshire, annual death rates in the early fourteenth century were running as high as 50 per cent. The cause was not an absolute excess of people in relation to resources (it has been calculated that the extent of ploughed land should have sufficed to produce suf-ficient bread for an even larger population) but a series of weaknesses which short-term difficulties, such as bad weather and crop failure, could render fatal. The demographic trend in the early fourteenth century was still upward, but at the local level contrary shocks were experienced in many parts even before the advent of the Black Death in 1348. Disease also struck at animal populations at this period, often with catastrophic effect upon the small-scale peasant economy. Moreover, particular storms aside, the British climate turned a little cooler from the end of the thirteenth century until around 1500. Yet, terrible as the combined effects of these extraneous forces were, they were greatly intensified by prevailing social structures, which seriously lowered the resistance of the peasantry who made up 90 per cent of the population.

The life chances of the early fourteenth-century peasantry were, in general, poor. Demographic expansion in many areas had led to a fragmentation of land holdings to the point where self-sufficiency was impossible. In parts of Norfolk (admittedly the most densely populated part of the British countryside) around 1300,

three-quarters of the tenants of the land held less than five acres—
whereas ten acres would have been the minimum for a household to
be able to feed itself. In any case, as rents rose with the increasing
pressure on land, and as the English and Scottish crowns increased
their own fiscal pressures in order to fund foreign wars, peasants were
increasingly compelled to sell much of their crops in the market,
simply in order to raise the necessary cash. Much has been made, in
recent scholarship, of the commercialization that already marked the
British economy by 1300. But since the hundreds of markets scattered
unevenly across the countryside served largely to enable increasingly
impoverished peasants to subsidise the extravagant consumption of a
tiny minority of landlords, it does not appear that the marketplace
yet represented a significant source of economic growth. In these
circumstances, it is not surprising to find families near Glastonbury
forcing their children out of the homestead to become servants in
husbandry to their better-off neighbours. Landless wage labourers of
this kind were certainly becoming numerous in other areas for long
before the demographic losses of the fifteenth century which in the
past have often been identified as bringing them into being. Other
peasants in this climate sold their land, thereby turning themselves
into hired hands. The very active peasant market in land at this time
should be seen for what it was: the route by which small farmers,
responding to a particular bad harvest or the loss of a cow to
murrain, gradually and reluctantly parted with their holdings. While
personal mobility was doubtless attractive to some, detachment from
ancestral land also brought risks and anxieties which should not be
underestimated. To say the least, personal hardship could come
equally to the half of the peasantry who were personally free as to the
half who, as villeins, were bound to their lords. Another means to
generate cash in the short term was through credit, which was often
available within the village from wealthier tenants—who thereby
established their own power over their neighbours—but which
tended to dry up in hard times. These difficulties could be com-
pounded by shortage of currency, such as was experienced repeatedly
throughout the later Middle Ages when silver became scarce, and
surrogate, token coinage entered into widespread use. All of these
circumstances encouraged a growing differentiation of prosperity
amongst the peasantry. Lords appear to have been content to witness
the loss of poorer serfs, to the advantage of a minority of more

Map 3 Movement of labour for the building of Welsh castles, 1282–3.
Source: A. Taylor, *Studies in Castles and Castle-Building* (Hambledon, 1985).

successful tenants who consolidated more extensive and efficient holdings at the expense of the rest.

Peasant farmers were often highly knowledgeable about their land and its productivity, and in East Anglia around 1300 could be found diversifying their crops and improving their outputs by more intensive manuring. Nonetheless, weakness is apparent in the small size of medieval farm animals, compared to those both of the Roman and of later periods, which suggests malnutrition; crop productivity was relatively low; and there is some evidence that by the early 1300s the soil was showing signs of having been progressively leached of vital goodness. In general terms, there was simply not enough manure produced to fertilize the cultivated lands effectively. Yet, the economic system being largely divided into single family landholdings, organized to enable the profits to be creamed off by an unproductive class of landlords, the potential for serious investment and expansion was negligible. Meanwhile, these hard times bred criminality, as the incidence of illegal gleaning in the fields after harvest, and of unjust profiteering from inflated food prices, increased on various manors such as Brigstock, Northamptonshire; economic tensions have also been blamed for social violence in contemporary Scotland; and in much of post-conquest Wales, and in parts of Ireland too, the assertion of English lordship over forests and mills, tenantry and rural trade, was deeply resented. The quality of health at the social level of the majority of the peasantry was low, and worsening. At this time in the West Midland village of Halesowen, richer tenants entering into land for the first time had a further life expectancy of twenty to thirty years; poorer residents could look forward only to ten more years before death.

Such bleak generalizations call for some qualification. The ability of lords to exploit their tenants was significantly affected by the structure of the manor. Where manor and settlement coincided, as they commonly did in the Midlands, the weight of lordship could be heavy. Where the multiple fragmentation of the land had broken this neat relationship, creating open settlements typically divided between several manors, as was the case in East Anglia, the hand of the lord could be much lighter. The manor itself, as an instrument of social and economic organization, was absent from the western parts of Wales and Ireland and from northern Scotland. In these areas of lower population density, where a little more pasture could always be taken in for sowing if the need for bread required it, the early fourteenth century was characterized by far less tension over resources than was the case in the south and south-east of England. For whereas peasant holdings in East Anglia were generally no bigger than two hectares, in the west and north peasant farms often ran to twelve hectares. There were other possible responses to pressure on food supply, including recourse to eating birds and animals, such as the rabbits which became a particular feature of the sandy parts of the East Anglian Breckland. On the other hand, both the Welsh and the Scottish Marches saw endemic violence in the later thirteenth and early fourteenth centuries, with serious consequences for the local economy. Thus when, after 1282, English immigrants were attracted to the new lordship of Denbigh, created in north-east Wales by Edward I, some Welsh proprietors were expelled from their lands and not all were compensated with property elsewhere—and those that were often received poorer or less accessible land. In 1322, when a Scottish army swept through Embleton, near Cockermouth, the lord of the manor was killed and almost half of the manor's peasant holdings were burned and destroyed. Moreover, the state of communications was not such as to make it easy to relieve such localities struck by violence; networks of roads and markets were a good deal more efficient in south-east England than anywhere else in fourteenth-century Britain or in Ireland. Despite the qualifications, the overwhelming impression of rural society in the early fourteenth century is of real or feared shortage, and of mounting anxieties. Over the whole region, the extremes of deprivation are likely to have been experienced in the areas of most intensive settlement.

Plague and population

Into this already tense and unequal world there irrupted, in 1348, the horror of plague. In the first outbreak alone, between a quarter and two-fifths of the total population of Britain died; in Ireland, the colonists' settlements in the east may have been hit hardest. In certain villages in Hampshire, Cambridgeshire, and Worcestershire, the death rate was 50 per cent. The impact of this catastrophe upon both economy and society was complex, but certainly enormous. Nor did the 'divine scourge' rest with this single ghastly visitation: in the 1360s and 1370s it returned, bringing local destruction sometimes on an even greater scale than the first time. Moralists claimed that few were spared; once more, however, social circumstances significantly affected the experience of the Black Death. Calmer observers noted that the aristocracy escaped more readily than their inferiors from the pestilence. An eyewitness in Aberdeen noted that 'this sickness befell people everywhere, but especially the middling and lower classes, rarely the great'. At Oxford the wealthier citizens, likewise, who possessed country properties, retreated to these and so evaded death. Less prosperous townspeople, packed as they were into unhealthy tenements (a group of twenty-seven properties in Norwich in 1333 was occupied by some 250 people), were sitting targets for the plague: the victims less of bacilli than of social injustice. On the other hand, in Wales 'the Great Mortality' (as it was known) cut seignorial incomes dramatically. In the short term, the economic effects of the plague were modified by the number of landless people who, if they survived the epidemics, came forward to enter vacant landholdings. Moreover, the population went some way to regenerate itself, so that by 1390 it would appear that in some places the pre-plague level had been almost recovered. But in the first decades of the following century there are clear signs throughout Britain and Ireland of empty tenements and abandoned holdings, indicating that some force, presumably endemic disease, was grinding the population down to a level in 1450 which was perhaps little more than half that of 1300. Given that the monks of Canterbury Cathedral priory were evidently recruited from a population—and that not the least privileged—which had a life expectancy at birth in the mid-fifteenth century of only twenty-two years, the prospects facing most of the contemporary peasantry would appear to have been grim. Not until the 1470s would the first signs of demographic recovery appear; and in some places renewed growth was delayed well into the sixteenth century. It seems, therefore, that the century from 1350 to 1450 was a watershed in the history of these islands.

Yet the precise impact of population change upon the living in late medieval Britain is difficult to assess. During the past century, historical accounts have tended to be very positive. It has been said that the thinning of the population created greater prosperity for the survivors, and even that some of these exploited new opportunities to create the basis for a capitalist 'take-off' of the economy in the early modern period. Yet if we retain our focus on the quality of life, it is hard to escape a sense that the century and a half after 1350 was for many a hard time to be alive. Although delayed marriage by women entering the workforce may have depressed fertility at this time, the principal reason for the evident slump in the population level in the fifteenth century is most likely to be recurrent disease, a view which gains support from the frequent references to 'plague' in contemporary chronicles. Moreover, in bad harvest years, like the 1430s, the poor—even in the south-east of England—could find themselves reduced to eating bread made of ferns and bracken. Nor did population losses make it easy, as has sometimes been assumed, for servile tenants to throw off their chains. On the contrary, with the help of the monarchs, lords in various parts of Britain tightened the screws upon their surviving labourers. Typical conservative landlords were the Benedictine monks of Westminster Abbey, who continued until the end of the fourteenth century to insist on the full performance of labour services on their estates, concentrated in the Home Counties, notwithstanding tenant deaths from plague. Contrary to modern assumptions, the issue was perceived by the monks not in economic terms, but as a question of due reverence for authority. On the other hand, there were some pronounced changes in the conditions of land tenure and management practices. Thus, the abbey of Couper Angus on Tayside was a vigorous and enterprising landlord in the later fifteenth century, though the Scottish writer John Major (1467–1550) came to the general conclusion at the end of the century that 'the country people [of Scotland] have no permanent holdings, but hire only . . . at the pleasure of the lord of the soil'.

The loosening of bondage, which did come about gradually over the course of the later Middle Ages, was no automatic consequence of the demographic recession and labour shortage. The emancipation of the serfs in the manorialized parts of Britain was a social, cultural, and economic achievement, often won by the peasants themselves in the teeth of resistance. The economic consequences of population change were thus determined as much by cultural and political considerations as by calculations of profit and loss. The peasants' desire for freedom may often have been more ideologically than materially driven, as is suggested by the passionate outburst of an old bondman of the abbot of Malmesbury in the 1430s, whose ambition was to achieve freedom for his family before he died: 'and if he might bring that aboute it would be more joifull to him than any worldelie goode.' To realize his dream by purchasing his liberty, he borrowed the huge sum of £10 from another peasant.

Yet some historians have felt convinced that a few, at least, of those peasants who benefited from cheaper leases to expand their holdings in the fifteenth century were evincing a fresh, capitalistic attitude towards their farms, and were thus sowing the seeds of a new phase of economic growth. One who has been advanced as a candidate for this role is Roger Heritage (d. 1495), who held the demesne of Burton Dassett, Warwickshire. The inventory of his goods compiled at his death lists two teams of oxen, two ploughs, 40 cattle, 12 horses and 860 sheep, together with a number of servants. His six-room house and his large quantity of pewter vessels declare him to be, in fifteenth-century terms, a 'yeoman': a comfortable peasant who prefigures the gentleman farmer of a later age. Of Heritage's modest prosperity there is no doubt; whether he represents a new force in the social and economic landscape is debatable. For one thing, such relatively rich peasants are to be found as easily in 1300 as in 1500. For another, his motives remain elusive. It is true that, as an economic enterprise, his farm depended upon hired labour. But it is no less true that neither Heritage nor any other yeoman of his day could afford to expand much, if at all, beyond the second plough team: the wages bill would have precluded it. While it is true that the conditions were in place for a more flexible market in land, the capitalist investor and the proletariat were both still centuries away. In the observable behaviour of such a man as Heritage, as of the similarly *arriviste* Paston family in East Anglia, and other substantial peasants in Scotland and Wales at the same period, there is little to distinguish them from the narrow-minded, grasping landlords of previous generations; only a residual commitment to finding harbingers of 'modernity' in the late medieval period could persuade one otherwise.

It has been suggested that one consequence of labour shortages in the post-plague period was the participation of many more women in the workforce. It is certain that women are found in almost every economic sector in the later Middle Ages; but it is less easy to be sure that they had any greater scope in this period than previously; still less that any increased role for women in the late medieval economy had a lasting significance. The prevailing pragmatism which governed attitudes to female work is epitomized in the witness of a Malmesbury Abbey chronicler in the 1350s: 'By the time the plague ceased at the divine command it had caused such a shortage of servants that men could not be found to work the land, and women and children had to be used to drive ploughs and carts, which was unheard of.' Indeed, on the manor of Alrewas in Staffordshire, women tended to dominate less specialized crafts and trades rather than specialized or capital-intensive ones. Insofar as need for their work gave them an opening in the fifteenth century, the subsequent recovery of population levels and renewed pressure upon employment by men forced the women once more into a secondary position. Regrettably, and notwithstanding recent claims to the contrary, this was neither a turning point nor a golden age for women in British society.

From arable to pasture

Of economic adjustments to late medieval circumstances, the one most commonly identified in all parts of these islands by historians is a shift from arable farming (because costly in labour, and less profitable in a context of reduced demand for basic foodstuffs) to pasture. The trend was a real one, but its impact varied across the territory. In the upland zones, including the west of Ireland and the north of Scotland, a predominantly pasture economy already prevailed, with transhumance to high pastures in the summer months. In woodland areas, there was usually scope to enclose additional sheep- or cattle-folds without affecting existing agriculture. Elsewhere the change was rarely wholesale. Animal manure was ploughed into arable, so that the farming types were ideally complementary. And the demand for meat was limited, after all; the change in general was made to save production costs, not to make unprecedented profits, which in any case, in a diminished market, were not there to be made. But in a previously arable-intensive area like the West Midlands, such a change was indeed apparent, as landlords or their lessees took a succession of economic decisions which transformed the landscape, from perhaps 10 per cent of pasture land in the 1340s to 33 per cent in the 1490s. It transformed social relations, also. Here we find that on the Catesby estate in south-east Warwickshire, arable tenants were evicted around 1400 to create a vast pasturage for cows and (by 1476) 2,742 sheep. For the same reason, at Billesley Trussell, near Stratford-upon-Avon, the earl of Warwick's chaplain, John Rous, briefly recorded that 'all the inhabitants were expelled'. The social costs of enclosure in this area during the fifteenth century were lamented at the time by Rous, who denounced 'the plague of avarice' of greedy landlords. He made the telling point that thoughtless abandonment of grain production left the poor defenceless; the argument was borne out when in the winter of 1520–21 Coventry suffered a major food crisis, which the region could not relieve.

It is fair to observe that, in at least a few instances, a landlord's decision to enclose followed the evident decay of the settlement in question. The wholesale and abrupt abandonment of villages was less common at this time than a piecemeal process of readjustment. Thus, if at Little Newton, Northamptonshire, the eighteen families of 1347 had by 1449 fallen to only four, the parish church nonetheless endured to become the new focus for the adjacent settlement of Great Newton (whose own church was allowed to decay). However, a great number of settlements did, over time, disappear in such marginal areas as the high fells of Cumbria, the lowland parts of Wales like southern Glamorgan, and more particularly the formerly heavily overpopulated zones of southern and eastern England. In the towns also, population losses created more space. Tenements in multiple occupancy in 1300 fell into neglect and in some cases were cleared to create gardens or, in the case of Oxford and Cambridge, colleges. The overcrowding of the towns in the mid-fourteenth century had exacerbated the effects of the plague; the indirect effect upon health of this clearing of the air must surely have been beneficial.

There is a little evidence that diet improved with the reduction of pressure on resources, although it might be simplistic to assume that meat consumption, which appears to have increased in the fifteenth century, was always regarded at the time as a sign of improved living standards. Because of labour costs, bread and cheese might in some parts have been a more costly source of energy than certain kinds of meat. Nor is it easy to be sure, given the scarcity of data, that material standards of living improved in any other respect in the post-plague world. From the piecemeal survivals of domestic timber houses, notably in Essex, the Midlands, and the Welsh March, there is some indication of the emergence of a more solid and spacious peasant, or yeoman's, farmhouse—though in Gaelic Ireland many houses remained insubstantial structures in the sixteenth century. Peasant inventories add a little substance to the picture, showing a few creature comforts such as bedlinen and pewter vessels in the fifteenth century. Meanwhile, because wages rose, labourers have been thought to be fortunate; but it could be argued that to be landless was never a desirable condition in the Middle Ages, for all that many were more or less compelled by circumstances to take this course.

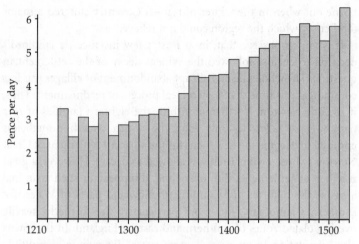

Figure 1 Daily wage rates of a carpenter in England, 1210–1520.
C. Dyer, *Making a Living in the Middle Ages* (New Haven, 2002).

The family

We should beware of idealizing an imagined former stability which was supposedly subverted with the onset of 'modernity'. None the less, the generations after the late thirteenth century in many parts of Britain witnessed an intensification of personal mobility which was to have profound consequences for family life. The study of family structures during the fourteenth and fifteenth centuries has revealed that this was for many a period of significant change in the experience of family life. Already in 1300 a distinction was apparent between those parts of these islands—still by far the majority—in which an individual could expect to count among his or her neighbours relatively large numbers of family members, and those—notably in the crowded East Anglian counties—where personal mobility was so common as to have greatly reduced the contact with kin. Comparison between villages in the West Midlands and Norfolk around 1300 illustrates this marked difference between levels of local kin density. Yet by 1450, after the disruptions of mid-century, the Midlands villages were also manifesting a fragmentation of the family, as members moved away, either forced off the land or deliberately seeking better wages elsewhere, perhaps in the towns. Similarly, in the Essex village of Birdbrook, in the course of the fourteenth century a formerly close-knit family élite of community officials was replaced by a far more diverse body of newcomers. At the poorest levels, the household itself came under pressure to contract, as has been documented in the Polden Hills of Somerset around 1300. In Celtic society, which in 1300 was still very strongly marked by family and kindred loyalties, the family was also coming under pressure in these centuries. For example, in Wales during the first half of the fourteenth century, the English conquest had eroded the old, kindred-based settlements of free peasants, as English lords confiscated hereditary holdings, imposed cash rents, and introduced new markets in planted towns which displaced traditional patterns of negotiation.

The effects upon the quality of life of these substantial changes within the family invite further thought and investigation. It is striking, for example, that when the English royal government conducted an enquiry into fraternities in 1389, by far the greatest concentration of these, to judge from the 500 surviving returns, lay in East Anglia; hardly any are recorded in the West Midlands. The fifteenth century, on the other hand, produced evidence of a great number of such societies throughout most parts of Britain. Guilds or fraternities, voluntary clubs having a variety of male and female participants, offered to their members, amongst other attractions, a sense of surrogate family membership. In the formation of such guilds it may, therefore, be possible to recognize a common response to a sense of dislocation or vulnerability which can be identified in the crowded manors of East Anglia by 1300, but which was intensified elsewhere by increased personal mobility consequent upon population losses after 1350. In other ways, also, means were found to substitute for what was becoming a less coherent extended family, weakened both by migration and by increased mortality. Contracts made by elderly tenants to secure their retirement from work, which around 1300 were usually made with younger family members, by 1400 were commonly entered into as business relationships with non-relatives.

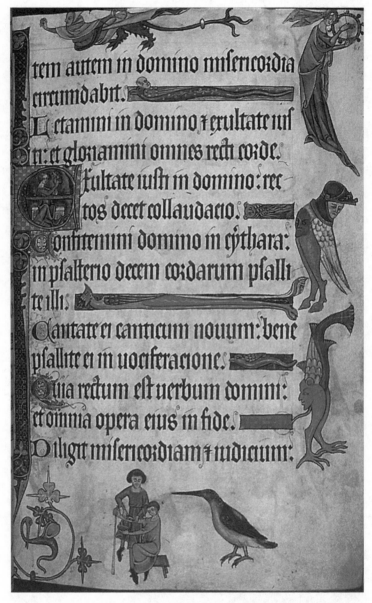

Plate 4 A doctor drawing blood from the arm of a sick patient, a common method of treating illness: one of the illustrations of English life from the early fourteenth-century Luttrell Psalter, written for Sir Geoffrey Luttrell (d. 1323) of Irnham, Lincolnshire. BL Add MS 42130. © The British Library.

A commercial culture

Could it be said more generally that human relationships came to be seen at this period as threatened by an all-pervasive culture of commerce? Such a claim would be controversial, for money had spread throughout society well before 1300, and few in Britain were untouched at that date by the market. Social distinctions within the peasantry and between townsmen already rested upon differences of wealth and economic enterprise. Nonetheless, an impression that the transformative power of money came to be widely debated in secular society in the later fourteenth century may have some validity. In the aftermath of the Black Death, moralists were quick to condemn those peasants and artisans who tried to capitalize on the labour shortage by demanding higher wages: 'The workers were so above themselves and so bloody-minded that they took no notice of the king's command. If anyone wished to hire them he had to submit to their demands,' recorded Henry Knighton (died c. 1396), a canon of Leicester. As lords turned to the crown for backing, workers not only intensified the pressure for better rewards but began in some cases to apply their new-found prosperity to apeing their superiors. The sumptuary legislation of the period, which vainly attempted to check (for example) the wearing of furs or fashionably pointed shoes by craftsmen and women, bears witness to the contemporary social reading of economic change. Langland was not the only contemporary observer to feel that in circumstances such as these, cash threatened to dissolve sincerity, obscure truth, and subvert the quality of life. Chaucer's *Shipman's Tale* offers another critique of this late fourteenth-century world. The plot is triggered by a merchant's wife, who desires fine clothes and so gets into debt. A single sum of money which is then loaned and borrowed becomes the fateful means whereby a marriage and two friendships are corrupted. The merchant himself is so caught up in reckoning his profits in his counting-house that he loses all human contact:

> His bookes and his bagges many oon
> He leith biforn hym on his counting-bord.
> Ful riche was his tresor and his hord,
> For which ful faste his countour-dore he shette;

> And eek he nolde that no man sholde hym lette
> Of his accountes, for the meene tyme;
> And thus he sit til it was passed pryme.

The cost of the merchant's social isolation is piquantly demonstrated when, even as he sits locked away with his gold, his wife makes up to his friend, the monk Dan John. She has ceased to love her husband, and tells Dan John with piercing irony:

> ... he is noght worth at al
> In no degree the value of a flye.

Like Langland, although with less explicit hostility, Chaucer observes the ways in which social values can be transformed by money— which itself is nothing. Whether one liked it or not, the currency of the commercial culture, as a rival value system whose centre was hollow, affected the quality of life throughout late medieval British society.

It is important to emphasize, however, that the incursion of the market into every corner of the land did not mark the transition from one phase of human history to another. Rather, different modes of exchange were practised concurrently, and historians would be well advised to reject the conventional teleology which sees the cash nexus as more 'developed' than other, allegedly 'primitive', forms of social negotiation. Alongside the many dozens of royally licensed markets scattered unevenly across the British Isles by the early fourteenth century, there existed unknowable quantities of unofficial places of exchange. Here, for example, enterprising cornmongers might meet on a quiet stretch of the River Severn to complete major transactions without having to pay the tolls required in the monopolistic borough markets of Gloucester or Bristol. Deals struck at crossroads and in remote country inns were never registered with the authorities, and remained part of the 'black economy'. Nowhere was the political purpose of the official markets more transparent, and their rejection more public, than in the English boroughs planted in Wales. Most towns in medieval Wales were of English foundation, and the English made up the vast majority of their inhabitants. By many of the Welsh they were both rejected as unnecessary and hated as the symbols of imperialism. Some of these towns suffered extensive damage in Owain Glyn Dŵr's revolt at the start of the fifteenth century, 'for that they stood for the king of England'. Just as vulnerable were the towns of Ireland, mostly of Anglo-Irish foundation; they suffered from

Gaelic pressure and economic misfortune—though, as happened in Wales, some of the indigenous peoples were not averse to acquiring property within their walls.

Beyond the circumvention of official trade, an infinite variety of exchanges was conducted without any reference to the market whatever. The world of the guilds is again relevant here, for their meetings provided occasions for the negotiation of private business arrangements, often no doubt without the need for money to change hands. The mutual trust fostered in the guilds was an essential ingredient in a diversity of social and economic relations which marched beside, often without touching, the public procedures of the marketplace. Guild funds sometimes functioned as banks, as in some Suffolk guilds of the fifteenth century which made loans, at preferential rates of interest, to male and female members. A great deal of work, too, not least in childcare, will have been arranged as a straight exchange of services. In such ways a shadow economy was appropriated to create social credit and to build human relations in a broader sphere.

A similar argument may be made about the investment of merchant capital in the larger towns. The criticism has often been made by economic historians that the successful medieval merchant typically used his gains, not to pump-prime capitalistic growth, but to buy his way into a more elevated lifestyle, thereby, it is alleged, merely propping up a retrograde social order. One of the greatest of all historians, Fernand Braudel, indeed, described the mercantile acquisition of country estates and coats of arms as 'the betrayal of the bourgeoisie'. Yet closer consideration of mercantile strategies may suggest that the claim is short-sighted. For one thing, merchants who bought land rarely abandoned the financial practices to which they owed their wealth. Adam Fraunceys in fourteenth-century London, and the Cely family in the fifteenth, exemplify the pattern of investment in country houses close to the city which symbolized a certain status, served as a security for loans, and was completely compatible with the continuance of a metropolitan financial career. What is perhaps called into question is the modern assumption that the sole objective of such men should have been to generate ever greater financial profits. Chaucer's fictive merchant is the victim of this very obsession; but historical merchants can be found making more creative use of their material resources, investing in the symbolic capital of urban and rural property in order to consolidate their public standing and political influence. Typically, Adam Fraunceys, who had bought a fine out-of-town house at Edmonton, nonetheless chose to be buried in London, in the nunnery of St Helen's Bishopsgate, where he had, after the manner of a knight in a country church, founded a chantry and so would be both admired and gratefully remembered by later generations of Londoners. Likewise, Adam Forester (d. 1405), a prominent Edinburgh merchant, acquired substantial estates outside the city, whilst the Redes of Carmarthen and Bristol were an acquisitive commercial family in Carmarthenshire, equally at home in both towns. The letters of the Cely family, meanwhile, underline at every point the crucial importance of credit. The scale of credit in international commerce in the later Middle Ages was enormous. The ledger of Gilbert Maghfield, a merchant of the time of Richard II, shows how iron was brought from northern Spain, woad dye from Genoa, wine from Bordeaux, and herrings from the North Sea, all on a dazzling fine mesh of credit. In that world, the creditworthy businessman was one who had appropriated at least some of the trappings of the old aristocracy, with their connotations (however misleading) of durability, chivalry, and trust.

To question whether medieval people should, or could, have pursued the god of profit further than they did is not to deny the possibility that, within the social and economic structures of the period, there existed at least some potential for future economic growth. Research on this theme has hitherto been largely concentrated on agrarian 'proto-capitalism'. But although British towns until relatively recently have been treated as immature and marginal to an essentially rural economy, a very different view can now be sustained. Although the British Isles contained only one centre, London, on a metropolitan scale, the hundreds of smaller towns (many containing just 1,000 or even 500 people) which existed especially in England, lowland Scotland, and the anglicized areas of Wales and Ireland represented a major potential resource. Because the majority of smaller urban centres in medieval Britain lacked constitutional independence, they have in the past been deprecated both by British historians of the rural sector and by continental students of the great city-states of late medieval Flanders and Italy. Paradoxically, however, the political situation, and specifically the relative weakness of such provincial British centres as Glasgow, York, Bristol, and Cork, were a key to the region's economic potential. In the Flemish and

Map 4 The overseas trade of Drogheda in the later Middle Ages.
Source: T. B. Barry, *The Archeology of Medieval Ireland* (London, 1987).

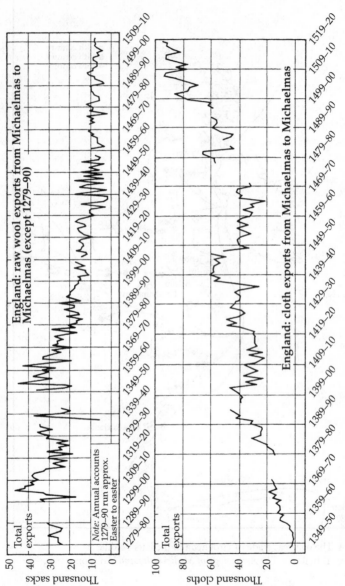

Figure 2 Comparative trends in the export of wool and cloth from England in the later Middle Ages.
Source: E. M. Carus-Wilson and O. Coleman, *England's Export Trade 1275–1547* (Oxford, 1963).

Italian cases, voracious cities devoured their hinterlands without check, creating short-term wealth but long-term economic stagnation. In Britain, however, the authority of the Scottish and English crowns was more than sufficient to contain the larger cities and towns within bounds, leaving outside them far greater freedom for the creation, by lords or by their enterprising tenants, of urban and industrial initiatives in the countryside.

If the sources of England's and Scotland's precocious 'take-off' into economic growth in the eighteenth century are to be traced back to the medieval period, particular attention should be given to this feature. Indeed, certain individual cases of late medieval small-town prosperity have long been noticed, such as the cloth-weaving centres of the Pennines or Castle Combe in Wiltshire, or Saffron Walden in Essex, which owed its rise to the dye used, once again, in cloth production. Paisley, founded in 1488, developed as a cloth-making burgh, whilst in Wales regional administrative centres like Carmarthen, Brecon, and Denbigh retained an importance when other towns were losing theirs. And in Ireland, there were similar contrasts in fortunes between, for example, the declining towns of Wexford and Cork and the relatively buoyant Waterford, Carrickfergus in Ulster, and, of course, Dublin, which was the centre of royal government and the largest port. On the other hand, a review of the British economy at the end of the period covered by this book can find remarkably little to celebrate in terms of financial prosperity and expansion. Most of the larger towns were economically depressed, and lacking in purpose. As Langland was cited as noting at the outset, economic life was largely driven by consumers; yet these did not yet represent a sufficiently large market for any product to make heavy investment in industry even remotely viable. Indeed, the demographic depression, from which many areas only began properly to emerge well into the sixteenth century, acted as an additional brake on entrepreneurial initiatives. So the household remained the unit of production, and production remained small-scale. Nor, of course, was the upturn in the population, when it eventually came, of itself any guarantee of prosperity; as it turned out, the early modern period was to see at least as much economic hardship as had any previous epoch.

At no stage was the medieval economy transformed by technological innovation. Modest technological initiatives there were, yet it is striking that they were more typically applied, not to improve efficiency when the economy was under pressure, as in the years around 1300, but rather to make life more comfortable in a time of economic stagnation in the fifteenth century. An instance would be the adoption by many peasant lessees of horses to work the land in place of oxen. Many of the English peasantry, having gained their hard-won freedom from serfdom, desired nothing better in the later medieval period than to enjoy at leisure some of the time (between a tenth and a half of the total available) which they had previously been compelled to devote to ploughing and weeding the lord's ground. A study of medieval workers in the lead-mining industry has revealed, similarly, that miners—who were usually seasonal or part-time employees—worked just hard enough for the minimum period required to make a living wage, and then stopped. The owners of land evinced a concern for a good return, but were evidently content to stop short of maximizing their profits. The absence of a work ethic or profit motive is, so far as one can tell, entirely characteristic of the generality of the late medieval population of these islands. To claim to identify, and then to build up, exceptional individual cases is arguably deeply misleading. Given the choice, as many were in the fifteenth century—a quality-of-life option *par excellence*—most peasants or artisans, who together made up over 90 per cent of the population, preferred to work just hard enough to keep their families and to fund what was probably an increasing range of leisure choices.

Leisure

Modern assessments of the quality of life take notice of the possible choices of leisure activities available to the individual. Nothing is more impressive than the seizure of the chance to gain freedom by the serfs of late medieval Britain. But no less striking is their evident preference for leisure rather than for maximal profits. One symptom of this tendency is the commercialization of leisure itself, exemplified in the proliferation, towards the close of the fifteenth century, of public archery butts and bowling greens—or again the import through Newcastle upon Tyne of Flemish tennis balls and printed playing cards. Another are the signs, in personal testaments, of more widespread literacy, book ownership, and reading. And yet another may be the exceedingly rich evidence of parish life at this period. The economic recession of the mid-fifteenth century coincided with a period of very little substantial building across Britain as a whole; yet in a few instances the generous commitment of time and money on the part of lay congregations produced, against the material odds, a set of stained glass windows, an opulent rood screen, a series of chantry chapels, or a new belltower. It appears that the laity concerned were prepared to devote a larger slice of a smaller economic cake to the communal life of the parish. So, beyond leisure, one may add participation in the life of the community to the indicators of an enhanced quality of life as it was experienced in at least some cases.

Charity and change

This all too fleeting account of some aspects of the quality of late medieval life began by underlining the vulnerability of the contemporary population. At its close, a word is called for on the theme of charity. It has been alleged that to an early, collective, and indiscriminate approach to charitable aid there succeeded in the later Middle Ages a more calculated and prejudicial treatment. However, the evidence indicates instead that already in the thirteenth century villagers and townspeople were fully prepared to apply their own assessment of need in response to appeals for charity, and that they gave priority to the local poor and to people like themselves. As the pious laywoman of King's Lynn, Margery Kempe, put it around 1400: 'It was more alms to help those whom they knew well to be well disposed folk and their own neighbours, than other strangers whom they knew not.' This sense of a primary obligation to one's own neighbours has been deprecated by modern historians; yet its common sense is rooted in an evident consciousness of the power of economic relationships to build social ones: a recurring theme of this chapter. Both the givers and the receivers of charity saw its power to preserve the standing of the individual and of the community alike. Hence the emphasis in countless guild statutes upon helping first the members of the society; and hence the requirement of a good reputation for admission to many contemporary hospitals and almshouses. Poverty was for all too many a matter of intolerable deprivation and suffering. Yet to the extent that it was identified as an indictment of the local community, it could elicit some response. Once more, economic behaviour was guided by perceptions of the quality of life.

The fourteenth and fifteenth centuries saw great changes in the local and individual response to economic circumstances. The adaptability and creativity of the inhabitants of these islands are apparent in many ways, from the means (not always violent on the national scale of the English Peasants' Revolt of 1381, yet always contested) by which personal freedom was wrested from lords to the introduction, at least on a modest scale, of fresh techniques and new products in industry (such, to mention a single example, as the making of cloth caps, which from around 1500 would become a staple of English cloth manufacture). Yet it is not evident that the potential for future economic growth was significantly greater in 1500 than it had been in 1300. The small scale of production, and the limits to demand imposed in part by the depressed level of the population, were significant constraints upon economic expansion. On the other hand, the period witnessed the advent, for perhaps the majority of the population, of a less high-pressure economic environment, within which individuals could make an enhanced range of life choices. This picture should not be romanticized, not least because life expectancy appears to have been significantly worse at the end than at the beginning of the period. Moreover, even at its best, choice may be experienced as a liability as much as a liberation. The descendants of many a villein found themselves, at the close of the fifteenth century, enjoying new-found personal freedoms yet, as tenants by the new 'copyhold' title, in some ways more vulnerable than ever—as was already being demonstrated in cases of eviction by lords creating sheep-runs or fashionable parks symbolic of their social pretensions. The wage labourers, who, although a significant presence in the economy in 1300, had become more numerous two centuries later, benefited at the later date from improved wages in relation to the cost of living. But they too had to weigh the gains of liberty against the loss of that stability which could be experienced through the hereditary tenure of land in close proximity to supportive family relatives. The great lords of the land, meanwhile, had suffered a reduction in their standards of living, as their general inflexibility in response to the late medieval changes left them forced to settle for reduced returns from their estates.

Yet for all the attendant hazards, many in the late medieval population experienced the reduced pressure upon resources as an opportunity to extend their range of choice in the conduct of their lives. A cost of the dissolution of the ties which had formerly bound most peasants to the land was a reduction in the available support from networks of kin. But the later fourteenth and fifteenth centuries witnessed, in the creation at the local level of hundreds of new fraternities, a creative response which put in place a surrogate family capable of providing material assistance, political influence, and an environment both for sociability and spiritual life. For some, the material conditions of the fifteenth century provided the chance to acquire fashionable goods as the mark of social aspiration, as conservative critics like Langland and, in Scotland, Robert Henryson (c.1425–c.1506) sharply observed. Yet while economic developments thus gave new life to an old moral debate about possessions, for most people between the small élite of the aristocracy and the larger body of the very poor, late medieval conditions offered scope for meaningful choices in a greater range of fields than had been available to their predecessors in 1300. These choices extended to diet (an improvement in which is likely to have contributed to the eventual abatement of endemic disease and the recovery of population levels from around 1500), housing, and clothes, but also to less material considerations, such as education and the life of the spirit. The evidence for the spread of popular literacy and schooling in the later Middle Ages becomes comprehensible in the context of the reduction of the time which artisan or peasant families had to devote to survival. The elaboration of lay religious lives in the environments of the parish and the guild, which is so richly demonstrated in the century and a half after 1350, needs to be understood, not as an overflow of material prosperity, but as a deliberate experiment in the creation of lives which could be experienced as meaningful. Experiences were too diverse to be reducible to neat generalization. But the conclusion to be drawn from this review is that, in any assessment of the material lives of the people of these islands in the fourteenth and fifteenth centuries, we shall come closer to their own perceptions if we focus, not on supposed evidence for an alleged profit motive, but on a multifaceted consideration of the quality of their lives.

Plate 5 Brass rubbing commemorating John Hawley (d. 1408) and his two wives, Joan and Alice, in St Saviour's church, Dartmouth, Devon, whose chancel he built. Hawley, possibly the model for Chaucer's shipman, was an enterprising merchant and soldier who invested in land, and was mayor and MP for Dartmouth under Richard II and Henry IV. V & A Picture Library.

Ranks of society

Philip Morgan

Social changes

When, in 1381, John Ball preached a sermon at Blackheath on the familiar text, 'Whan Adam dalf, and Eve span, Wo was thanne a gentilman?', he had questioned the existence of social rank and distinctions before the Fall. A century later, likewise using a common idiom, the three hollow-eyed skulls conjured by the Scots poet Robert Henryson asked of the viewer, 'Or quhilk of us kin was gentillar?' But, of life on the mortal sea which lay between the Fall and death there was little doubt. Although medieval societies are popularly seen as stable and straightforwardly hierarchical, social relations in the British Isles in the later Middle Ages were both dynamic and marked by a plethora of distinctions of rank and status which might exhaust the contemporary enumerator as much as they bewilder the present-day observer. 'I am alle wery, Of so many Names to name, Of so many craftes, So many offices, so many servises; I wyll reste me', as the author of an anonymous text printed by William Caxton observed.

Although we shall come to such lists, the immediate problem for the modern reader is that the context of naming or describing in the later Middle Ages was both variable and changing. One of the great changes was in the very number of people who occupied the British Isles. At its medieval peak around 1300 the population of Britain—of whom perhaps as many as 70 per cent were English—may have been around seven millions. Thereafter (as we have seen in Chapter 1), first a period of demographic stress and later a collapse under the impact of the Black Death of 1348 and 1349 reduced the population by between a third and a half. Recovery in mere numbers, inhibited by deteriorating climatic conditions and characterized by widespread low fertility, was slow until the early sixteenth century, and population did not again approach its pre-plague levels until the early seventeenth century. These trends seem to have applied in England, Wales, and Ireland, although levels of plague mortality may have been lower in Scotland, and recovery faster. Intuitively we look for great changes and a new society which must inevitably have arisen after such a catastrophe.

For historians too this collapse of population following the Black Death remains the great fact of the later Middle Ages. But, if the plague stands over the corpse of an old society, there is some doubt as to how long the victim had lain there, and even as to whether this was the fatal blow. In reality many of the features of later medieval society—notably the opportunities afforded by land, service, and labour—had been first mapped in the context not of a collapsing population in the fourteenth century, but of a rising population during the economic expansion of the thirteenth. There were, as in all expanding economies, beneficiaries and victims, amongst whom wealth and status were no longer nor necessarily coincident. A vigorous land market had greatly altered traditional boundaries in agrarian local societies, creating great disparities in wealth amongst those who worked the land. There were increasing opportunities amongst those who sought to prosper by service in the law and at war, and amongst the many who acted occasionally as agents of the state. Increasingly a pattern of royal commissions or appointments, sure indicators of connection and opportunity, may be used to supplement the land transactions which otherwise constitute the known biographies of thousands of knights and esquires. Equally importantly, by 1300 the landless—those who made their livings as hired labourers and as servants, as well as those who were truly destitute—had increased markedly, to perhaps 13 per cent of the whole population. To this now swollen 'labouring' population we might also add that army of parochial stipendiaries, chaplains, and bedesmen and women who made up the growing clerical proletariat of the later medieval Church, mostly men with some status but little wealth. The demographic collapse initiated by the Black Death may have deepened these trends, arrested or diverted others, but the plague was neither the father, mother, nor even midwife to the new society of the later Middle Ages.

Amongst all groups the connection between individuals, land and the locality was greatly weakened, most markedly in those parts of the British Isles which were urbanized and to which the poor and ambitious were often drawn. About 15 per cent of the English population were town dwellers. London, then as now, was an international city, with perhaps 40,000 inhabitants in 1350. Dublin, with a population of around 8,000 at the same moment, was the sixth largest city in the British Isles. There were other Irish towns, principally the ports on the south and east coasts, but in general urban functions thinned greatly from London to the north and west, in Wales, Scotland, Ireland, and northern England. Fewer than a handful of towns had populations above 5,000. Exeter, at about 3,000 souls, was the largest town in the south-west. Edinburgh, if size matters, was a mere provincial town; other Scottish burghs were little more than glorified villages. Oswestry was apparently 'the London of Wales' to its poets, but 'small' and 'tiny' are the more usual epithets applied to Welsh towns. The Black Death meant that there were to be fewer townsmen in the British Isles, but most towns survived; a few continued to prosper. All were marked by a diversity of social ranks, but many were perhaps not socially distinct from their rural hinterlands.

Later medieval Britain, with around 15 per cent of the population over sixty, enjoyed a similar ratio of old to young as today; the norm is reckoned to be around 5–8 per cent. However, male life expectancy, in contrast to our own experience, was higher than female. Such are what might be described as the demographic facts. However long those facts might endure, and they did for most of the later Middle Ages, contemporaries whose opinions survive looked for the world to get better and preferably to return to what it had once been, often employing an archaic vocabulary to recommend what could only ever be anachronistic social policies, and frequently calling on the old world to redress the balance of the new. Such, for example, was the tone of most parliamentary labour legislation from the 1380s into the fifteenth century. It is with such thoughts in mind that we should approach the contemporary official and literary descriptions of social rank. Much of this record was concerned either with personal status—distinguishing between the free and the unfree—or with tenure—that is the terms on which land, the principal resource, was held, and with personal wealth in the form of land or goods. The forms of written record were traditional, but medieval society was perceived as having changed, and changed not necessarily for the better.

Personal status

In the occasional surveys of great and small landholdings, in the statutes and tax lists of states, their agents and the law, and in the frequently homiletic literature of social comment and criticism, social labels would nevertheless appear faithfully to record contemporary inequalities of status, tenure, and wealth. By 1400 many labels in common use had been coined centuries earlier and were now frequently anachronistic. Marginal groups, amongst whom one might include women and children, were also frequently excluded. Outside Gaelic and Gaelicized Ireland, and despite a great regional variety of descriptive terms elsewhere, the British Isles had belonged to a wider European zone of common social organization in which most social relationships had long been negotiated on the basis of lordship, land, or labour. The rise of lordship in the early Middle Ages had brought with it legal definitions of personal status, principally between the free and the unfree: villeins or serfs in England, neyfs in Scotland, betaghs—often Gaelic Irish, in colonial Ireland—and taeogau in Wales. The unfree, as indeed the free, were born to their condition; they were tied to the land and to a lord, and commonly owed labour or other services across the most significant social boundary of the early Middle Ages.

Personal status continued to provide the backcloth against which much of the later medieval record should be read, but personal unfreedom was now in retreat across much of the British Isles, just as slavery had earlier withered away. It had virtually gone from Scotland by 1300 and was a fading concept elsewhere during the next two centuries. By the mid-sixteenth century, English courts treated insults such as calling a man 'a villein knave' as defamation rather than trespass; servility, real or perceived, had become a social rather than a legal disability. Nevertheless, attempts to enforce and even restore villein status had continued as regressive acts of lordly utopianism and in parliamentary legislation throughout the fourteenth and fifteenth centuries.

Estate surveys further labelled their tenants according to the size of their holdings and, to the extent that land was the traditional source of wealth, might be expected to provide a guide to the ranks of rural society. On the estate of Coldingham priory at Fishwick on Tweed about 1300, for example, the 500 acres of peasant arable were shared between sixteen husbandmen, each with a notional thirty-acre holding, and six cottars with six acres each. This distinction between the more substantial peasants and those whose holdings were barely adequate to sustain a family was almost universally repeated in extents and rentals, but such a view of society in Coldingham as elsewhere was probably more imagined than real. Uniform land-holdings had long been interrupted by an active peasant land market, and a man's 'name', whether peasant or gentle, might not adequately communicate his status, or determine the range and quality of his social relationships. More significantly, by 1400 ever greater numbers were also dependent on income from their labour, both the indigent who were dependent on charity and occasional paid work and the ranks of agricultural labourers, and urban and rural crafts-men who rarely featured in traditional surveys. Status and tenure were nevertheless important elements in the negotiation of social relationships.

The judgement of the archbishop of Canterbury's tribunal against customary tenants at Wingham, Kent, who had chosen to perform their historic labour services secretly in 1390 is justly famous, not least because it was illustrated with a drawing in the archbishop's register. Archbishop William Courtenay, indignant that his tenants were ashamed to fulfil their obligations openly, sentenced them to parade like penitents around Wingham church, each carrying a sack of hay and walking barefoot with slow steps. More pragmatic was the advice of Thomas Goding of Ealding, proffered in hope of prompt payment of his fee, to the prior of Christ Church, Canterbury, in the early sixteenth century to search his records, for 'there be bondmen longyng to the manor of Blackham (on the Kent/Sussex border) and they be richemen'. In the 1540s Henry, Lord Stafford, clearly following similar advice, gloated on identifying two of his tenants as bondmen, 'wheche shalbe a good matier for me to sease there lande to my hande and not to sue theym in any courte'.

In response to similar speculative attempts at lordly oppression, unfree tenants on manors across England and Wales sought increasingly to challenge what they perceived as novel, unreasonable, or excessive burdens imposed by lords. The unfree tenants of Penrhosllugwy on Anglesey were to protest on numerous occasions after publication of a new rental and valuation of their services in 1294, even petitioning Parliament in 1315. Likewise, in the Wiltshire Ogbournes, near Marlborough, tenants pursued a campaign of ancient demesne lawsuits against their monastic landlords for over a century between 1309 and 1416. Similar, often highly localized narratives provide the background to the English Great Revolt of 1381 and may have contributed to the Glyn Dŵr outburst in northern Wales in the early fifteenth century. Interestingly, there was no great peasant rising in Scotland, although in other respects landlord fortunes exhibited similar trends across the British Isles. The exploitation of fossilized definitions of personal status and tenurial obligation merely gave lords a residual power over a proportion of the overwhelmingly rural population; but in all such conflicts it is clear that the basis of relations between lords and peasants was changing. Wealth in unanticipated places, as Thomas Goding had realized, was invariably the root cause, and personal status or tenurial obligation was often a faulty guide to its whereabouts.

Social implications of wealth

A kind of social hierarchy arranged according to wealth had long existed in the fiscal system of the English state operating in England and Wales, which seems to have shown a greater awareness of changing economic realities. Yet, like the estate administrators who drew up the records of personal and tenurial status, royal and local officials also clung to traditional distinctions and the conviction that rank and status should hold a place in assessments for taxation. The English state continued to ask what you were, when it was really interested in what you were worth. The Staffordshire county community, for example, broke up into smaller discussion groups by social rank when discussing the subsidy of 1337.

The standard form of English taxation, the fifteenth and tenths, was initially one of taxes on moveable property but had evolved into standard assessments by individual township. The existence of the poor had been formally recognized in England in 1225, when those without land or whose labour was insufficient to have provided them with material possessions worth more than 6s. 8d. (33p) were exempted from the tax of a fifteenth on moveable possessions. Thereafter, although the thresholds varied, only the destitute who lived by begging were consistently beyond the reach of the state. Possession of land or fees and the value of moveable goods were seen as the principal indicators of wealth. From 1512 people were taxed either on a graduated scale of incomes from land or fees or on a graduated scale of the value of their goods and chattels. Occasional and novel taxes were driven by the suspicion of concealed wealth, and provide an enlightening commentary on contemporary perceptions of the lack of homogeneity in traditional ranks. The English poll tax of 1379, for example, introduced subdivisions within particular ranks, distinguishing between esquires who held enough land to support the rank of knighthood, those who did not, and those who held no property but who were in service. The arrangements for the poll tax of 1380 further included descriptions of the lesser ranks amongst whom the township assessments were to be divided. Alongside the usual division between substantial peasants, the cultivators and farmers, and the less substantial landholders, the cottagers, were large numbers of labourers and servants. The community in Rugeley, Staffordshire, for example, included sixteen cultivators and one cottager, but also twenty-one labourers and twelve servants, as well as seven widows' households and twenty-eight others headed by craftsmen such as bakers, cutlers, and hosiers. Many of these would not have featured in estate surveys. Wage earners were to be brought within the orbit of taxation in England again in 1450, and in 1512, when 'labourers, journeymen, artificers, handicraftmen and servants, both male and female', were to pay a poll tax of 4d.

For most writers, however, discussions of social rank were invariably contained within an organic framework. Whatever the number and nature of social distinctions, medieval society mostly saw itself metaphorically as a body with members, each mutually dependent on the other, but nevertheless assigned separate roles as the head, heart, or feet; the allegory could work within this simple framework, or be extended to include a long list of body parts. Other models were common: the faith in a divinely ordained hierarchy daily witnessed by cosmology, and expressed in similar allegories, whether the ship of state or the game of chess, and all were marked by the conviction that an ideal and balanced society had existed in the mind of God. This imagined society of reciprocal and interdependent roles, traditionally a three-way symbiosis between those who fought (the nobility), those who worked (the peasantry), and those who prayed (the church), has frequently been mistaken for social description, with medieval society seen at a cursory reading as monolithic and resistant to change. In fact, the faults and failings of contemporary society were keenly felt, and much comment was precisely concerned with social change and with social criticism, and with the ways in which a stable and traditional society might yet be restored.

Social hierarchies

Such concerns were not merely the language of social commentary, but frequently provided the framework for social policy. An anonymous author at the Cistercian abbey at Vale Royal, Cheshire, drawing up a memorandum of legal pleas concerning the abbey's estates in the first third of the fourteenth century, occasionally embellished his record with judgements on the characters of the parties involved. His frequently indignant narrative is thus a barometer of social relations on the abbey's estates. That, to modern readers, his villains might now be our heroes is equally a guide to the writer's radically different vision of the social landscape. His world was seemingly filled with knights and peasants who refused to behave according to their rank. At Kirkham, Lancashire, Sir William Clifton, a member of the county's greater gentry, embroiled in a dispute with the abbey about the tithes of his lordship, had stood aloof and approvingly as an abbey clerk was beaten in Preston; he had disrupted services in the church, and had marooned the abbey tithe-collectors' cart in the fields for a month, 'mockingly using the cart-horse as a palfrey for himself'. Since a palfrey might be worth between £10 and £50, and a cart-horse as little as 2s. 6d., his was a piece of unseemly foolery for the crowd. Only excommunication had returned the wayward knight to amity with the abbot. In Cheshire, close to the abbey itself, tenants had waged a campaign against their villein status over several years, claiming to be freemen; they remained unchastened by shackles at courts at Weaverham and Over, and had been willing to pursue their case by pilgrimage to Hereford, by personal petition to the king, Edward III, who was on the Scottish border, and by assaults on abbey servants in

Nottinghamshire. Henry Pym, a peasant from the hamlet of Swanlow in Over, who had been the campaign's leader and appears as the narrative's accidental hero, was finally brought to heel on 15 August 1336, when he was forced to stand barefooted and bareheaded before the monks to offer a candle in token that 'he and his would continue in villeinage for ever'.

The Vale Royal author's world seemed to him to be out of balance, and he reserved his criticism for those who had disturbed it: the knights who behaved like peasants and the peasants who behaved like freemen. Like other polemic, homiletic, and descriptive writing, his text is tinged with nostalgia for an apparently real but now lost world with an aboriginal balance in the social polity. Yet in 1336 the abbey was scarcely sixty years old, and its modernizing estate administration was seeking to impose an archaic pattern which, had it ever existed, had long passed from that particular landscape, and certainly pre-dated the abbey's own lordship. Late medieval Britain was thus less like Éamon de Valéra's Ireland, an old world armed against the threat of the new, and more like John Major's Britain, a new world seeking authority in illusions of the old. Certainly, like present-day Britain, its medieval counterpart seems also to have been a society ill at ease with itself, nervous at what seemed at best a loosening of traditional bonds and at worst a threatening degree of atomization. Public policy and official preaching were thus deeply conservative, often regressive, and commonly designed to inhibit social mobility whilst still maintaining a hierarchy of social relations.

The most familiar mechanisms of social closure were laws which attempted to control the external signs of social mobility, wages, dress, and consumption. There were regional differences within the British Isles, yet the nuances of English, Welsh, Scots, and Irish experience were also matched elsewhere in Europe. The precocious English state, for example, may initially have arrested wage rises which followed the Black Death in 1348. The parliamentary statute of labourers of 1351 sought to enforce wage levels 'against the malice of servants who were idle and unwilling to serve after the pestilence without taking outrageous wages', although it also admitted that an earlier ordinance of 1349 had been ineffective. Reissues of the statute in 1388 and in 1414 further set out to inhibit the mobility of the labouring population, complaining that labourers and servants were fleeing from county to county. In Ireland, however, an English statute, which had been part of Sir Thomas Rokeby's Ordinances of 1351, was replaced by a more realistic Irish version in the Statute of Kilkenny in 1366, which effectively licensed local wage negotiations and daily hiring, 'since food and the cost of living were dearer than they used to be'. Similar concerns are also to be found in the Parisian Grand Ordinance of 1351, suggesting that Irish experience was closer to the European norm than was that in England.

Other sumptuary legislation, on the consumption of food, the wearing of clothes, and the pursuit of field and other sports, had been popular since the 1330s and is equally revealing of the charged atmosphere of changing social relations. If the slight evidence of enforcement is a guide, most sumptuary projects had a symbolic value for threatened social élites rather than a practical policing role. Since the externals of dress and consumption were thought to signify the state of the soul, so rising artificers, labourers, servants, and grooms were at least guilty of the vice of *luxuria*. Most sumptuary laws prohibited particular qualities of food and dress to specified social ranks, but Scotland's earliest legislation of this sort in 1429 instead prescribed appropriate minimum dress standards for lords and knights, gentlemen and burgesses, and yeomen and commoners. As one moved further from the wealth of the south-east of Britain so, one suspects, the signs and steps of social gradation grew simpler. In Scotland, as in many other parts of Britain, the issue was as much of lords who dressed below their status as of yeomen who dressed above theirs.

If there was an expectation that you could tell a man's rank from his external appearance, then it was possible to see not merely what he was, but also where he came from. The anxieties about social mobility which underpinned social comment and legislative action inevitably embodied a language of geographical precision which often added ethnicity to concepts of status and class. Although lordly cultures in Wales, Scotland, Ireland, and England came ultimately to resemble each other, albeit that their immediate roots lay firmly in southern England, and though other social ranks and relations seem to outside observers to be variations on a European theme, ethnic pluralism has remained a critical and often divisive element in the British Isles. The later Middle Ages has been called the ebb tide of the first English empire, a period of disengagement and divergence in which the British Isles were increasingly marked by a pattern of mutually exclusive national mythologies. Race relations in Britain have always had the propensity to be antagonistic and discriminatory.

Ethnic and regional distinctions

It is worth remembering, for example, that the English gentry who framed parliamentary legislation on social relations also argued for a parallel body of statutes which placed civil restrictions on Welshmen. If that was what men supported in a national assembly, they took similar views in their own locality. The townsmen of Newcastle upon Tyne reserved the most severe fines not for guildsmen who called each other fools or rogues, but for those who called each other Scots. Similar examples are legion. The nations of the British Isles could and did trade ethnic abuse. Most also marked their own internal frontiers. The Aberdeen chronicler John of Fordun (c.1320–87) famously distinguished between two peoples of Scotland, the wild Scots of the west Highlands and Isles and the domesticated Scots of the Lowlands, just as the Irish Church explicitly recognised the two nations of the island, the Gaelic and the Anglo-Irish; distinctions between north and south Wales were commonplace. England too was marked by its own moving frontier between north and south. Everywhere intense localism and regionalism frequently added an edge to social relations between apparent equals. Close to the year 1400 the east Cheshire author of *Sir Gawain and the Green Knight*, for example, heaped contempt on the men of west Cheshire, remarking that few dwelled in the wilderness of Wirral who loved either God or man with a good heart. Likewise, it was probably a Scot in the following of Edward Bruce who had earlier penned the Irish Remonstrance of 1317 and cruelly reminded the English in Ireland that they were a 'middle nation . . . so different in character from the English of England'. Homilists, like the Dominican John Bromyard (active 1350–91), railed at those who spoke divisively of northerners and southerners as citizens of the Devil's State. An Irish proverb even optimistically prophesied that the defeat at Bannockburn (1314) might remind the English of their own ethnic diversity, 'born as a people from Welsh-born Scotswomen'. Such apparently encouraging stories are sadly rare. Certainly the oddest was perhaps the Anglo-Scots treaty of

Edinburgh of 1474, which offered peace, love, and tenderness between the two nations, improbably wedded to a novel concept, 'the noble isle of Great Britain'. In the end it is almost impossible to speak of British society or social ranks and relations in the later Middle Ages in an exclusively British context.

As John Ball's text on the English rising of 1381 implied, however, the significant social boundary was that between lord and peasant, between the world of the dependent cultivator or labourer and that of the landed aristocrat. The division also held true in colonial Ireland, throughout most of Wales, and even in large parts of Scotland. The situation may have been radically different in Gaelic Ireland, but the distinction does allow us to speak at the same time of the several societies of the British Isles.

Such descriptions are not straightforward. Words like 'aristocrat,' 'noble', or 'titled' are much more restricted in modern usage than was the case in the later Middle Ages, when they were also applied to the lowest levels of the gentry; whilst the word 'peasant' equally conflates a heterogeneous group of social ranks. But the cultural boundary between lord and peasant remained profound. It separated less than 10 per cent of the population from the remainder. It has been suggested that a ratio of 1:33 between lords and their tenants was close to the national average in England, decreasing somewhat if we include a lord's whole kin group. Indeed, holding the lord's family within the class was a perennial concern. Agnes Barry, a gentry heiress who had married William Paston of Norfolk in 1420, later worried that her younger sons had so little from her husband's will that 'they might not live without holding the plough by the tail'. William's family had probably been servile; in 1448 Agnes had been told so during an abusive quarrel in Princess Street, Norwich. Her eldest son, John Paston I, tore out the offending word, 'churls', from the letter which he received describing the fracas, but left in the report that his wife and mother had also been called 'whores'. The Pastons had recently crossed the boundary and remained sensitive to its limits; better whores than churls, as John must have mused.

The essential dynamic in social relations in the British Isles was that negotiated between these two classes, lords and peasants. As John Paston had realized, birth defined both groups. The fifteenth-century English translation of the *Liber Armorum*, a manual of heraldry rather than theology, nevertheless glossed the story of Genesis as offering instruction on 'how gentilmen shall be knowyn from ungentill men and how bondeage began first in aungells and after succeeded in man kynde'. A peasant lineage could be drawn from Lucifer to Cain, the churlish murderer of his brother Abel, and thence to Ham, the youngest son of Noah, who had published his father's drunken nakedness and been condemned, he and his heirs, to eternal servitude. It was perhaps the new society's response to claims of aboriginal social equality, and may suggest that status by birth was under attack, from one side by peasantries which sought to discard the stigma of a debilitating heritage, from the other by lords who, with equal energy, sought to embellish and sharpen its contours. The gentry, or to be more precise the English gentleman, the principal beneficiary of genealogy and family history as political activity and an enduring cultural icon, will dominate much of the remainder of this chapter, although whether by 1500 England, and to some degree Britain, was a culture more gentle than yeomanly is a moot point. We must needs return to the counting game, and to the naming of parts.

The English gentry

The higher reaches of nobilities in Britain, 'a land of two and a half aristocracies', in one historian's memorable phrase, came ultimately to resemble each other during the later Middle Ages, and to do so upon an English model. Leaving kings aside, as also the traditional determinants of inherited name and lands, and an assumed military prowess, the nobility in England, Scotland, and the Anglo-Irish lordship in Ireland was defined by parliamentary summons. The existence of this parliamentary peerage, a nobility which defined the continuance of its titles by regular personal summons to a representative assembly, differed markedly from continental models of *noblesse*. In Scotland it had emerged only under the early Stewart kings, and was recognized by an act of 1428 which identified the 'lords of parliament' and dispensed with the future attendance of 'small baronnis'. In Ireland 'peers of the land', in effect the Anglo-Irish ruling class, were summoned from the 1340s. Owain Glyn Dŵr, consciously imitating English royal practice as prince of Wales, called a Welsh nobility to the brief series of assemblies in 1404–5 which marked his revolt against English rule. Parliamentary peerages had originated in England during the thirteenth century; in the British Isles only Gaelic Ireland stood aloof. In each nation the quality of nobility varied, but they shared a common role as the great men (*proceres*) of their kingdoms, distinguished from other noble but lesser men. Scottish lords were, on average, fewer in number and generally between a half and a third poorer than their English counterparts; those summoned to the Irish Parliament, usually no more than fifty men, were often of knightly rank.

Knighthood remained crucial to the ranks of nobility beneath the parliamentary peerages, but where once it had united the whole of noble society from kings and earls to the humblest warrior, late medieval aristocratic society was far more variegated. The roots of nobility were threefold: a nobility by practice and service, as for example service in war; a nobility by lordship, that is by possession of lands and estates as a landlord, but also by the exercise of legal authority over others as a law lord or lord of men; and a nobility by birth, that is by membership of a lineage. These adopted self-images are, no doubt, simply a way of dignifying what in origin and practice had been the mere possession of the bigger stick, which was now protected by tradition. But, one effect of the accelerated social mobility which marked the two centuries after 1300 was that such traditions were continually renovated and enlarged.

In England, amongst several titles, for example *scutifer*, sergeant, and *valettus*, which had implied military service in the early Middle Ages, and which were generally applied to the lower ranks of the nobility, *armiger* or esquire had come to predominate after 1300. But whilst the label remained attached to the lower ranks of the nobility, it had migrated from the battlefield. The customary description of the non-infantry soldier, the 'man-at-arms', was generic and socially non-specific. It appears in the records of English, Scottish and Anglo-Irish armies, and as a description of the followers of Owen of Wales, the last heir of the royal house of Gwynedd, in the armies of the French crown in the 1370s. Warfare continued to be a reliable and well-worn route to social advancement throughout the later Middle Ages, notably in the campaigns of the Hundred Years War. For example, John le Ward of Sproston, the holder of a few parcels of land near Middlewich, Cheshire, prospered in an exclusively military career which he began as a mounted archer in the Scottish wars of the

1330s, continued as a royal sergeant-at-arms in the households of Edward III and Edward, the Black Prince, and ended with an endowed knighthood in 1347. But whereas in the early Middle Ages such titles had frequently grown from military practice, the relative lack of warfare in the British Isles meant that innovation in social nomenclature was rooted in other more peaceful areas of service.

Only in Gaelic Ireland did the connection between aristocracy and real warfare remain close and necessary. Here a period of intense localism and fragmenting political authority encouraged the proliferation of Irish lordships with new roots in war. Irish chiefs and minor lords of the fourteenth and fifteenth centuries were again war captains of competing military lordships of varying size and independence; 'creaching' or cattle-raiding added to the opportunities for political violence. Such men were often the leader or *taoiseach*, rather than the *rí*, 'king'. Prominent in armed bands of the period were lightly armed mercenaries known as 'kerns', originally perhaps displaced Gaelic landowners and often household troops, and the heavily armed *gallóglach* or 'galloglass', usually foreign vassals from the Western Isles and Highlands, who often received lands in return for military service. Both groups began to a limited degree to harden as social ranks. The leadership of household 'kernety' was often hereditary. Likewise, the MacSweeneys, a galloglass family in the service of the O'Donnell hegemony in the north-west, became lords of Fanad, Donegal, in the fifteenth century, founding the Carmélite friary at Rathmullan in 1516, and adopting all the cultural symbols of a settled nobility. But if the relationship between war and nobility in Ireland appeared atavistic, its hybrid society shared with its neighbours many other features of a nobility acquired by service outside war.

Prominent amongst these new ranks of nobility were those groups which have been termed the gentry. Although, as we shall see, it was possible to rise to gentility through a variety of routes, the title itself often carried only the implications of birth and lifestyle. Unlike the knight or the esquire, the gentleman's title was sufficiently socially ambiguous to imply neither service in war nor lordship of any distinction of land or men. Indeed, the fact that it might safely be applied to the whole range of men, from the most modest to the most powerful, who shared a common pattern of cultural practice and lifestyle, was ultimately the guarantee of its widespread adoption and dissemination. It seems to have been adopted first in England during the earlier fifteenth century as the generic label for those members of the nobility who bore no other title, possibly in response to a parliamentary statute of 1413 requiring that defendants in legal cases be described, in addition to their name, by 'their estate, degree or trade, and the names of places and counties where they reside'. The first known gentlemen were thus so named by their accusers as the alleged perpetrators of crimes which carried the threat of outlawry. But gentility, and indeed the gentleman, were an already old concept.

The earlier contexts were often poetic. The late twelfth-century Middle English *Proverbs of King Alfred* speaks of both the 'gentile man' and of 'genteleri' almost at the same moment that men were recorded carrying the byname 'le gent'. The related surname, 'Gentleman', appeared shortly afterwards during the thirteenth century. These were, however, attributes rather than titles. Historians now commonly speak both of Anglo-Saxon and of post-conquest gentries in England, and of other gentries in the remainder of the British Isles, but the later Middle Ages remains the golden age of the gentleman. Whatever their regional contexts and often different origins, the later medieval gentries were local ruling élites who claimed superiority largely through the value placed on their 'name'. In the prologue to his version of the classical tale *Orpheus and Eurydice*, Robert Henryson, the Scottish poet of the second half of the fifteenth century, counselled that the recitation of genealogy inclined men the more to virtue and worthiness. 'It is contrary to the laws of nature', he added, 'for a gentleman to be degenerate'— that is, to have fallen from his ancestral status. Such a man would be *rusticat*, a boorish peasant, and a 'monster in comparison'. Henryson's youthful poetic convention was nevertheless widely practised amongst contemporary gentlemen.

The Englishman, John Devereux, Lord Ferrers, claimed of an accusation by his neighbour, Sir William Mountford, that it would 'depryve the said lorde Ferrers of his name, the wheche John hath been enheretyde in and all his auncetours out of tyme of mynde, the wheche shulde put a way all the wordely ioy that the saide lorde shulde have in his person'. In 1491 Ferrers had only recently been restored to the title held by his father, Walter Devereux, Lord Ferrers of Chartley, killed fighting under Richard III at Bosworth field in

1485, and later attainted by Henry VII's first Parliament. In fact John had continued to enjoy the name held by his paternal ancestors; the name in peril was that acquired through his mother's family, Ferrers of Chartley. There is an important lesson here on perceptions of family and personal identity.

Other local élites—of substantial peasants for example—exercised authority by possession of land or wealth, by power, as it were, in the present; the gentry claimed a further authority from their ancestors in the past. Gentry lordship thus extended across both space and time, and generated its own rhetoric of perpetuality. Heraldry, chivalry, and lineage, even the architecture of hall and church, all served as chapters in a 'handbook' of gentle culture which exemplified the nature and permanence of gentility. It was a rhetoric that helped paper over, often literally, the accidents of inheritance and rebellion, of barren marriage, and of the obliteration of name implicit in the production only of daughters; it underpinned the reproduction of a social élite and smoothed the recruitment of new members in the straitened demographics of the years after 1350. Of new members, of lawyers and doctors and such, indeed of the troubling concept of newness in general, there is much to be said in the age of service that was the later Middle Ages. But, just as significantly, it allowed the gradual assimilation of the regional noble élites of the British Isles, especially those in Wales and Ireland which had long valued lineage and ancestry as the true expression of nobility. It was the age of the 'time lords'.

The word 'gentleman' slowly colonized Wales, Scotland and Ireland, replacing or acting as a serviceable translation for other labels. Welsh experience is instructive. For John Trefor (d. 1410), bishop of St Asaph, translating a French heraldic treatise into the vernacular as the *Llyfr Arfau* (The Book of Arms), the man of noble birth of Welsh stock, who could claim a coat of arms from his ancestors, either by prowess, wisdom, wealth, or numbers of near kinsmen, was a *bonheddwr*, a 'man of stock'. In England the same man might be described as a squire or a gentleman, although the mere existence of a large kin-group would not there have carried the same value. Trefor might perhaps have chosen *uchelwr*, the 'high man', the usual name for free-noble Welsh, but he clearly chose to stress those elements of gentility which seemed to him to inhere by birth rather than position or power.

Such qualities are, of course, relative, and we should perhaps ask whether the noble in England was the same as his counterpart in Wales or Scotland. A consideration of the title 'baron' is indicative of the problem. By birth Owain Glyn Dŵr could claim to be a 'baron of Wales', but in the 1380s he took English pay in the garrison at Berwick-upon-Tweed as a simple *armiger*. Had an English clerk intuitively applied a notional exchange rate to Welsh titles, or straightforwardly awarded a suitable title to a man who had not been knighted? In fact Glyn Dŵr's inherited nobility belonged as much to poetry as to politics. Certainly his Welsh title did not easily migrate from its regional context, and even there it was already something of an anachronism. This is also true of the English title, although here its mere oldness guaranteed its survival in some noble families, occasionally with disastrous results. In the aftermath of the battle of Shrewsbury in 1403 Henry IV executed two Cheshire knights, indistinguishable from others of their peers and fellow rebels except by possession of the antique title of 'baron', as the most elevated of their class in the county. But, most English barons tended to be of the grander sort. In Scotland the term survived longer, and the 'small baronnis' who had been excluded from summons to the Scottish Parliament in 1428 constituted the lowest ranks of Scottish nobility, mostly holding baronies within a single parish.

In Scotland these small barons formed the society later described as of 'poorer gentlemen'. In England historians have commonly used the term 'parochial gentry', to distinguish such men from those with wider interests, the greater gentry. In Wales the word *uchelwr* has occasionally been translated as 'squirearchy'. The shifting and imprecise nomenclature of gentility in the British Isles seems to have been largely redundant in defining social relations between nobles and non-nobles. The fact rather than the quality of nobility is what granted authority in the locality. Elsewhere, relations between nobles were governed by a plethora of subtle gradations which reflect the expansion of the ranks of the gentry after the early fourteenth century. Who then were the new gentries of the new society?

For John Trefor, a Welsh bishop who had served on heraldic commissions in England, it was not necessary for arms to have been inherited. Any who had risen in rank 'by learning, knowledge, or wisdom and bravery or by graduation' could bear a coat of arms. He was here writing in the vernacular for a Welsh audience, anticipating by decades the first English vernacular writing on the same theme. The English translator of the mid-fifteenth century *liber armorum*, the 'book of arms', distinguished nine ranks of gentlemen, of whom only two were gentlemen by ancestry and blood. The remainder were recruited from amongst those 'made up', the sons of peasants who had become priests, the sons of gentlemen who had done the same, yeomen granted lordships by the crown, and servants. The years after the demographic collapse of 1348 had multiplied the opportunities for social rise which had now found their way into heraldic manuals. As well as those who had risen to gentility, however, there were others who had fallen from the class, like the biblical heirs of Judas Maccabaeus whose kindred had 'by succession of time fell to poverty', or whose nobility seemed under threat through the accidents of inheritance. Those, like John Devereux, who claimed nobility through the female line were reassured that Christ himself 'was a gentleman of his moder'. The implied manuals of social rank in the later Middle Ages were practical and serviceable.

Avenues to gentility

Prominent amongst the ranks of new gentry, at least in England, were lawyers. Early medieval England is said to have been a land without lawyers. The rise of the common law had led to a massive increase in the profession by the end of the thirteenth century, recruiting partly from amongst the yeomen and scriveners who kept the records of manorial courts. Such origins generated social tensions from the outset, and in 1381 the rebels claimed that the land could not be fully free until all the lawyers had been killed. In England modest provincial families, as Michael Bennett has shown, were investing in a legal education for their children from at least the early fourteenth century. In 1323 Thomas de Hale was prepared to support his daughter, Anyne, and her husband, Richard de Bruche, for five years, one at Oxford and four amongst the apprentices at the court of Common Pleas, 'in the manner that a gentleman and gentlewoman ought to be maintained'. The brass of Robert Skern at Kingston on Thames (1437) argued that 'making a living from the king's law brought honour'. But the rise of the professional lawyer is an English phenomenon. Scottish lawyers remained clerics, and although the continuing rise of written records gave greater opportunities to the literate, Scottish experience of legal careerism was different.

The longer-established freedom trail lay within the Church, where a modest level of education might lead to social advancement, occasionally as a priest but more often as a secular clerk and administrator, although both servility and bastardy were technical bars to ordination throughout the Christian world. Manumission and dispensations may have been relatively common. And, opportunities within the several churches varied enormously. Local churches in Gaelic Ireland remained largely in the hands of lay guardians or *erenaghs* and promotion to the parish clergy was frequently hereditary. Kinship links also often took precedence over supposed illegitimacy. In Scotland, where there was a high and growing level of appropriation of local churches to ecclesiastical institutions, a significant proportion of the wealth available to clerical careerists lay instead within the gift of a small minority of churchmen. Those who staffed local churches here were amongst the most poorly paid in Europe. They nevertheless attracted the usual anti-clerical sentiments of the period. Sir David Lindsay's portrayal of the relationship between the vicar and the pauper in his play, *Ane satyre of the thrie estatitis*, first performed in 1552, is justly famous. Having lost three cows in death duty in quick succession, Pauper complains to Diligence, 'In good faith, sir, I thought he would cut my throat. I have no goods except an English groat that I will give to a lawyer.' The comment drives Diligence to the heartfelt remark, 'You are the daftest fool I have ever seen.'

In Scotland the gap between a small group of senior ecclesiastics, and royal and noble bureaucrats, who frequently held the greater proportion of rectories and swallowed the income from teinds (tithes) and other parochial revenues, and a clerical proletariat of mercenary priests and stipendiary chaplains, who staffed local churches and sang masses in the chaplainries or chantries of the dead, could be cavernous. There were perhaps between 10,000 and 11,000 churches in England before the Reformation, with perhaps a tenth of that number in Wales. But to the numbers of clergy who served as resident priests in parish churches and chapels we must add that army of chantry chaplains who could be rented by the mass. This latter group had multiplied across much of the British Isles in the later Middle Ages to create the lowest ranks of 'spiritual gentry'.

Many in what must be seen as the local church seem to have been recruited from amongst the middling ranks of wealthy peasants and craftsmen. Those who eked a perilous living from masses for the dead may have enjoyed a barely perceptible 'superior' status; others may have lived their lives as parochial gentry, wealthier and more comfortable than their neighbours, but bound by the same horizons. Testators asked for chaplains 'of honest fame and conversation' with an emphasis which might suggest a scarce commodity. Whether Scottish clergy were more rapacious than their English, Welsh, or Irish counterparts, as has been claimed, or Irish clergy more prone to concubinage, as has also been argued, are perhaps moot points. Anti-clericalism was a leitmotif of the period, as often born of the permanent cold war which marked the collection of tithes as the consequence of clerical defects. Social relations between local clergy and community were up close and personal, and prone to ill temper. Most did not move up the career ladder, and, like the 500 or so resident clergy in north-west England in 1379, stayed close to home. Real social advancement came as clerks moved from—perhaps even escaped altogether—this respectable but poor pond, and swam in the deeper pools of national churches, and in the households of the crown and regional nobilities.

Across the British Isles, then, such social advancement implied mobility and service. Such mobility might carry the ambitious to ecclesiastical centres, to the households of lay and ecclesiastical lords, to the armies and garrisons of France, and to towns; but of these, London far outstripped all centres of attraction. The records of London probate courts are full of bequests to the remote parishes of origin of those whose wills were made in the city and its environs, migrants whose connections to an old country had never quite been severed. That of Geoffrey Downes, gentleman of London, which established a fraternity, library, and cow trust at the moorland chapel of Pott Shrigley in Cheshire in the 1490s, is rightly well known. Downes's service as head of the household of Sir John Tiptoft's daughter, Joan Ingoldsthorp, was in part the key to his wealth. That the gentry everywhere were serviceable may be a truism, but it is worth stressing to a modern audience which imagines itself to be exploring the novelties of a service economy.

Nobility and service

Service began in the locality, but permeated the wider spread of social relations. In part it stood in apposition to ties born of land and lordship, often supplementing rather than supplanting traditional bonds. The contrast has often been drawn between this feudalism of the first sort and a bastard feudalism of the second, the latter bearing a heavy implication of decline and social disorder. In reality, service for payment or patronage was far from novel in the fourteenth and fifteenth centuries, but it did increase in societies in which the ties of landed authority had weakened, from the multiple links which kings maintained with regional gentries as effective rulers of their localities, to the formal bonds of retinue by which lords organized their affinities, the so-called indentured retainers of the later Middle Ages. But it reached too to the lowest ranks of the parish gentry, as such minor lords often hired their estate and household servants using formal written agreements, either on annual contracts granted at hiring fairs, or on a more random and local basis.

Such links bound many local and regional societies, creating expectations and undertakings of 'gode maystreshippe' at every level. Sir John Mainwaring of Over Peover, one of the greater gentry of Cheshire, was, for example, retained for life by Humphrey, earl of Buckingham, in September 1441 'to do him service (in peace and war) and with him to sojourne and ride'. Eighteen months later Mainwaring in turn retained the services for life of a local lawyer, Thomas Alcumlow, 'in such occupation as he most useth, that is to say with penne and inke and counsell'. The importance of the household, as both a physical and a conceptual space, was crucial to both contracts, and marked both Buckingham and Mainwaring, the former with his castle at Stafford, the latter with his knight's chamber in the hall at Over Peover, as lords.

Bastard feudal relationships of this kind seem to have developed later in the north and west, in part because kinship links underpinned lordship and social relations more strongly in Wales, Ireland and Scotland. Elsewhere the personal contract of service embodied a curiously imprecise language of connection and friendship which reflected a growing degree of socially corrosive individualism. The occasions on which service was withheld with catastrophic results are many and well known, from Sir Robert Holland's abandonment of his lord, Thomas, earl of Lancaster, at Burton Bridge in 1322 to the more spectacular treachery of Sir William Stanley towards Richard III at Bosworth in 1485. Holland was himself murdered some six years after his betrayal: the old world briefly reasserting its values against those of the new. But the trend in England was firmly set towards calculating self-interest, and towards the creation of a moneyed as well as a landed ruling élite. It was increasingly possible for an English earl, for example Thomas Percy, earl of Worcester, to hold modest landed estates but to maintain his wealth and lifestyle through grants and other incidents of patronage.

The language of retaining in Scotland was strikingly similar to English models. The marriage agreement between Alexander Stewart, earl of Mar, and Alexander Comyn of Altyre in 1408 held that the latter was 'oblist to be lele man and trewe . . . agayne all dedelike'. True and loyal men, like good and honest priests, may have seemed hard to find, but the earl's bond presumably sought to establish the normal parameters of a new kinship bond. More indirect relationships, common in England, developed later as bonds of manrent and maintenance, formal contracts of friendship and support, usually for life. They survive in large numbers from the mid-fifteenth century, although the system may have been evolving from the 1370s. However, the vast majority were sealed by those between whom few kinship links existed. The affinities of Scottish lords, it seems, continued to be based on land and tenure. Certainly the following of Archibald, 4th earl of Douglas, in the early years of the fifteenth century, contained few permanent members, and only one, Herbert Maxwell, granted a bond of retainer. The loyalty of most was guaranteed by the traditional resources of land grants. Perhaps Scottish nobles were simply short of cash, but land, locality, and lineage, rather than money, may have held their allure longer here.

The great service industries of the later Middle Ages were to be found in the Church—notably amongst the ranks of those who served the dead as chantry priests and chaplains—in the law— amongst those who worked in the great hierarchy of local, regional and royal courts—and in royal and lordly service—amongst those who served as clerks, soldiers, and men of business. The English crown, in England itself but also in Wales and Ireland, took many thousands into its service on local commissions, its ambition and reach greatly extended by the local grasp of its agents. Social relations in the locality were frequently given an added nuance because this or that gentleman was a servant of the crown. The Scottish crown, less precocious and with fewer resources, ruled a much less centralized kingdom. Here, as in Ireland and the north of England, magnates retained a more prominent role and ruled their regions in kingly fashion. The courts of Percys, Mortimers, Douglases, and Kildares were not, however, greatly different worlds from the households of English kings. Service revolved around the court and the household. Medieval élites did not float in a global nowhere; everybody, in the end, had to be somewhere, and that somewhere was frequently a central place, most often a castle, hall or house.

Picard, one of the Norman colonists of the Usk valley in Brecon during the eleventh century, had built a castle in the Rhiangoll valley at Tretower. His successors had extended the castle in later centuries, but around 1300 the castle was abandoned for a new house, Tretower Court, built less than a hundred yards away and itself extended and modified throughout the later Middle Ages by the Vaughan family. The words 'abandoned' and 'new' are misleading. In reality Tretower Court drew its authority, as did its occupants, from its proximity to the 'old' castle. The rhetoric of perpetuality applied to buildings as much as to genealogies, and across the British Isles 'new' gentry and noble dwellings frequently stood in suggestive proximity to their predecessors. Great Codham hall at Wethersfield, Essex, successively the house of the Coggeshall and Tyrell families, likewise sits a few yards from the moated mound of the former manorial *caput*. One suspects that as families came and went following the inevitable accidents of inheritance, the place retained its authority. Joan Armburgh, gentlewoman of Mancetter in Warwickshire, commented on attempts to dispossess her of a manor house at Radwinter: 'that maner hath been a habitation and a dwelling place for many a worthy man of myn ancestors from the conquest to this time and a long time before.' Perpetuality with knobs on.

Lifestyles

There is little wonder, then, that an important part of gentle rhetoric was expressed in lifestyle. For new and rising families, and for those who prospered in service, living in the traditional places of gentlemen and living like gentlemen was the quickest route to adoption and recognition. But of the classes who lived like gentlemen, the most notable was that of townsmen. Throughout most of the British Isles there was a marked absence of social difference between town and country, and, of course, no separate sphere of merchant families. Country gentry frequently maintained—occasionally even built— town houses. Chaucer's testimony in the Scrope–Grosvenor heraldic dispute of the 1380s, which concerned two provincial knights of Yorkshire and Cheshire who claimed the same arms, described the poet's confusion on visiting the wrong gentle town house in London. Although merchants, like lawyers, did buy country estates and live as country gentlemen, they also built town houses and lived as what can only be described as urban gentry. Pippard's 'castle' and Hatch's 'castle' in the Market Street at Ardee in County Louth resemble the tower houses built by local lords in the Irish countryside during the fifteenth century. The demographic crisis also allowed some townsmen to build town houses which included large walled gardens, a kind of proto-*rus in urbe* colonized from vacant plots and tenements. But many continued to live over the shop, the upper rooms of urban tenements resembling the knights' chambers of rural manor houses, the lists of their possessions in inventories revealing their gentle tastes.

Were, then, the societies of the British Isles in the later Middle Ages a model of Smilesian self-improvement? If gentries ruled everywhere, was there an undignified clamour amongst those looking to rise to join them? By 1500 was England—and to a degree *trends in* the other nations of the British Isles—more gentle than yeomanly? Peasantries were certainly familiar with their own descents, and used them to trace the tenure of holdings which, like gentry estates, had no direct heirs. Naming patterns suggest also a unified sense of the historic family. Some, if the remarkable carved stone from a house in Chipping Dassett in Warwickshire is to be believed, even marked

Plate 6 Aberconwy House, a mid-fifteenth-century house within the late medieval walled town of Conwy, north Wales. It has a timber-framed upper storey over a stone-built lower storey and basement, and was probably owned by a prosperous Anglo-Welsh merchant. It is the earliest identified town house in Wales. Crown copyright: RCAHMW.

their houses, just as gentry hung their arms from town houses and embellished the gatehouses and porches of their manors. Here a carved stone door-jamb bearing the family name Gormand, tentatively identified as a house-name plaque, was placed to the right of a door in Newland Street in the New Market of Chipping Dassett sometime after 1267 by a member of the family of locally prosperous peasants. The fact that it was a name, rather than arms or a rebus, like the Stafford knot which the Stafford family painted on signs outside the Swan Inn in Stafford, is suggestive of a different and independent culture.

The differences, however, are profound. Yeomanly or even peasant culture generally, and the social relations which it engendered, remained firmly rooted in the locality, even where peasants moved from manor to manor, and from manor to town. Gentility, even whilst it inevitably remained rooted in particular places, sought by subscription to be part of an increasingly national and even island culture. Of relations between the two cultures, gentle and peasant, we need look no further than one of the great conversations of English history, that between Agnes Paston and her neighbour in Paston, Warin Herman, in 1451 on the subject of the blocking of a processional way around Paston church. Herman showed little deference to and even less respect for gentle space; he berated Agnes, leaning across the parclose screen of her private pew, and pursued her into the churchyard. Like the report against Henry Pym, a peasant leader on the estates of Vale Royal abbey with whom this chapter began, the story is all the more delicious for being in the voice of the supposedly aggrieved party.

Is it possible that yeomanly social relations were more practical and more neighbourly? Peasant élites were frequently as wealthy as their gentle neighbours. No doubt they treated their inferiors no better than the gentry did theirs. But one suspects that the gentry-free communities of the British Isles—of which there may have been many, since there were not enough gentry to go round—may have been freer and more humane societies. John Palmer, a Warwickshire gentleman, wrote to his mother in an undated letter of the 1440s in response to an impending maternal visit. After prevarications, excuses about litigation and lordship, the burden of fines, and the costs of building new houses and the repair of old, he warned that should she come, 'it schall not lye in oure power to resceyve you and refresh you, neyther to your worschip nor to our worschip, but and ye wolle tarye your comyng a litill lenger . . . the which is litill more than a yere and a quarter.' We know much less about peasant family culture, but they must surely have been freed of the great English gift to social relations, the business of keeping up appearances.

Plate 7 The nave of Exeter Cathedral, Devon, looking east. Built in the early fourteenth century, it is the longest unbroken vista of Gothic vaulting in the world. The solid and elaborate pillars and exuberant vaulting create a symmetrical avenue of what appear as towering palm trees. The nave was completed by 1360, mainly by Bishop John Grandisson (1327–69). Photo A. F. Kersting.

3

The Church

Richard Davies

The Universal Church

By 1300 all parts of the British Isles were in communion with the papacy, organized into dioceses and parishes and—as four Irish kings irritably informed a tutor appointed by Richard II in 1395 to civilize them—fully acquainted with the key tenets of the Catholic faith. This homogeneity of formal organization and of fundamentals of faith continued, even the latter barely contested until enforced reformations in the mid-sixteenth century. The British Isles were amongst the most loyal parts of Catholic Christendom in this period; it was even such fidelity that led to what friction there was between the papacy and English crown in the fourteenth century and again in the 1420s, as the latter sought a legal formula to protect its control of its own ecclesiastical officers and lay rights of patronage without offending the spiritual authority of the pope. The papacy's own problems, of trying to recover a secure base in Rome whilst it was installed in Avignon (1305–78), of schism (1378–1417), of challenge by conciliarists in the mid-fifteenth century, and then of entrenchment in domestic Italian politics, meant that money and at times political support were what it most often sought from the British Isles, rather than any active attempt to influence the internal conduct of religious life there. Whilst from the 1340s every bishop but one before the Reformation was papally provided in England and Wales, the number of bishops actually chosen by the pope dwindled rapidly; England in particular was not to be a resource base for cardinals and others working in the papal curia. The onset of the Great Schism, when two—eventually three—competing popes claimed the allegiance of the Catholic Church, likewise ended what opportunities such men had had to enjoy preferment in cathedral dignities and prebends. When a brief trickle of Italians acquired bishoprics around 1500, it was purely because the Tudors thought them a useful contact with Rome. The papacy, for its part, received a pay-off in revenue and patronage from each episcopal appointment, whilst the crown found it far easier to gain the bishops of its choice by papal provision than by soliciting the votes of recalcitrant or small-minded cathedral chapters. As to direct taxation of the clergy by the popes, this was a considerable bone of contention in the late fourteenth century, especially during England's own war with France, and in the following century the tap was virtually turned off altogether.

It was all done with little formal agreement and certainly no great concordats of the kind that the French crown concluded with the papacy. It might even be argued that it was such amiable coexistence, leaving difficult matters of principle to lie dormant, that underlay the fateful crisis of the 1520s and 1530s, when the pope's spiritual author-ity, usually so benign, proved uncontrollable by the crown. 'We are so much bounden unto the see of Rome that we cannot do too much honour to it,' Henry VIII chided Sir Thomas More. In 1378 England and Wales had rallied with swift conviction to the side of the Roman pontiff, Urban VI, and more than once it was this realm's obstinate support which was held by others, especially in France, to be blocking any attempt to resolve the Great Schism; indeed, in 1408 Thomas Arundel, archbishop of Canterbury, publicly admitted as much. At the Council of Constance the English delegation paid lip-service to reform but was eventually the catalyst for Pope Martin V's being elected well-nigh free of specific limitation. There was, however, one crucial exception, the pledge to call general councils at fixed intervals: at the Council of Siena–Pavia the English delegation openly blocked any reform inimical to the pope, whilst, marginalized and mainly absent from the far more determined Council of Basle, the English government and Church supported Eugenius IV firmly in his battle to frustrate that radical experiment.

Urban VI's opponents had never made headway in Wales; even Owain Glyn Dŵr, with a background in the English court, showed no initial wish to join the anti-pope and tried instead to compete against the English for the favour of the pope in Rome. For a while this seemed promising. When Bishop Trevor defected to Glyn Dŵr in 1404, he was not challenged by a royal nominee to St Asaph. There were rumours that the pope was prepared to translate Guy Mohun from St David's to make way for one of Glyn Dŵr's men. Very soon after, there was a serious crisis between King Henry IV and the pope over the execution of the rebellious Archbishop Scrope of York, but there was never going to be a full parting of the ways, and Gregory XII had to realize that he could not keep both the Lancastrian king and Glyn Dŵr under his roof. Glyn Dŵr was forced to switch: he needed the political and military backing of France, a principal supporter of the Avignon popes, and Owain's own ecclesiastical advisers were insisting on the creation of an enlarged Welsh province of the Church coterminous with the planned Welsh principality, under an archbishop at St David's, and with themselves installed in the existing four Welsh sees at the expense of Lancastrian incumbents. This no Roman pope could dare authorize. In the event, even formal adherence to the Avignon line led to little advance of such ambitions: Gruffydd Yonge was named bishop of Bangor and John Trevor's reluctant fidelity held, but there were no appointments of anti-bishops to Llandaff or even to St David's. With the calling of the Council of Pisa and, more especially, the waning of the rebel's fortunes, his ecclesiastical advisers fell into the *demi-monde* of the refugee, drifting around Scotland and other parts of the fading anti-Romanist world in forlorn attempts to recover a dream.

The native Irish, like the Welsh, had never thought to use the Great Schism to advance their hostility against the English colonists. The Gaelic lords and bishops had no complaints against a papacy which had always responded well to local cultural variants requiring grace, and which had not been exploited by the English crown for decades as a means to destabilize their own heartlands. Unlike the Welsh, the chieftains controlled their local bishoprics. Arguably, any switch to the Avignon obedience might have provoked the Roman pontiff into a series of counter-appointments of English loyalists, who would stand little chance of gaining possession in most places but could have caused instability in some marginal areas and provided a focus for any internal conflicts. Clement VII used Thomas MacEgan, prior of Roscommon, as an envoy, who reported a favourable response from the archbishop of Tuam, three other bishops, and (so he claimed) many priests, monks, and laity. More certainly, the bishops of Killala and Elphin opposed the Clementist cause sternly. There is evidence that people from Connacht looked to Clement for favours, and some appointments were made, but there was no success as regards the senior positions in the Irish Church. By 1393 even Tuam had been cleansed. Neither the Gaelic chieftains nor indeed the Church in their areas had the unified structure to take any binding decision to change sides. Had there been any significant civil wars between them, no doubt there would have been some who went over. As it stood, all a fragmented society had in common was that they had long enjoyed direct and friendly relations with the Roman papacy and had every reason to avoid throwing it into the arms of the English crown. The Urbanist popes made sure to nominate members of leading local families wherever there was a Clementist pretender.

Without an archbishop, the Church in Scotland answered directly to the pope as 'most special daughter' and the papal schism affected it closely. Scotland supported Clement VII and his successors more doggedly than simple obedience to France or hostility to England can explain. Because it was so long under a regent, the kingdom was perhaps especially influenced by senior churchmen such as Walter Wardlaw, bishop of Glasgow (1367–87 and cardinal, 1383), his nephew Henry Wardlaw, bishop of St Andrews (1403–40), and Gilbert Gren-law, bishop of Aberdeen (1390–1421 and chancellor of Scotland from 1397). Sodor and Man split, but otherwise the Urbanist cause made little headway, and Scotland was almost the last country to abandon the Avignon line and recognize Martin V in August 1419, almost two years after his election. Relations thereafter were much like England's, with friction over the pope's over-helpful response to supplicants, including implication in barratry (that is, undermining incumbents), and the cash outflow for his graces, but this was a practical issue, not one of principle. The government could be confident that all major appointments would be to its liking. However, the political factional-ism following the assassination of James I in February 1437 did become directly identified with sharp preference for either the pope or the Council of Basle, undermining Scotland's stance diplo-matically and making for more than ten years of bitterness within the Scottish Church before the pope's friends won the battle at home and settled the country's ecclesiastical stance their way, even as the conciliar cause waned generally. As to the papacy's influence on the persistent political instability around the crown, it was in absolute terms very little, just as in England. Scotland was an emerging society of considerable potential, as was England: whether coincidentally or not, both found themselves with an incestuous political super-structure that was deeply inadequate at first to maintain stability and which was engulfed in one crisis after another. In both countries, the monarchical and aristocratic hierarchies managed to survive in power, having come to terms with the nearest socially of the emerging elements, mainly through a shared ambition to centralize direction of, and kick the ladder down on, the rest of society. The Church, which had never really been the master of the old order, would be used more explicitly as an instrument of this new order; and more intrusively and punitively than ever before. Whether 'the rest of society' could be so persuaded, or brought low, is another question in another era. It was by no means an inexorable flow.

Accordingly, the elevation of St Andrews to metropolitan status by Sixtus IV in August 1472 has been much debated, as between being a signpost of rising royal ambitions to control the Church in the realm and the independent ambitions of Bishop Patrick Graham which, like those of his uncle Bishop James Kennedy, were certainly not modest. According to the pope, the elevation was intended to sharpen up the Scottish episcopate as a whole, which was often founded in its highest reaches on personal and political nepotism and in its lower by well-meaning mediocrity in personnel and effect, and to make ecclesiastical jurisdiction more accessible; and eventually the latter aim did prove successful. For whatever reasons, however, the early years were confused: Graham lingered abroad, exercised no active rule and was finally removed from the see in 1478 by papal order, possibly by reason of mental collapse rather than hostility at home. In January 1492 Glasgow was elevated and given four dioceses to form its own province. Again, this can be (and has been) interpreted very differently, whether as a further refinement in consolidating the Church or as a surrender to an abrasive major see. Certainly, especially when Archbishop William Scheves had lent strong political support to King James III and been left isolated after that king's death in 1488, there had been resistance to St Andrews' hegemony; Bishop Thomas Spens of Aberdeen had gained a personal exemption in 1474 and his successor, Robert Blackadder, in 1488, as too had Andrew Stewart of Moray, when the archbishop's canonical authority had been further enhanced. The two provinces bickered a good deal hereafter. Most notable, however, was the crown's ability and intent to insert members of the royal family, laymen indeed, into major bishoprics and then to supplement that income with grants of leading abbeys *in commendam*. Even Cardinal Wolsey, who was at least in orders and could offer some justification for amassing leading sees and abbeys into his own hands, must have blinked—but he probably understood.

Bishops and dioceses

Internally, England and Wales had been divided between two ecclesiastical provinces since the eighth century: Canterbury by now with its thirteen English and four Welsh suffragan sees, York with just Durham and Carlisle. Scotland's complement was still evolving alongside the working out of the kingdom's frontiers, but was settled at thirteen in the later fifteenth century in the two provinces. The diocesan structure of Ireland was more fluid, because for political reasons the English crown sought to unite or absorb some of the smaller units, especially in Gaelic areas, but a figure of around thirty-three or thirty-four sees is not misleading, divided among no fewer than four provinces—Armagh, Dublin, Cashel, and Tuam, the only one in the Gaelic west.

English dioceses varied enormously in size and population, and so too in their financial worth to their bishops: Lincoln stretched from the Humber to the Thames at Dorchester, with heavy settlement all the way, whereas Ely barely reached the few miles south to Cambridge and no further in any other direction across the fenlands, an immensely fat sinecure and created as such by Henry I in 1108. The bishop of Winchester's sway from Southwark on the south bank opposite London (whose straitlaced civic policies made him the unembarrassed principal landlord of the city's red-light hinterland) through Surrey and across Hampshire left him with only Milan as rival as the richest prelate in Catholic Christendom. At least half of the other twenty bishoprics, headed by Canterbury, York, Durham, and Ely, made their holder as rich as an earl, and only three in Wales and Rochester and Carlisle in England might be termed modest in this respect. Size and wealth made English bishoprics unusual in western Christendom. As a consequence, although often based upon ancient political and administrative territories, they were

Map 5 The pre-Reformation dioceses of England, Wales, and Scotland, and the archdioceses of Ireland.

beyond the realistic ambition of local clergy and (usually) of local magnates to dominate and enjoy, and had even been designed by the crown as such. Durham, for example, was a royal bastion in the north of the kingdom, usually—if the king had sense and authority—reserved for a leading civil servant. In the civil conflicts of the fifteenth century it was contested hard. Broadly speaking, if a son of an earl went into the Church, he would get a see if he survived his teens. The son of a lesser lord might well become a bishop in time but only after a sound career. Much the greater part of the later medieval episcopate was not drawn from such exalted backgrounds at all, but dominated by university doctors in law who had risen through royal service alongside a miscellany of theologians, confessors, canon lawyers, and diocesan officials in the minor sees. The early assertion of royal authority and the size of the bishoprics meant that they could not easily be subsumed into local power structures, even though the magnates would have liked them to be.

Such local ambition was strong in Wales. St David's was quite well endowed, if only of third-division rank in English terms; it had a fine cathedral and episcopal palace, mainly thanks to Bishop Henry de Gower (1328–47), and was no more isolated in terms of an English and anglicized Welsh society for company in its lowland parts than its several Scottish counterparts, which divided up the Highlands but had most of their populations comfortably to hand along the coastal strips. It had enough to attract royal servants as bishops, with a mixed record of absenteeism and attention, and was beyond any local aspirant or his lord. Indeed, it was not in a region dominated by ties of kinship and petty lordship. It is the three other bishoprics— Bangor and St Asaph in the north, Llandaff in the south—which catch the eye. All three were very poor financially, certainly insufficient for any civil servant to give up his plurality of benefices to take, and Bangor, at least, very much in Welsh Wales. It is clear that the crown had no wish to see native Welsh clergy fill these sees, and since the concept of 'stepping-stone' promotion of aspiring prelates, beloved of the eighteenth century, could not be applied in the later Middle Ages, an assortment of ageing confessors, scholars, monks, and erstwhile officials in the papal curia were promoted, to enjoy status and a reasonable sustenance for men of their kind but not with the expectation of their giving their dioceses much personal attention.

The moral dimension has often been raised here. It is true that these bishops could not speak Welsh. On the other hand, the local clergy were very ill-equipped in Latin, and in medieval terms that was much the greater failing in terms of organization and conversation within Church circles. Most especially, there is no reason to suppose that local Welsh society had any significant moral reasons for wanting Welsh bishops anyway. It came down to local power structures. The *uchelwyr*, with their careful pedigrees and extended kinship systems, were accustomed to controlling the meagre resources of their areas along such family lines, be these property, persons, or offices under absentee great lords and English kings. The property and offices of the Church could not be exempted from this trawl, nor did there seem any reason why they should be. The Church's wealth and social influence demanded that it be sucked in, and parish benefices, stewardships and farms of church lands, cathedral prebends, and membership and headship of religious houses all had been. Parish clergy and senior monks alike were appointed by genealogy, not moral fervour. As far up as dean of cathedral or archdeacon, the Welsh gentry had control. The crown could still arrange to perch its English colonial bishops on the top of this hierarchy. The question has to be whether this infuriated the local Welsh establishment or whether, as in much else, they were intent only on wrapping their tentacles ever more tightly around local patronage and administration in the service of alien, absentee headship, especially at a time (it has been argued) when they were finding their hereditary expectations challenged from below.

In the time of Glyn Dŵr, there was a group of ambitious Welsh clergy—all from substantial northern kin-groups—who formulated the rebel's ecclesiastical programme for an autonomous province under St David's to match his secular design for a greater (as it would have to be) Wales, and took possession of the four present bishoprics as and when they could. By political definition and personal ambition, they naturally excluded English from this scheme. It is true also that, occasionally in the fourteenth century, Welsh cathedral chapters elected one of their own number in vain when a bishopric fell empty. But English chapters were inclined to do that too, often even when it was explicit whom the crown wanted and clear that the crown would get its way. Possibly there was some symbolic gesture of ancient independence intended, some well-known 'favourite son' gesture not intending any insubordination to the king. At any event, the choice was usually woefully unimaginative to fill so great an office. In Wales, of course, the bishoprics being so much smaller in real substance (if not always in territorial size), the electors may have felt that the office did fall within the competence range of a local candidate and hence did vote more meaningfully for him; but it would take much more evidence to prove that there was any consistent and authentic Welsh protest and ambition *per se*, save to privatize the bishop's office into some local kinship hands from which it might never emerge. True, the bishops would then reside rather more, but only to answer to their kin's demands. Bishop John Trevor of St Asaph, whom the pope had placed in his native see in 1394 for services in the curia, tried bravely to mediate between the English crown and Welsh rebels for three years before succumbing, probably with a well-founded sense of doom, to the compelling call of his kin; led by Glyn Dŵr, they were destroying him, his home, and his bishopric.

If the *uchelwyr* of Wales, self-conscious concerning their descent from royal blood, did not have formal control of local bishoprics, the local kings and lords of Gaelic Ireland certainly did. Like their Welsh counterparts, they were not as secure in their authority in the later Middle Ages as they might have liked, especially as demography, economic recession, and social mobility went against them, heightening the tension between ancient claims by blood and upstart claims based on effectiveness and ambition. The contrast with Wales, of course, is that the *uchelwyr* worked within a society in which, because English culture was gaining ground after Glyn Dŵr and crown rule was politically effective, they worked by infiltration, whereas in Ireland, the territorial rule of the crown was in scarcely interrupted retreat all through the later Middle Ages, and never had been total.

In broad terms in this period, the bishops of the province of Tuam were exclusively Gaelic in all eight of the dioceses; Armagh's twelve dioceses divided equally into Gaelic and Anglo-Irish strongholds; Cashel's nine divided between five Anglo-Irish, two Gaelic, two swaying between; Dublin's five remained firmly Anglo-Irish. It was a mirror of the political divide, often an unpleasant one in the many areas of mixed affiliations, where the English attempted to exclude Irish clergy and monks by legislation in the fourteenth century. For his part, Archbishop Richard O'Hedian of Cashel (1406–40) was accused locally in 1421 of excluding English clergy in favour of Irish whenever he could. There could also be pragmatism. The archbishops of Armagh, for example, accepted that even in their own diocese their effective control and residence was restricted to the eastern parts, using Termonfeckin, County Louth, as their home and St Peter's, Drogheda, as their seat, whilst a quasi-autonomous organization ran its Gaelic west, embracing even the cathedral. (Probably this is why no Gaelic Irishman had the archbishopric after 1346.) Pilgrims to St Patrick's Purgatory had to obtain the archbishop's licence, but in practice had also to be handed over gingerly for inspection and approval by the O'Neills for the final stage of the journey. In fact, although Raymond, viscount of Perelhos, found their society alarmingly uninhibited in dress and lifestyle in 1397, they were generous hosts to him. The archbishops had to look to such secular chiefs to interest themselves in clerical provision in their area. It was simply too dangerous for the archbishop to attempt any visitation of the dioceses of Dromore and Ardagh between 1417 and 1471, and in 1427 the archbishop reminded the deputy lieutenant to exclude the dean and chapter from government councils because they would betray confidences. Few if any Gaelic bishops attended Parliaments as the century wore on. On the other hand, Archbishop Colton received all due hospitality and authority when he visited the Gaelic see of Derry in a vacancy in 1397, conducting a hugely attended outdoor mass in the city.

The crown did recognize that attempts to infiltrate candidates into Gaelic sees were fatuous. Although there were always Englishmen, usually friars, carrying Gaelic titles and certainly consecrated, these eked out mundane lives as suffragans in England, relieving diocesans of the mechanical *ex ordine* functions of episcopacy. The papacy made no attempt to destabilize the custom of the Gaelic areas. Hence, what failed to happen in Wales was certainly the case in Gaelic Ireland, namely that dynasties of clergy—often father to son—occupied many of the sees. Thirty-three or thirty-four sees in a relatively small country, much even of that sparsely populated, meant that each episcopal seat (some indeed so desperately poor, such as Clonmacnois and Dromore, that no one would take the latter in 1487 and 1511) was not only well within the ambition of the leading local family but, once secured, would be held onto as a part of that family's hegemony in the area. In 1425, 1441, and 1461, for example, a bishop was killed in a family feud, whilst William O'Faull, bishop of Ardagh, usurped a chieftainship by imprisoning a kinsman. Raymond of Perelhos found it hard to tell the bishops and the layfolk apart. In this respect it is worthy of note that, commencing with the archbishoprics and descending steadily to the least of sees, papal provisions superseded chapter elections in Ireland no long time after they did in England, and as amenably to local secular interests. As in Wales, the Irish chiefs had much influence in the local chapters but were not slow to recognize, as all European princes did, that the papacy's expanding claims to patronage were little more than a commodity for sale.

As with Wales, a poor society dependent on kinship networks for organization of fragmented assets found Catholic precepts of clerical celibacy alien and unhelpful, just as it did those of strict monogamy, difficult divorce, and a sharp, morally condemnatory divide between legitimacy and illegitimacy. All these had been created by the Catholic Church under self-interested pressure from dominant lay societies in earlier centuries, and not from any special moral or spiritual purpose. The Gaelic powers accordingly were driven to offend against them to a spectacular degree. An impressive number of sons of clergy headed to the papal curia to obtain dispensations from illegitimacy in order to continue their dynasties' careers within the Church, and the papacy obliged. Not a few Gaelic bishops and other senior churchmen had numerous children, whom they placed either within the Church or by marriage back into the family's political kin-groups. Roger Maguire, bishop of Clogher (1450–83), son of a king of Fermanagh, had at least ten childen. Lochlainn O'Gallagher held the see of Raphoe from 1420 to 1438, a grandson and namesake from 1443 to 1479, and a grandson of Lochlainn II from 1534 to 1543. These are examples, not scandals. The mothers in such families came from the same networks and contributed, not forfeited, their status to the children. There were, in effect, hereditary clerical families at the most senior levels, such as the O'Farrells around the bishopric itself of Ardagh, and the O'Gradys across the four significant dioceses of Kildare, Cashel, Cloyne, and Tuam. As in Wales, the local abbeys were drawn firmly into these systems. They had, after all, been first founded (even if subsequently 'reformed') by the ancestors or predecessors of current lords and kings, to act as spiritual, symbolic, political, and material bedrock for the regime. It is pure anachronism to introduce the term 'abuse' for an endowment that had always been intended as possessive and kin-based and remained so.

This explicit control of so many local sees by Gaelic families extended down to the hereditary control of many Irish churches by *coarb* and *erenagh*. The former enjoyed a higher status as the claimed descendant of a founding saint, but both were basically stewards and farmers of the parish church's lands, responsible for the church fabric and for certain of the obligations, such as hospitality or visitation dues—and yet something more than that, with some residual sense of being themselves within the clerical order, and thus much more than, say, an English churchwarden or farmer of a glebe. These officers were numerous, if unevenly distributed, across Gaelic Ireland, again marked out by their tenaciously hereditary nature and by their close synonymity with the dominant local families in secular life. The O'Grady family were coarbs of St Croman's, Tuamgraney, County Clare, from 1189 into the sixteenth century.

Religious orders

Although there were old traditions of monasticism in each country, these had been subsumed everywhere by the familiar orders of Catholic Christendom. Monasteries have often been seen as part of colonization processes, alongside the military and merchants, staking out the ideology of the conqueror into pious fortresses in the new territories, and often his economic and political overlordships too. In England, William the Conqueror had reformed or established large-scale Benedictine houses, especially in the outlying areas and, almost unique in Western Christendom, made cathedrals of some of them. Magnates founded and adopted others likewise as family mausoleums. The later medieval history of Benedictine houses in England is a significantly quiet one; but it is not to be forgotten that the order always included a majority of the biggest and wealthiest houses, especially those whose heads were summoned to (albeit rarely attended) English Parliaments. The enormous regional importance of houses such as Durham, Bury St Edmunds, Norwich, St Albans, Tewkesbury, Bath, Chester, Westminster, and at least twenty more is too easy to overlook. As against this, each house recruited its monks very locally and elected their abbots for life from within. There was a provincial structure but it was feeble. Thus the order had no capacity to punch its weight nationally or drive through any coherent overall strategies in the face of the insularity of each house. Within each convent, the Rule of the order promoted theoretical autocracy and practical factionalism. Yet generally it worked well. Although bishops sought keenly for defects, most houses continued to perform as they had been meant to. Only changing society marginalized them. There is a current attempt to show that some houses realized this, and sought to advertise themselves more aggressively as social workers and centres of holiness in their local communities; it is not convincing.

The Cistercians made the bigger impact in the north of England with their perceived austerity (sometimes hard to sustain) and greater emphasis on ascetic and spiritual individuality, and likewise in the Scottish lowlands, Wales, and the English parts of Ireland. In Scotland, houses on the March played an aggressive part in mustering ideological and physical support for resistance to the claims of Edward I and his successors over their country. Neither that loudly pious king nor his equally devotional great-great-grandson, Richard II, paused for a minute before savaging such places. In Wales, houses had become exclusive to one or other race, the Welsh houses in particular now firmly bound into the family nexuses and bastions of Welsh tradition and culture. In the time of Glyn Dŵr's revolt, the houses were seen by both sides as fully politicized and treated accordingly. Even the abbey of Cwm-hir, in the central March, the burial place of Prince Llywelyn the Last, was attacked by Glyn Dŵr and may never have recovered. However, whilst many did suffer damage, the scale was sometimes nothing like that often asserted then and since. It is a familiar tale: those houses that had been in a bad state before the revolt were those that complained longest and loudest afterwards, and those with a vigorous abbot bounced quickly back to health in a way that others were still bewailing as impossible decades on. Apart from local outrages, there was no such large-scale conflict in Ireland, but the racial divides across the religious map were just as sharp. Repeated fourteenth-century legislation forbade the admission of Irishmen into houses under English control. Such formal exclusion only reinforced a natural parting of the ways. Although efforts were made to keep the Cistercian order together, even (belatedly) creating a separate Irish province in 1496, most of the thirty-five or so houses had 'gone native', not merely in an ethnic sense but in obeying the imperative of fragmented localism in the country; the newly created head of the province, the abbot of Mellifont, dared not even attempt a visitation of many such houses. In his house and in Dublin, the conventions of liturgy, dress, and corporate life were maintained, but in few other places. Ireland's characteristic church families swept up the abbacies into their collections. Given that an order like the Cistercians did have a universal Rule, such practice does, of course, imply corruption of the ideal; yet, equally, it gave more sense to the houses in their own local contexts.

In contrast to England, too, the Austin canons flourished in

Ireland, especially in their Observant form, initially in English areas but extending significantly in the fifteenth century into solidly Irish zones. Such religious, less scholarly than some other orders but more explicitly aiming to promote religious knowledge amongst the laity, had an obvious and appropriate role for that society, their openness making them much more relevant. Great insulated houses of worship had their time and place, but not here. Most especially, the fifteenth century saw striking advances by all the mendicant orders—again especially in their Observant form—in both Wales and Ireland, and especially a very dramatic swing from confinement to the English areas (towns being their natural milieux as critics of materialism) to a predominantly native role. In both countries, as in England and Scotland, they had not always worked well alongside the secular clergy, and some prelates like Archbishop FitzRalph of Armagh (1346–60) had been openly hostile to them; but they now received considerable encouragement from the native lords and chiefs, and as a result were housed in numerous small units to reflect the proprietary right of each founder. It has been proposed that they had a double appeal in their poverty and in the role of shaman, both traits long prized in Irish religion. A 1515 report declared that the sheer inadequacy of the parish priests meant that the friars were the only preachers in Ireland. This, of course, must carry the familiar warning label that preaching was not customarily accorded the highest priority in the work of parish priests as against liturgy and social work. More to the point, perhaps, the scattered and often still impermanent nature of settlements in those Irish parts made formal parish structures difficult to sustain, and a friar seeking out his audience was more likely to be effective than a priest needing his congregation to come to the church. It does seem likely that the religious orders were still more central to the religious life of Wales and Ireland at the time of their reformations than in either England or Scotland, where the secular clergy had much stronger cohesion overall, clearer lines of authority, and more settled and integrated populations to work with. Nonetheless, it is thought, for example, that there were no more than some 275 monks, nuns, and friars in Wales in 1536, and by then scarcely any monastic house could muster the theoretical minimum for viability of twelve—many even once large houses operating on no more than six. In Ireland it was reckoned that there were only six houses with more than six monks at the time of the Tudor Reformation.

Parish clergy

The parish structure was meant to be universal by this time; and although still indeterminate in some parts of native Ireland, generally it was. Much of this structure had evolved piecemeal as a mirror-image of the manor, and had been endowed by the lord of the place. The superstructure of the Church as a whole had to be based upon this fact, and how this was achieved has caused much unfavourable comment. Principally, rectories were appropriated to support other priorities—episcopal *mensa*, cathedrals and their staffs, religious houses, hospitals, university colleges, collegiate churches, chantries, and guilds. The duties of the rector in the parish were then delegated to a vicar, who received an arbitrary portion of the revenues, sometimes quite handsome but too often no better than subsistence. It is almost impossible to avoid being subjective here. A Church composed entirely of parishes is an unreal concept in all truth, both from an organizational viewpoint and in respect of the need to promote piety in its fullness. In more worldly terms, able men required career structures in a wider scene than one village, and there had to be a leadership capable of defending the Church at national level, with the resources and status to match.

In Scotland, the effects of this support of a superstructure were extraordinary. Although the Church was reckoned to have ten times the income of the crown (a disingenuous comparison admittedly), by the sixteenth century 86 per cent of all the thousand or so parishes had had their rectories appropriated—in the dioceses of Caithness and Ross there was not one left independent, in Moray only five out of seventy-nine. Principally, these had been taken to support the bishoprics themselves, many of which were poorly resourced, others to support cathedral chapters, and yet others monasteries. The same process had occurred in England, and university colleges at Oxford and Cambridge had been endowed as well, but England's 9,000 parishes and their relatively greater wealth made for an easier overall burden. Despite contemporary satire and complaint, this wealth and the scarce labour market meant that the majority of vicars and other deputizing stipendiary priests in the parishes could obtain tolerable terms and even provoked several unsuccessful attempts in the Convocation of Canterbury to impose ceilings. It is generally reckoned that, by contrast, many of their counterparts in the other three countries had to settle for desperately low wages. In Scotland a vicar was supposed to have a minimum of £10 plus house and glebe, but devaluation and non-payment affected this badly. True, this used to be said about England until record material showed otherwise, but everything points towards the parish deputies in the other countries indeed having to settle for a small slice of a small cake; in parts of Ireland parish priests averaged only £2 per annum. Although this might be set against the fact that they mainly lived and worked amongst comparably poorer societies, their economic status has been thought to have declined.

In each country the intellectual élites complained of the poor formal education of the parish clergy, but in each country recent historians have wondered how much this mattered. It has been proposed that, whilst parishioners were by no means unconcerned with their priest's performance, their criteria did not demand high levels of academic training but, rather, due performance of the rites and a good heart—a depressing lack of interest in the man's degree results. The principal duty of the priest was the performance of the liturgy. Since this was ordained to be in Latin and thereby incomprehensible in terms of text to the laity, the Church could not be thought to be overly concerned whether the priests understood it either. The text was only part of a ritual of signs, symbols, movement, and sound, all made comfortingly familiar to celebrant and congregation by weekly repetition and involvement—the 'bowings and beckings, kneelings and knockings' which were so to distress Bishop John Bale of Ossory (d. 1563), and the less official 'keenings' at funerals which were by no means restricted to Ireland. As a bonding act of community, it had obvious merits over the one-way didacticism offered by early Protestantism, especially but by no means only for a non-literate congregation. Ideally, as in lowland England, the parish should congregate, at least on Sundays; but even where this was impossible, as in the scattered settlements in Wales, Ireland and the Scottish Highlands, the priest could continue with the mass, vicariously representing the parish to God even when so few individuals could be with him in person. Again, a Protestant service would lack this capacity to reach out beyond those actually present.

In all regions the rites of baptism and of consolation of the dying were regarded as an essential part of a priest's duty. Although other expectations were also shared, they were weighted differently from one area to the next. Hospitality from the holder of the rectory and/ or the priest in charge, for example, was certainly expected in lowland England, but more in the sense of occasional alms and relief to the immediate parish, whereas in Ireland especially, and predicated once more on acknowledged networks of distant kin and practice amongst the laity, it amounted to provision by the incumbent or the *erenagh* of lodgings and board when required. Wales, where parish clergy were likewise bound into kinship structures, was not dissimilar. It is perhaps significant that what secular resistance there was to the dissolution of the monasteries in England came mainly from the north, where extended kinship remained a social priority and raised the loss of hospitality and charity as a problem.

In lowland England and Scotland the priest worked as reconciler in his parish, and also contributed, if by experience as much as formal literacy, to such basic bureaucratic and legal needs as the making of wills and testaments. There was much wishful thinking about his role as a teacher: in practice, the seven virtues, seven vices, Lord's prayer, and ten commandments would often constitute the available curriculum. In short, his role was moulded to help bind a community that had to work together, and it was important for the priest to be independent. In native Wales and Ireland and in the Scottish Highlands, with less day-to-day integration within a village community and far smaller penetration of the localities by formal instruments of authority and hierarchy, the balance of a priest's roles would be different. His liturgical functions remained essential, even pressed further towards his sacerdotal connection with the supranatural, but his social role could only work within kinship structures. Thus, in England and most of Scotland parish priests were celibate, and evidently informed on by their parishioners if they were not; in Wales many kept wives (or concubines, as their English-born bishops insisted on calling them); and in Gaelic Ireland marriage was in effect regarded as compulsory.

Map 6 The larger hospitals for the sick and lepers in the British Isles.

Shrines and pilgrims

Shrines based around artefacts such as a cross or tomb, or around a relic or some natural phenomenon such as a spring or cavern, were common to all the societies. Ireland's were ancient sites: St Patrick's bell, St Dympna's crozier, the Holy Cross of Ballyboggan. The Holy Cross of Raphoe bled in 1411. Inevitably, the custody of such places was often hereditary; the taboos and privileges of St Caithin of Fenagh were still being well sustained by coarb Tadhg Ó Rodeihe in 1516. Archbishop Richard FitzRalph's tomb in Dundalk was the centre for a *de facto* local cult which the papacy twice refused to legitimize in the late fourteenth century. St Patrick's Purgatory at Lough Derg, County Donegal, the freely intermingled real and allegorical terror of whose caves was never knowingly undersold by the prior in charge or by those who had been there, required the dedicated pilgrim to be locked up there overnight after lengthy rites of penance, settlement of life's affairs, and rejection of desperate pleas to desist; only the righteous would survive to be let out the next morning. By definition, the prior could not allow more than the occasional élite suppliant to endure the trial, such as the Viscount Raymond in 1397 or the Hungarian knight Laurent Rathold de Pesztho in 1411; and so this shrine could offer only vicarious relief to most of its pilgrims, who were held to be too fearful or aware of their sin to enter.

Such a religious experience was, of course, rare. In England, St Thomas Becket at Canterbury, declining but still the biggest crowd-puller, was fully accessible and marketed keenly by the monks. This shrine had reached maturity and respectability, less dependent on miracles than in its youth but still a compulsory visit for kings and leading aristocracy. St Mary at Walsingham was similarly 'establishment'. England was also notable for the development of *de facto* cults in this period, often political and occasionally durable too. Henry VI's remains, especially in the first years after their removal in 1484 from Chertsey Abbey to deliberately public access in St George's Chapel, Windsor, offered the much greater incidence of miracle-working usual in a successful new site. Whilst intended as an act of political reconciliation by the reigning Yorkist dynasty, its success might seem to imply popular rejection of them, but more probably it was King Henry's unique personal reputation which underwrote the success. Windsor was also very unusual in having a major supporting star in John Schorne, whose shrine in North Marston, Buckinghamshire, had been but a minor attraction for many decades but had sprung to wider fame, for some reason, especially amongst wealthy woolmen, in the early fifteenth century. His successful transfer to Windsor for blatantly commercial reasons (to help pay for the new chapel building) adds to the peculiarity, in that he had no previous connection with the place, usually a prerequisite for a saint's success, or any special track record for healing.

St David's had a steady strength as a place for pilgrimage. By geographical definition it drew mainly inhabitants of Wales (even Canterbury had a distinct south-of-England weighting to its catchment), but there were no malignantly ethnic or political subtexts in its appeal. The English crown and the English in Wales did not regard St David as dangerous. Had Glyn Dŵr achieved his intended purpose of making the cathedral metropolitan, this would no doubt have changed in order to promote the new order. However, the bland, uncompelling nature of St David's primacy bears witness to the general fragmentation of pious loyalties in Wales. Although the Normans had displaced native Welsh saints as patrons of parish churches in their own areas of dominance, in favour of a handful of the customary 'great saints' of Catholic Christendom, elsewhere the great majority of Welsh parishes preferred to have a saint peculiar to each or just a few places close by, a saint of great antiquity, usually austere, preferably of royal, aristocratic, or native blood, and usually directly associated in his own lifetime with the parish as its missioner or priest. A by-product of this extreme localism was that these saints could readily give a practicable place name to the whole settlement in a way the over-common saints in England could not, a distinction shared (unsurprisingly) with Cornwall and still prominent in the index to any gazetteer. It would, then, be dubious to suppose that this also reflects any stronger adherence to piety, even or especially to the cult of saints, in these areas than in England; similarly, the additional widespread prevalence of *llan-* ('church') in Welsh place names, usually with a topographic or personal description, is evidence purely that early medieval church buildings were permanent at a time when few other structures were.

Saints had been notably political in Scotland and refashioned accordingly over time. Columba had emerged from the original four holy men to represent Kenneth MacAlpine's integration of different native peoples, with Andrew coming to stand for universality under the MacMalcolm dynasty: their banners went together into the seminal, nation-myth battle of Bannockburn (1314), with Andrew emerging, significantly, as the prescribed hero of the two. St Margaret, the second wife of Malcolm III (1058–93), had already been pushed forward from 1250 as the mother of a pronounced Christian form of kingship and dynasty in the realm: a weak or emergent régime usually clothed itself in piety. St Andrews, the place, provided both a shrine to the unity of the realm (after a century and a half of dawdling, its cathedral was finished within four years of the victory at Bannockburn) and a wider interest in the Cross in Scotland. The Virgin Mary was as favoured as elsewhere, with a particular centre at Paisley. However, there remained considerable and enduring diversity of local affiliations, even a reversion to such in the fifteenth century, prompted by bishops sharing in the general revival of assertive nationhood. William Elphinstone (d. 1514) tried to collect more than seventy native saints into his Aberdeen breviary of 1510 in an attempt to construct a shared heritage all across the Church in Scotland and integrate it into the most recent and fashionable Marian and Passion feast-days from Catholic Europe. He was not especially successful in either respect. Unlike Ireland (*pace* some modern wishful thinking), Scotland did not have a bitter internal divide between Gaelic and the rest, reflected in its religion and church organization. It was in every sense a multicultural and geographically diverse society, and its religious map was a mirror which generally reflected contented faces. Elphinstone's ideas were, willy-nilly and like Dean Colet's efforts at clerical reform in England, a well-meaning portent of the far less kindly faces of secular government at Edinburgh and Westminster just around the corner.

Belief and heresy

Whilst shrines and pilgrimages played a major part, centrally in parts of Wales and Ireland, more as optional extras in England and Scotland, it is in the parishes and communities that the central

Map 7 The more important pilgrimage centres in the British Isles.

features of late medieval religion must be located. There was a notable rebuilding of parish churches in England in a distinctive Perpendicular style, sponsored by the laity. It would be simplistic to identify the higher nobility as the fourteenth-century leaders in this, the gentry, merchants, and urban guilds taking over in the fifteenth century, even though this is often the impression left by their greatest benefactions. Scotland, for reasons of economy as much as lack of awareness, witnessed rebuilding on a thinner and much less ambitious scale. In both countries, however, the conversion of parish churches into collegiate churches staffed by secular clergy and at the behest of aristocracy or urban oligarchies, was a notable phenomenon of the time. So too was the provision of grammar schools, in which clerical founders joined, with a willingness to educate boys who had no intention of joining the clergy but with, especially in lay-dominated foundations, very conservative curricula.

This last point can be made general. Although it can be demonstrated in many different ways that the upper orders at least were interested and active in developing their personal piety and involvement in the Church, and likewise, as many historians see it, the lower orders too, it is hard to support the perennial assertion that this led to much anti-clericalism at any social level, certainly not as regards tithes (*tiends* in Scotland) or aggressive attacks on the status, office, and property of the clergy. Heresy made no great headway in any part of Britain, but not because of vigorous prosecution. Capital punishment was belatedly introduced in both England and Scotland, but more as a sign of the state's growing interest in ideological control of its subjects than out of any religious fears. Nonetheless, Lollardy did establish roots in the late fourteenth century in places in southern and Midland England, mainly through family networks, and these were still alive when the Henrician Reformation came. Some slight evidence suggests a few similar cells in Scotland. These groups became sectarian very quickly as against any realistic alternative church. Wales was scarcely touched, outside a brief early flurry in the marches of Herefordshire and Shropshire, whilst a few earlier prosecutions in Ireland were unconnected and based essentially in local factional fighting.

Lollardy had, however, tapped into a wide lay interest in the social and moral imperatives of theology in the later fourteenth century, with reference to individual response amidst, rather than against, collective ritual and conformist acts of piety. In the highest circles, this was shown in the endowment and support of Carthusian and Bridgettine houses, such as those at Mount Grace (Yorkshire) and Syon (Middlesex), and, under the patronage of James I of Scotland, at the Carthusian Priory at Perth. Although these orders attracted considerable interest amongst the élites of both town and countryside (and have attracted a disproportionate interest amongst recent historians), they were always too small in number and personnel to make a wide or deep social impact. They still reflected contemporary interest in pious opportunities for the laity, as witnessed too by the interest in the writings and lives of mystics (broadly defined), especially those who discussed and sought to reconcile the dichotomy of the contemplative and active life. As a matter of simple economics, one would not expect to find Carthusians established in Gaelic Ireland, but arguably they would not have suited the social religion of that region anyway.

Literacy, status, and economy ordained that the manifestation of piety would vary between social orders. On the other hand, the common threads remained unbroken. The strongest theme in the later medieval period was the increasing emphasis on Jesus Christ himself. In terms of his time on earth, there was some attention to his miracles, but—at least amongst the didactic who provide most of the evidence—much more on his teaching of social virtues, and, most of all, simply on his own lifestyle. The apostolic life became increasingly contentious: a stick with which to attack the material wealth and secular priorities of many contemporary clergy; hallowed turf over which friars and Wyclifites fought for exclusive ownership; and especially a fiercely disputed moral high ground in the intense debates over poverty and unemployment in this period. Steep demographic decline, with its opportunities for full employment at (in employers' eyes) outrageously inflated rates of pay, turned 99 per cent of 'the poor' from 'unfortunates' into work-shy parasites in the eyes of those hitherto willing to accept charitable giving as a pious duty. How Jesus and his band had supported themselves took some careful explanation.

However, the death of Christ loomed far larger, expressed not simply through the ubiquitous roods and other depictions of the crucifixion but in the intense focus on the week of his Passion, culminating in the great Easter day of resurrection, when Man was saved; every medieval man and woman had to devote the festival each year to confession and repentance, peace restored with neighbour and with God, to be worthy to receive that salvation. Traditionally, success in this was marked by lay receipt of the Eucharist for the only time in the year (as opposed to weekly or even daily witnessing of the priest's celebration). It was through the Eucharist, the infinitely portable and flexible symbolic representation of Christ's blood, body, and passion, that Jesus's personal pre-eminence waxed in the later medieval period. It lent spiritual credibility and metaphor to bodies social, political, or civic. In many ways it offered individual hope and consolation, most notably through requiem masses and chantries and, more generally, private masses in life for those who could afford it. Thereby it underwrote that great proletariat of chantry priests whose presence so skewed the character of the priesthood, for all the spasmodic efforts made to add some social utility to their role. It was an instrument by which the traditional haves kept the traditional have-nots in their place, and a much-needed one at a time when the hitherto have-nots were showing social and other aspirations of an unwelcomely brazen kind. Such currents, potentially contrary to the deliberately all-inclusive parish mass, attracted much criticism, but the tide was high, not least because those rising could seize and deploy it to declare their own advance. The Lollard heretics (with more conviction than Wycliffe, in fact) found the theology in itself irrational and the obsessive fascination at every social level with the powers of the Eucharist obscene; it cost them a lot of votes.

The deployment of Corpus Christi imagery is, naturally, far easier to see in England and Scotland, especially in urban environments where contests between interest groups were flagged more openly, for example through guild activities, procession routes, and the casting and performing of plays (these last much more an innovation of the end of this period than is often thought). English Wales and what was left of English Ireland—in both cases seriously restricted to protected towns by now—naturally produced mirror images of the same, perhaps even out of conscious anxiety to ape the mother culture. Not simply lack of evidence but also the different milieux of the Welsh and Irish societies make it much harder to know whether these too followed a Christocentric path and, if so, the same one. There is literary evidence, especially from Wales, to suggest vernacular interest, but as always this could have been didactic rather than proof of reception. It has also been noted that Wales still enjoys a remarkable number of surviving roods and rood screens of fifteenth- or early sixteenth-century origin, by no means confined to parishes or areas under the control of modishly anglicizing gentry or nobles, and indeed many from otherwise unremarkable churches well off the highway and, like those in the Black Mountains of Breconshire, in deepest Welsh Wales.

Nowhere in the British Isles are there clear signs of a Protestant Reformation to come, or why such a Reformation occurred in England, Wales, and Scotland, or how it was accomplished. Why Gaelic Ireland resisted would probably be the easiest phenomenon to explain, in both political and religious terms. Glib suggestions regarding the nature of the Reformations in the other three societies would be not so much hostages to fortune as suicide notes, for certainly both politics and religion were involved everywhere, with many layers of interaction. The apparent facts that the Scottish Church had denuded its parishes of wealth in favour of its higher institutions and corporations, that its metropolitan structures were still recent, its universities nascent and faltering, and the crown brazen in using its greatest preferments to support family members, provide significant context rather than explanation for the radical Reformation in Scotland, but not in any simplistic way. The English crown's persistent devotion to the papacy but quiet squeezing of ecclesiastical franchise, the first two Tudor monarchs' very personal enlisting of religion in their concepts of rule, the ancient metropolitan structures which Wolsey found cumbersome, the existence of two ancient universities, of which one at least was being paid eager attention by the highest in the land and giving some audience to new continental ideas (not necessarily synonymous themes): these too must be taken into account.

These features, however, mainly delineate how the Church was related to the civil power at the centre. As such they are of key importance, because the centres determined the formal structures across the land, especially as central powers were now encroaching decisively on localities. Localities had to adjust. Wales did without difficulty, its *uchelwyr* long attuned since Glyn Dŵr's debacle to persuading the local choir to hold back on the tenor-line whenever the English lord called in to hear a loyal chorus. Ireland had no reason to respond in religious terms, and no political imperative to make it do so. In England, despite much hair-splitting by historians, a long-integrated and homogeneous society continued its local varieties of interpretation of a state Church's demands. Scotland, with the greatest concentration of population in the direct paths of effective reform from the centre, had to think longest and hardest. The British Isles in the later Middle Ages saw English *imperium* in retreat. The Scots and Irish went their own ways, the Welsh equally cannily went for co-habitation. Christian religion offers itself as an impartial moral imperative and social code. In practice, it reinforced the secular imperatives of each society in the later Middle Ages. Designed to describe, underwrite and preserve a one-size-fits-all basic concordance and uniformity with the will of God—which, for a multitude of reasons, most of medieval Europe wanted—the Catholic Church's necessary and time-honoured local flexibility in practice had to allow each state, nation and society—when push came to shove—to do its own thing.

Plate 8 Painted alabaster panel representing the Annunciation, from an altarpiece depicting the Joys of the Virgin, a popular theme of English religious art and devotion in the later Middle Ages. English alabasters from the East Midlands became a major medium of English sculpture from the fourteenth century and were frequently exported. Ashmolean Museum, Oxford.

Forms of cultural expression

Michael Bennett

Cultural boundaries, c.1300

In 1278 Edward I presided over the exhumation and reburial of the remains of Arthur, king of Britain at Glastonbury. Early in his reign, a magnificent Round Table was constructed. Edward's interest in the Arthurian and British past was by no means antiquarian. It provided an ideological gloss to his ambitions in Wales and Scotland. His conquests had a cultural dimension. It is most striking in Wales, where there may have been some resolve to destroy the native culture. Edward made a triumphal progress through the defeated country-side and in a splendid ceremony was presented with various Welsh treasures, including a crown with alleged Arthurian associations and a celebrated relic of the True Cross, known as *Y Groes Naid*, subsequently displayed in the chapel at Windsor Castle. Meanwhile, the castle towns raised along the Welsh littoral seemed poised to throttle Welsh cultural life. Caernarfon Castle was consciously 'imperial' in style. Its polygonal towers and striped masonry were reminiscent of the walls of Constantinople, and the Roman imperial style was further evoked by the tribune arch over the gateway and the eagles on the battlements. In Scotland Edward I was likewise intent on pressing his claims to suzerainty. Given the cultural affinities between the kingdom of the Scots and the kingdom of England, the task was both easier and harder across the northern border. At the height of Edward's short-lived triumph in Scotland there were, as in Wales, signal acts of cultural appropriation. The 'black rood' was carried in triumph to Windsor, and the Stone of Destiny was moved from Scone to Westminster.

The notion of a 'British' culture was not without substance around 1300. Geoffrey of Monmouth's *History of the Kings of Britain* (*c.*1136) had given the peoples of the British Isles a seductive myth of common Trojan origins. Brutus, the eponymous founder of Britain, was the son of Aeneas, founder of Rome. His three sons had in turn divided the land into the components later known as England, Scotland, and Wales. The *Brut*, as the vernacular version of this tradition became known, moved to firmer historical ground with its account of Britain's incorporation into the Roman Empire. With the withdrawal of the legions, legend reasserted itself. The *Brut* gave pride of place to the deeds of King Arthur, but provided a framework as well for other legends like that of Joseph of Arimathaea, who brought the Holy Grail to Glastonbury, and Merlin, who prophesied the future tribulations and triumphs of the British peoples. All in all, it laid claim to a special destiny for Britain, and anticipated some modern constructions of British imperial identity. While it was as clear in 1300 as it was 500 years later that England would dominate this enterprise, it cannot be regarded as a narrowly English myth. The focus on Troy, Roman Britain, and King Arthur provided a framework for cultural integration that was both universalizing and accorded specific value to what would later be termed 'Celtic' traditions. It served well the interests of the Norman and Angevin rulers whose ambitions extended over the entire Atlantic archipelago, and who took some pride in ruling over diverse peoples with a multiplicity of languages.

The Edwardian conquests mark the high water mark in Britain of the process of cultural expansion which Robert Bartlett has termed 'the Europeanization of Europe'. During the twelfth and thirteenth centuries population growth and commercial expansion strengthened the heartland of Latin Christendom at the expense of the periphery. In the British archipelago it strengthened lowland England at the expense of the Celtic fringe, and underpinned the military conquest of Wales and Ireland. Christianization, the centralization of the Church, and the growing power and appeal of Christian learning and culture facilitated and consolidated the processes of colonization. Yet there is a sense, too, in which England was itself being colonized by Europe. In the wake of the Norman Conquest its language and culture were all but destroyed, and in the thirteenth century a newly emergent English cultural identity found it hard to make headway against the powerful cultural forces emanating from the continent. The culture that triumphed in Britain around 1300 was still very largely Latin-based and French-based. It would be anachronistic to talk too much in terms of English cultural imperialism.

In terms of 'high culture', Britain is most usefully seen as a region within Latin Christendom. While the major cultural influences tended to emanate from the European heartland, though, it must not be assumed that Britain was wholly provincial. Travellers from the continent would have found little that was positively alien, and a good deal to admire when they crossed the Channel. At Dover there was the great castle, 'built by devils', according to a Bohemian squire, 'so strong and well-fortified that its equal is not to be found in any Christian land'.[1] On display was the alleged skull of Sir Gawain, a mute witness to Britain's place in the imagination of European chivalry. The cathedral at Canterbury was familiar enough in shape and style to pilgrims from the continent, but impressive to all in the rich ornamentation of its principal shrine. St Thomas of Canterbury, after all, was not only England's most popular saint but the object of devotion throughout Christendom. In London there was much for all but the most world-weary to admire: old St Paul's, with its long nave and high towers, and the Tower of London itself. London presented itself as a heritage site: it was the 'New Troy', its cathedral was built on the site of a great pagan temple, and the Tower of London was allegedly the work of Julius Caesar. Meanwhile, in the city foreign visitors found a range of commodities and crafts equivalent to those in other cities of northern Europe. Italians as well as northerners wrote admiringly of the number of London goldsmiths and the quality of their work. At Westminster there was the royal palace and the abbey, home of the great shrine of St Edward the Confessor and rapidly developing as a royal mausoleum to rival St Denis in Paris.

At Oxford, England could boast a body of scholars engaged in the great philosophical, theological, and scientific enterprises of the age. The contribution of the British Isles to the intellectual life of Europe

[1] *The Travels of Leo of Rozmital through Germany, Flanders, England, France, Spain, Portugal and Italy, 1465–1467*, ed. M. Letts (Cambridge, Hakluyt Society, 2nd ser. 108, 1957 for 1955), p. 49.

in the first half of the fourteenth century is out of proportion to its population, and the history of scholastic thought in this period can plausibly be presented as a contest between two British giants, Duns Scotus (c.1266–1308) and William of Ockham (c.1285–1347). The leading exponents of 'realism' and 'nominalism' were both trained at Oxford before moving to Paris and other European studia. The same is true of two key thinkers of a slightly younger generation—Walter Burley and Richard FitzRalph (c.1300–1360)—whose work testifies to the intellectual vigour and creativity of Oxford before the Black Death. Richard de Bury, bishop of Durham, who wrote a remarkable treatise on the love of books, was a great champion of Oxford, claiming that Minerva 'has passed by Paris, and now has happily come to Britain'.[2] He could cite the high international regard in which Oxford was held for speculative philosophy and natural science. Bury himself was one of a number of English classicists whose work was recognized in southern France and Italy. It should be noted that Oxford at this time served as the training ground for scholars from all parts of the British Isles. Ockham may have been from Kent, but Burley was a Yorkshireman, Scotus was from southern Scotland, and FitzRalph from Ireland. Cambridge remained a backwater. There were no universities in Wales, Scotland, or Ireland. A fledgling university at Dublin—authorized by the pope in 1312, and inaugurated in 1320–1—failed to prosper.

The peripatetic royal court could prove elusive, but it seldom strayed far from the Thames valley. In the reign of Edward III, Windsor emerged as the major royal seat outside the capital. An ambitious programme of building and renovation was inaugurated in 1350 and continued through to the 1370s. Fresh from their triumphs in France, Edward III and his sons held great feasts and tournaments there in the 1340s and 1350s. The headquarters of the newly founded Order of the Garter, Windsor was the new Camelot. For a time Edward III's court was the most splendid in Christendom. Its language was French, its ambience was cosmopolitan, and its magnetism was felt throughout north-west Europe. Royal and aristocratic women played a major role in tempering the martial ethos of the English court, and in cultivating the arts of peace. The dowager Queen Isabelle (d. 1358)

[2] *The Love of Books: The Philobiblon of Richard de Bury*, ed. E. C. Thomas (1888), pp. 212–13.

owned a collection of French romances, while Philippa of Hainault, Edward III's queen, brought to England poets of the stamp of Jean de la Mote and Jean Froissart. The cosmopolitan milieu of the English court was greatly enhanced by the presence of two captive kings, King David of Scotland from 1346 to 1357 and, most especially, King John of France from 1356 to 1360. In the countryside around Windsor there was the prospect of hunting and dalliance. Further up-river, Woodstock was a palatial country retreat, where English kings had taken their ease for several centuries. Once celebrated for its menagerie, Woodstock offered in the bower and tomb of 'Fair Rosamond', Henry II's mistress, a site of romance.

Of course, some parts of Britain were more central than others. Once beyond the Thames valley, there was less that was monumental or impressive by continental standards. The king maintained a number of castles, not least the great fortresses built in north Wales, but none was sufficiently used to warrant major expenditure in the later Middle Ages. A number of private castles like Warwick, the seat of the Beauchamp earls of Warwick, and Kenilworth, a favoured residence of the house of Lancaster, assumed grand proportions, but none really bore comparison with the castles of European noblemen. For the most part the only significant buildings were ecclesiastical. During the thirteenth century the cathedral chapters and monastic corporations in England had the resources to build on a grand scale and to delight in the rich decoration of arch mouldings. In the early fourteenth century English Gothic continued to distinguish itself from French style by its exuberance and eclecticism. The Decorated style was the fruit of a new openness to continental ideas and cross-fertilization between England's still vigorous regional schools. It remained the dominant aesthetic in almost all the great building programmes of the first half of the fourteenth century. Its crowning glory is the octagonal tower and Lady Chapel at Ely Cathedral. Around 1300, however, there are already the signs of a new style better suited to the adverse economic conditions of the period after the Black Death. In the tracery grid on the outside of St Stephen's Chapel, Westminster, and in the design for the chapter house and cloister of St Paul's Cathedral can be seen the clear rectangular lines characteristic of the Perpendicular style.

Moving westwards or northwards from an imaginary line drawn between the Severn and Humber estuaries, the cultural patterns of lowland England still largely remained dominant. True enough, continental influences might be felt directly, not only along the southern and eastern coasts but also on the littoral of the Irish Sea. Scotland participated in a European culture in ways that often bypassed English mediation. In terms of military architecture, it was hard to avoid English influence. Caerlaverock Castle, occupied by the Scots from 1300, was actually built by the English. The rebuilding of Edinburgh Castle, begun by David II on his return from captivity in 1357, was doubtless undertaken in the spirit of emulation. With regard to church-building, the Scots showed greater independence. The thirteenth-century expansion which sustained ambitious building programmes throughout Britain was checked early and brutally in Scotland with the English invasion. It was not until 1318 that St Andrews Cathedral was finally consecrated. Drawing a considerable income from the shrine of Scotland's patron saint, St Andrews was one of the longest churches in Britain. It is a moot point, then, whether Scots disdain of English-style decoration is more attributable to national pride or to penury. The point remains that, in terms of the high culture of monuments and books, the lands to the west of the Severn and north of the Humber probably appeared as rather backward and impoverished versions of lowland England. The castles, towns, and monasteries looked more like plantations in a wasteland. Still, it was not until travellers moved—as they seldom did—into the fastnesses of Wales, the Highlands of Scotland, or beyond the Pale in Ireland that they came across ways of life which, rather than being a drabber and thinner version of what they knew, seemed positively alien. Even then it was still a map inscribed by the European imagination: the 'other' retained little capacity to surprise.

Metropolitan and provincial

Alongside this metropolitan and international perspective, it is necessary to have regard to the local tap-roots of culture. Throughout Britain, especially perhaps in Wales and Ireland, it is possible to posit the existence of numerous local, regional, even tribal cultures maintained largely by oral tradition. Even in lowland England populations were sufficiently immobile to exhibit considerable linguistic variation. Differences in the pronunciation—or, strictly speaking, the orthography—of Middle English have made it possible to construct interesting distribution maps showing variant renderings of a word like 'church'—'chirche' in the west, 'kirk' north of the Trent. Along with ethnic, linguistic, and dialectal diversity, differences in landscape, settlement patterns, and economic activity must have led to significant variation in popular culture. Communities whose livelihoods derived from fishing or mining differed culturally from communities engaged in pastoralism or agriculture. The differences between 'chalk' and 'cheese' in the south-west Midlands in England went beyond patterns of land use and nourished distinct lifestyles. Across Britain there was doubtless diversity in word usage, proverbs, storytelling, song, dance, children's games, village sports, drama, rituals, and superstitions.

The 'little traditions' which existed in the Middle Ages have largely gone unrecorded. On the basis of folkloric survivals into modern times, it is thus tempting to imagine a lost world of kaleidoscopic richness and diversity. Yet folk songs carefully recorded in modern times have often turned out to be popular ballads published in London in the seventeenth century, while many village festivals are clearly invented traditions. Village culture in the later Middle Ages may well have been as thin and plain as its gastronomy. One well-documented form of cultural expression is the naming of children. Since there are hundreds of saints, and indeed no restriction on using names from romance, name-giving provided real potential for variegation. Eccentric names can be found, but they are few and far between. Among the unusual names, some regional preferences can be discerned: Thurstan, for example, is largely restricted to areas of Norse settlement. What is remarkable is the astonishing level of conformity exhibited in the naming of children. In later medieval England the proportion of males sharing the five most popular names—John, Thomas, Robert, Richard, and William— rose to over 80 per cent. Only the linguistic frontiers—within Wales, Scotland, and Ireland—appear truly significant, and even then the boundary is more apparent than real, with some of the most common names being Welsh and Gaelic versions of John and other old standards.

The conditions of life favoured conformity. For most people life was short and hard. The struggle for survival left little scope for individual creativity. A great deal of folk culture reflected an engagement with the natural world, the rhythms of the seasons, and the colours of the countryside. It had to do with what seemed least mutable in the human condition: birth and death, age and gender. Above all, it drew on a broadly based belief system, which was sustained and constrained by the authority of the Church. Across the countryside, people shared a common culture with circles which far transcended their immediate kin and ken. Villages were less insular and more porous culturally than is often imagined. People looked outwards to the manor houses where rents were paid, to the towns where produce was sold and goods purchased, and to the monasteries, cathedrals, and shrines where education, spiritual guidance, and salvation were to be found. Drawing on the resources of the district, manor houses, towns, and major churches were able to support cultural production on a scale and of an ambition inconceivable at village level. They could likewise provide the conditions for effective transmission and survival. The process can be illustrated by the history of English drama. Drama had deep roots in the countryside. There is evidence of plays and interludes associated with the major rites of passage, church festivals, and the seasons of the year. In some local churches priests embellished the liturgy or enlivened their sermons with dramatizations. Yet popular drama craved re-enactment, and re-enactment with incremental elaboration. It was in the great hall of the lord at Christmas that interludes were staged with more elaborate costumes and props, and in the monasteries that performances were carefully scripted and recorded. Above all, it was in towns across England from the later fourteenth century onwards that whole play cycles were staged, under the auspices of the guilds but with a broad regional audience in mind, and that the foundations of a professional drama were laid.

If it is unwise to talk of highly localized folk cultures, at least in lowland Britain, it may nonetheless be useful to talk about regional cultures. In the remoter parts of Britain regional cultures were sustained by a degree of physical isolation, and ethnic and linguistic separateness. Even in later medieval England it is possible to map 'regional' dialects, though it must be stressed that the lines should not be regarded as deeply etched. Dialect forms, and presumably other cultural traits, shade into one another, and indeed cut across one another in a complex and rich pattern. If regional cultures were to flourish they needed some focus and core. Fairs and pilgrimage centres, noble households and monasteries, and, above all, urban centres, especially cathedral cities, might all contribute to this end. In some combination, they might provide the weight—in terms of population, wealth and stature—to hold in creative suspension local forms of expression and the powerful tide of metropolitan and courtly culture. The districts around Exeter, Hereford, Durham, and Norwich, for example, might have been able to sustain distinctive regional cultures. The diocese of Norwich, for instance, followed its own liturgical calendar. Distinct schools of East Anglian architecture, sculpture, painting and manuscript illumination have been discerned. In the shrine of Our Lady of Walsingham the region had its own major cult.

Generally, though, English culture was becoming more homogenized in the later Middle Ages. Population movement and the growth of the market served to create a common market of taste which was nationwide. Some cultural products were mass produced. Pilgrim badges, seals, and trinkets were disseminated from a limited number of centres throughout the British Isles. English coins constituted the main medium of exchange in independent Scotland as well as in the English colony in Ireland. Many precious items—illuminated manuscripts, embroidery work, and silverware—were likewise highly transportable. Booty from the French wars put some highly fashionable pieces into circulation in provincial England. Even building materials were transported considerable distances. Marble from the Isle of Purbeck in Dorset can be found right across the country. A point to bear in mind is that material culture transcended dialectal and even linguistic boundaries. Craftsmen and artists generally seem to have been highly mobile. Masons, in particular, undertook projects in different regions, and in the later Middle Ages as in earlier centuries architectural fashion passed very rapidly from place to place. The same point can be made with regard to music and dance. Musicians and other players moved round the country in generous circuits, and indeed English minstrels can be found across western Europe. Aristocratic sponsorship facilitated cultural diffusion: minstrels wore the liveries of their noble patrons, and dance troupes—and the particular dances they developed—were often known by the names of their lordly sponsors. During Lent, when there was no demand for their services, minstrels from far afield gathered at some central place to share their knowledge and skills. The city of London hosted a 'school' of minstrelsy in 1358.

The Black Death and the demographic collapse of the later fourteenth century accelerated this process. Population loss diminished the capacity of some regional cultures to sustain themselves. The royal court and the city of London assumed an even more marked predominance in English cultural production. High mortality rates among artists and scholars made consolidation the order of the day, and facilitated cultural integration at a national level. As Philip Lindley has observed, standards in architecture and building could be maintained, but only by drawing on a larger geographical area. There was a regrouping of masons to serve a national market, and an increasing homogenisation of style. According to John Maddison, the transition from the Decorated to the Perpendicular style in Lichfield diocese was surprisingly rapid, indicating less a gradual adaptation to the new architectural fashion from the south than 'the disruption and eventual extinction of the lodge of masons working in the Yorkshire manner' and the completion of their projects decades later 'by one clearly identifiable master mason whose experience was gained in a very different background'.

In the fields of language and literature there is a similar pattern. Writing in the 1380s, John Trevisa attributed the decline in the use of the French language to the plague, when grammarians of the old school were replaced by younger masters who taught Latin in the medium of English. The epoch-making change began in the schools at Oxford, but the men responsible for the change were, like Trevisa himself, Cornishmen. Poets as well as scholars were on the move. The remarkable body of alliterative verse in the dialect of the north-west Midlands is often contrasted with the writing of poets based in London. It certainly drew on its regional roots, and can be regarded as evidence of the vitality of regional culture. But the best of the work was written by and for men with a wider outlook. *Winner and Waster* is concerned with matters of public policy. *Parliament of Three Ages* shows an awareness of both geographical and social mobility. *Sir Gawain and the Green Knight* and *Pearl* may well have been composed and read by Cheshire men far from their native haunts. The last of the great poems from this school, *St Erkenwald*, was set in London and was written in honour of London's patron saint.

Retreat and revival, *c.*1330–1400

The demographic crisis of the later fourteenth century had a considerable impact on the cultural geography of the entire British Isles. The processes that weakened regional cultures in England had dire consequences for the English colony in Ireland. Even in the early fourteenth century its cultural identity was being defended with a shrillness which reflected its vulnerability. The Black Death hit the English towns of the east and south first and hardest. In 1366 stringent laws were enacted to prop up the colony. The Anglo-Irish living in England were ordered to return to Ireland, while forms of fraternization and assimilation with the Gaelic Irish were proscribed. Conversely, the changing demographic and social realities seem to have provided space for Celtic revivals in Wales and Ireland, and perhaps even in Cornwall and the Scottish Highlands. Meanwhile cultural consolidation in lowland England was matched by the consolidation of a distinct 'English' culture in lowland Scotland. The fourteenth century is a crucially formative era for these cultural traditions, and it is interesting to observe the rather different terms on which the various 'national' vernacular cultures were constructed.

In Wales and Ireland there seems to have been a conscious reconnection to a past almost wholly dependent on oral tranmission. The experience of defeat and changing social circumstances prompted a salvage campaign. During the fourteenth century some of the basic rules of Welsh poetic grammar were codified and set in writing. This achievement is associated in later tradition with Einion Offeiriad (*fl.* 1320s–1330s) and Dafydd Ddu of Hiraddug (*fl.* 1350s–1370s). The former seemingly enjoyed the patronage of Sir Rhys ap Gruffudd, who found advancement in the service of the English crown in south-west Wales. The latter was probably a canon of St Asaph who taught in the cathedral school. The work of the two grammarians fed into a broader enterprise, supported in a number of gentry houses as well as monasteries, to bring together classic works of Welsh verse and prose—most of which had survived over the centuries through oral tradition—in composite volumes of grammar, literature, and history. The most notable surviving books are *Llawysgrif Hendregadredd* (The Hendregadredd Manuscript), which may have been first compiled at Strata Florida in the early fourteenth century, *Llyfr Gwyn Rhydderch* (The White Book of Rhydderch) which was composed around the same time, and *Llyfr Coch Hergest* (The Red Book of Hergest), which was put together around 1400. The fourteenth century has been rightly regarded as the most important period in the recording of Welsh literature. As R. R. Davies has observed, 'the heritage of the past was being preserved and organised'.

In Ireland there are likewise few manuscripts from the century or so before the Black Death. A Latin chronicle maintained at the Franciscan friary at Kilkenny ends poignantly with Brother John Clynn's account of his 'awaiting among the dead for death to come'. It may be that it was the threat to oral tradition posed by the pandemic which prompted the Ó Ceallaighs (O'Kellys) in Connacht to gather together a large number of bards and poets at Christmas 1351. This assembly was later commemorated by Gofraidh Fionn Ó Dálaigh (d. 1387) in a poem, 'The poets of Ireland to one house'. The survival of many texts from the later fourteenth century may reflect better conditions of preservation in the stone buildings that Gaelic chieftains increasingly occupied. For the most part, though, it would seem to provide clear evidence of a Gaelic literary revival that reached its peak in the decades around 1400. This 'renaissance' spirit is best exemplified by Seoán Mór Ó Dubhagáin (d. 1372), the author of the *Book of Uí Mhaine*. He looked back to a Gaelic golden age prior to the Anglo-Norman invasion, and sought to retrieve and resuscitate that once proud culture. Written under the patronage of Muircheartach Ó Ceallaigh, bishop of Clonfert, probably before his election in 1392 to the archbishopric of Tuam, it is the first great monument of the Gaelic revival.

The 'great books' of Wales and Ireland were composed almost entirely of texts written centuries earlier. The contents were largely unintelligible to the uninitiated, and there was much in them that must have been wholly obscure to the men who compiled them. Still, they assured the survival of two great literary traditions, and provided the materials for revival and development. Above all, they were works of beauty and prestige. They can be seen as the heirlooms and talismans of peoples who, defeated and marginalized, clung to their culture and language.

It would be a mistake, though, to regard Welsh and Irish culture as wholly traditionalist and defensive. Alongside the bards, the friars, especially the Franciscans, played some role in the promotion of Celtic culture. The mendicant orders were especially prominent and well regarded in Gaelic Ireland. The Franciscan friary at Quin, County Clare, founded in 1433 and still surprisingly intact, lacked the fortifications considered necessary by Irish Cistercian houses. In Wales, as elsewhere, the Franciscans preached to the people in their own tongue, and encouraged vernacular verse. *Gwasanaeth Mair*, a verse translation of the 'Little Office of the Virgin Mary,' and *Ymborth yr Enaid* (Food of the Soul), a mystical treatise, seem to be fruits of their pastoral care. They reveal the rapid assimilation into vernacular culture of current devotional and spiritual concerns, but above all the expressive capacity of the Welsh language. In the fourteenth century, Wales enjoyed a measure of peace and stability, and many Welsh squires and clerks prospered in the royal service and in the French Wars. Dafydd ap Gwilym (*c.*1320–*c.*1360) is the most accomplished of a number of poets who, though well-schooled in the bardic tradition, were open to wider cultural influences, and felt constrained neither by the forms nor by the subject matter of old Welsh verse. His writings indicate a deep engagement with French literature, especially the lyric and the fabliau, and a preparedness to break the rules, not least the bardic prohibition against writing love poetry to married women. He travelled widely in Wales, and a love of the land, its people, and indeed its wildlife is evident. He showed little interest in, or animosity against, the English. It is doubtful that he regarded the great English organ, whose installation in Bangor Cathedral he witnessed, as an alien cultural import. In any case he was too busy ogling a pretty girl! It was in reflection on God's creation and the human condition, not in military defeat and the precariousness of cultural survival, that Dafydd ap Gwilym found poetic inspiration.

It was in Scotland, proudly independent since the triumph at Bannockburn in 1314, that a national culture was constructed which was most explicitly antagonistic to England. In pressing his claims over Scotland, Edward I invoked aspects of the *Brut* tradition. The Scots countered with a rival account of their origins. According to the Declaration of Arbroath (1320), the Scots hailed from Scythia and migrated first to Spain and then to Scotland, where after the defeat of the Britons and Picts they defended the land stoutly against all comers. In the 1380s John Fordun, seeking to confound 'the foolish babbling of the British people', elaborated the tradition in *The Chronicle of the Scots' Nation*. The Scots sprang from Gathelus, a proud Greek not an abject Trojan, and Scota, the daughter of the pharaoh of Egypt, and they settled first Spain, then Ireland, whence they brought the Stone of Destiny to Dalriada. Meanwhile, John Barbour gave expression to Scottish pride in vernacular verse. Barbour's *The Brus* (1375) is a celebration of the heroism of Robert the Bruce, and begins with the immortal line, 'Ah, freedom is a noble thing!' There is a sense, though, in which Fordun and Barbour protest too much. Their protestations reveal their real anxieties about Scotland's political, economic, and cultural weakness. Fordun was based at Aberdeen, but Barbour had travelled in England, and received a licence to study at Oxford. *The Brus* is a bravura performance, but in terms of its language and style it is very much indebted to the broader English literary tradition.

Conversely, what Basil Cottle has called 'the triumph of English' in the fourteenth century needs qualification in a number of respects. There was certainly linguistic chauvinism, most crudely evident in the English plantations in Wales and Ireland. Interestingly, though, the strongest affirmations with respect to the English language tend to be defensive, even plaintive, rather than triumphalist. If the Edwardian wars between England and Scotland stimulated national feeling on both sides of the border, it was the humiliating defeat at Bannockburn in 1314 that prompted the most significant English literary response. Even more important in England was the continuing sense of cultural inferiority to France. In war propaganda it was regularly claimed that the king of France was seeking to destroy the English tongue. The charge was groundless, but it reflected a deep-seated and well-founded anxiety about the status of the English language and culture. Robert Holcot (d. 1349) alleged that William the Conqueror had sought to abolish 'Saxon speech' by making French the language not only of the law courts but also of the schoolroom. He might have noted the wholesale capitulation of English culture to Norman fashion in respect of personal names. Only two Anglo-Saxon personal names—Edward and Edmund—are well-evidenced in later medieval England, and they were not survivals but revivals. Edward, in particular, was re-introduced from the top down, from members of the royal family to their godsons among the nobility.

By the time of the Black Death, Old English was long dead. A study of the copying of Anglo-Saxon charters in the later Middle Ages reveals progressively less interference from the scribes, indicating their growing incapacity to understand the exemplars. English did have more of a literary tradition than the Scots. *The Owl and the Nightingale*, a poem of subtlety and charm, *King Horn*, a lively romance in simple rhyme, and Layamon's *Brut*, a vernacular verse rendition of 'British' history, for example, were written in the early thirteenth century, and still found readers a century later. The alliterative poets of the west and north-west Midlands seem to have had some consciousness of a metre and a poetic language passed down over a longer time-frame. Still, the overwhelming impression is that the English poets of the later fourteenth century were wholly cut off from their Anglo-Saxon roots, and paid scant heed to more recent experiments in the vernacular. While Dafydd ap Gwilym had access to a venerable Welsh literary tradition, his counterparts in England had little in English to build on. For Geoffrey Chaucer and the Chaucerians, Old English was not only a closed book, but a book that they showed little interest in opening.

The new English literature owed much to regional impulses. The Harley Lyrics survive in a book compiled near the Welsh border. In the west Midlands, poets schooled in the alliterative tradition found sources and sponsorship in local monasteries and gentry households. It was under the auspices of Humphrey Bohun, earl of Hereford and Essex (d. 1361), that the French romance *William of Palerne* was reworked as an English alliterative poem. William Langland (*c*.1330–*c*.1388) was probably a native of south Shropshire, born within sight of his beloved Malvern hills. His *Piers Plowman* is a work of considerable originality and energy. It gave urgent voice to the deep religious and social concerns which, long pent up, were clammering for expression, and proved a popular and influential work. Unlike most of the religious art of the later Middle Ages, it won the approval of the reformers and escaped the fires of the Reformation. The fate of the alliterative masterpieces of the north-west Midlands was less happy. Written in what increasingly seemed an alien language and metre, they failed even to become tributaries to the mainstream, and survive only in solitary manuscripts. British Library Cotton MS Nero A x (*c*.1400) comprises the only known copies of four alliterative masterpieces, notably *Sir Gawain and the Green Knight* and *Pearl*. It survived by the skin of its teeth, probably in a monastic house in the north of England, to reveal a poet or group of poets producing work in the north-west Midlands dialect of rare technical sophistication and courtly refinement.

The growing importance of the court and London as centres of cultural production, and the decline of some of the noble households, abbeys, and provincial towns which had nourished cultural life at a regional level, took their toll. Still, the picture should not be overdrawn. The great translation projects which helped to create a serviceable English prose were largely undertaken in the provinces. John Wycliffe (d. 1384) began his translation of the Bible at Lutterworth (Leicestershire), and his disciples continued his work in a number of regional centres. In the decades around 1400, Thomas, Lord Berkeley supported John Trevisa at Berkeley Castle in Gloucestershire in the translation into English of a number of Latin works of history and science. At the same time, the institutions of 'metropolitan' England—the royal court, the bureaucracy, the inns of courts, the universities—were infiltrated, even dominated, by people from the provinces. The city of London was not only the home of Chaucer and Gower, whose families were migrants from further afield, but also the adoptive home of William Langland and the author of *St Erkenwald*. Indeed, the form of the English language which became standard in the fifteenth century owed less than might be imagined to London. It reflected the language of a much wider circle of immigration into the capital, not least the dialect of the many clerks from the north Midlands who staffed the chancery and privy seal offices.

In literary terms the rise of English is associated with the Chaucerians. There is irony here. Geoffrey Chaucer (c.1340–1400) and John Gower (c.1330–1408) began their careers writing in French. Though the son of a vintner of London, Chaucer spent his formative years in court circles which were francophone in language and taste. His decision in the late 1360s to write a major poem in English is the more remarkable in that it was, in part, an elegy for Blanche of Lancaster, the wife of John of Gaunt, duke of Lancaster. For all its borrowing from Machaut and other French poets, the *Book of the Duchess* (c.1370) is experimental in form and has considerable imaginative power. It is linguistically self-conscious: Chaucer uses a higher proportion of English words in this work than in his later œuvre. Over the following decade his confidence in the capacities of his mother tongue and his ambition as a philosophical poet grew in step with a growing engagement with the works of Dante, Petrarch, and Boccaccio. *Troilus and Criseyde* (*c*.1385) is a long and accomplished poem, displaying a wholly unprecedented psychological depth. It can be regarded, not too fancifully, as England's first novel. It reveals, too, an author conscious of his place in history. Though he is oblivious of his Anglo-Saxon forebears, he feels himself part of a literary tradition rooted in the classical world. He is all too aware of the mutability of language, especially his own. Like the poets of antiquity and in emulation of the poets of the Italian *trecento*, he nonetheless writes for the future as well as for his own time.

By the late 1380s English had won acceptance at the English royal court, and English poetry and translation enjoyed the highest sponsorship. According to the original prologue, John Gower began work on the *Confessio Amantis* at the specific request of Richard II. A late convert to the vernacular, Gower almost certainly wrote the poem, too, in emulation of his younger friend's *Troilus and Criseyde*. By this time Chaucer had moved on from the 'dream vision', the ideal device for the ambitious writer seeking a voice but uncertain of his reception. It is not quite clear when he first conceived of the notion of a company of pilgrims telling each other tales on the long road to Canterbury. The device of the frame-narrative was not new, and many of the stories have French or Italian sources. Yet it provided Chaucer with limitless scope for invention—in the characters of the pilgrims, in their interaction on the road, and in the matching of teller to tale. The work seems quintessentially English in its dramatic quality, its rich characterization, and its variously ironic and earthy humour. A merchant's son, a bureaucrat and a courtier, Chaucer was socially amphibious. On his death in 1400 he was buried at Westminster Abbey, partly perhaps because he was already acknowledged as one of the kingdom's cultural treasures.

The literary achievement of the age of Chaucer reflects not a defensive self-absorption, but a confident engagement with French, Italian, and classical models. In other areas of cultural life, England in the later fourteenth century was likewise open to foreign influence. It is true that in church-building England remained stubbornly attached to its own dialects of the international Gothic language. The Perpendicular style which became fashionable in the middle decades of the fourteenth century held the field until the early sixteenth century. It provided a magnificent frame, too, for English schools of glassmaking and wood-carving. Yet in secular architecture there is plentiful evidence of continental inspiration. A number of noblemen and soldiers who had served in the wars in France, and won fortunes in the process, sought to build elegant castles—like Maxstoke in Warwickshire, Bodiam in Sussex, and Cooling in Kent—in the latest French style. They decorated them with Flemish tapestries, some acquired by pillage in France. An increasing taste for brick building from the later fourteenth century onwards reflects peaceful intercourse with the Low Countries. Originally the bricks themselves were imported, perhaps as ballast, but brickworks were soon established in and around London. The memorial brass—one of the best-known items of England's later medieval cultural heritage—is likewise an import from Flanders. The earliest and most fashionable exemplars are all to be found in eastern England, where, despite the ravages of the Puritans, the highest concentrations still survive.

Aristocratic and courtly circles were most open to international influences. Women may often have set the pace. England's fourteenth-century queens were all foreign-born, and had circles of relatives and friends across western Europe. A number of noblewomen—like Marie, countess of Pembroke, and Elizabeth de Burgh, lady of Clare—were discerning patrons of letters and learning. Like Chaucer's prioress, who learned French at finishing school and read romances, many women may have been more literate and refined in their tastes than were their menfolk. In the reign of Edward III many English nobles and knights served in France, and some deepened their engagement with French culture. Henry of Grosmont, duke of Lancaster (d. 1361), military commander and author of the *Livre de Seyntz Medicines*, acknowledged the limitations of his own Anglo-French. William Montagu, earl of Salisbury (d. 1344), a comrade-in-arms of Edward III, brought back from the French wars a collection of French romances. His grandson, John Montagu, earl of Salisbury (d. 1400), wrote French poetry and enjoyed the esteem of Christine de Pizan. John of Gaunt, duke of Lancaster, should be regarded as a European prince, not a provincial nobleman. After a lifetime of political and military adventurism, Gaunt became a convert to peace in 1389, and led English delegations in a number of peace conferences which were characterized by courtly display and emulation. Gaunt recruited into his household a number of notable musicians from northern France, assisting the process of musical cross-pollination.

Above all, it was the court of Richard II that provided the setting for cultural exchange between England and the continent in the late fourteenth century. Richard's marriage to Anne of Bohemia in 1382 brought the English court into contact with the 'imperial' style and cultural eclecticism of the house of Luxembourg. The great coronation portrait of Richard is reminiscent of work commissioned at Prague by the Emperor Charles IV. French influences remained predominant. Richard certainly took his cue from the Valois court, and seems to have run up large accounts with Parisian *ateliers*. Still, he was also a king who took pride in the traditions of English kingship. He used a remarkable team of English architects and craftsmen, most notably Henry Yevele and Hugh Herland; his great building projects were in English Perpendicular style; and the highlight of his greatest monument is the remarkable hammer-beam roof which spanned the remodelled Westminster Hall. The splendid double tomb of Richard and his queen in St Edward the Confessor's Chapel was likewise English work. Since Richard spent lavishly on clothes and jewellery, it is a pity that so little survives to illustrate his aesthetic taste. The Wilton Diptych (*c.*1396) is a richly evocative representation of Richard, supported by his three saintly sponsors, including Edward the Confessor and Edmund the Martyr, kneeling before the Virgin Mary and the Christ Child, from whom he receives a banner symbolizing the kingdom of England. An intensely private work, it speaks to his deep identification with his royal office. Stylistically, it is at the forefront of north European painting. Since there is no record of its commission, the Wilton Diptych remains at heart a mystery, but must be taken as in some measure indicative of the quality of the art work produced for Richard in the 1390s.

Attenuation and consolidation, *c.*1400–1470

The triumph of the vernacular in England, so evident in the early decades of the fifteenth century, seems to reflect an increasing provincialism and insularity. The deaths of Geoffrey Chaucer in 1400 and John Gower in 1408 took from the scene not only the two literary giants of the later fourteenth century but also two men who, though writing in English, were very much part of an international literary scene. The deposition of Richard II in 1399 led to the dissolution of a court which, at its height, had a strongly cosmopolitan flavour. The courts of the Lancastrian kings, by contrast with their predecessors', appear somewhat lacking in vitality and panache. The Chaucerians of the fifteenth century seem decidedly derivative and second-rate. This cultural malaise is a little hard to explain. To some degree it presumably reflects the continuing demographic and economic decline. It may be that it is a matter of more contingent factors. Henry IV (d. 1413) never enjoyed his kingship. Henry V (d. 1422) was in war harness for most of his short reign. It is perhaps significant that women were not so much in evidence at court as they had been in Edward III's and Richard II's time. Henry IV was a widower when he came to the throne. Henry V married late, and the royal couple spent only a few months together in England. Still, it is a remarkable fact that the most interesting verse written in English around the 1420s and 1430s came from the pens of prisoners of war in England: James I of Scotland (d. 1437), the author of the *The Kingis Quair*, and Charles of Orleans (d. 1465), the last great court poet of the Middle Ages.

Yet in its own way the Lancastrian court was open and innovative. Henry IV and his sons were literate, even bookish. Even if they presided over a public culture which was increasingly finding expression in English, the Lancastrian princes commissioned works in French and Latin, and patronized scholars and craftsmen from right across western Europe. In the field of music it may even be said that they set the pace. Perhaps more than most art forms, music crosses boundaries. While the English always took pride in their music, especially church music, they were open to new influences and talent from the courts and cities of Europe. John of Gaunt built up his chapel by heavy recruitment in the Low Countries. England could give as well as receive. Henry IV was a noted musician, and was probably responsible for the compositions attributed to the 'Roy Henry' in the Old Hall Manuscript. His sons seem likewise to have been musically inclined. Henry V's chapel royal became the envy of his contemporaries, and his brothers, Thomas, duke of Clarence (d. 1420), and John, duke of Bedford (d. 1435), maintained this musical tradition. From the Lancastrian stable came a number of singers and composers who later found service in the household chapels of other European princes. The most notable of this cohort was John Dunstable (*c.*1385–1453), whose flowing rhythms and sonorous harmonies revolutionized European polyphony. By the 1440s the *contenance Angloise* was greatly admired. A musicologist of the 1470s enthused that 'the possibilities of our music have been so marvellously increased that there appears to be a new art ... whose fount and origin is held to be among the English, of whom Dunstable stood forth as chief'.

English cultural influence in Wales and Ireland was less welcome. The rebellion of Owain Glyn Dŵr in Wales in the early fifteenth century both reflected and built on the revival of Welsh culture apparent in the later fourteenth century. Interestingly the rebel programme included the establishment of two universities in Wales. In Ireland, too, the Gaelic resurgence continued, and the English colony survived only in attenuated form. The high water mark of English colonization in both countries had long since passed. In an age of demographic decline, the English found it hard to maintain their cultural ascendancy. During the Glyn Dŵr rebellion the Lancastrian regime seemed bent on suppressing the use of the Welsh language. In Ireland the English authorities faced an even greater challenge: the tendency of some Anglo-Irish to go native in language, dress, and lifestyle. Government measures to maintain English cultural ascendancy met with only limited success. In the Welsh heartlands the bardic schools continued to flourish, and in 1450 a major festival or *eisteddfod* was held in or near Carmarthen. Welsh poetry in the fifteenth century exhibited a freshness and vigour wholly lacking in England, while music may likewise have been a source of Welsh inspiration and pride.

Signs of a hardening of cultural boundaries between 'English' and Celt must be set alongside evidence of strategic accommodation. The Welsh continued to prove adept in taking advantage of broader opportunities in England, albeit sometimes forsaking their own traditions. A number of Welsh clerks achieved academic distinction at Oxford, and several Welsh clerks were promoted to bishoprics in England. In Ireland, too, the line between Gael and Saxon was rarely hard and fast. During the course of the fifteenth century, Irish literature was increasingly open to influence with translations of popular French and English works like Mandeville's *Travels* and Caxton's *History of Troy*. Anglo-Irish magnates like the Fitzgeralds, earls of Kildare, owned books in four languages, Latin, French, English and

Irish. The Irish bards, like their Welsh counterparts, sought patrons on both sides of the ethnic divide, and seem surprisingly free of rancour against the English. Indeed, the Welsh poets—the high priests of the 'matter of Britain'—had had some considerable purchase on the English imagination. Henry V was born in Wales, and his military success in France briefly lent some colour to the belief that he was the new Arthur. The Mortimers transmitted to the house of York a pride in their Welsh ancestry. In 1485 another Welshman, the great-grandson of one of Glyn Dŵr's lieutenants, ascended the English throne.

In England and Scotland the major achievements of the fifteenth century were more prosaic. One solid advance was the development of a serviceable vernacular. Despite prohibition by the Church authorities, religious writings in English proliferated. Wycliffe's Bible was beyond the reach of ordinary folk, but Lollard sermons and other tracts were kept in circulation by networks of dissenters. Most vernacular literature was scrupulously orthodox. Two of the most popular works of the age were a translation of the *Legenda Aurea*, a collection of saints' lives, and *The Prick of Conscience*, a devotional work for the laity. The great cycles of plays staged at York, Coventry, Chester, and other towns from the later fourteenth century until the Reformation—which laid the foundations of an English dramatic tradition—had their origins in liturgical celebration and had a clear didactic function. Reginald Pecock, bishop of Chichester (d. 1460), sought to meet the challenge of Lollardy by writing theology in English. His concern to create a vernacular capable of high scholastic abstraction led him to replace Latinate words like 'impenetrable' with ungainly Germanic compounds like 'un-go-through-some'. Secular writers likewise played a role in expanding the capacities of the vernacular. If Bishop Pecock saw ordinary people floundering in the faith because of their lack of Latin, Sir Thomas Malory (*fl.* 1460s) saw the gentry in want of chivalric refinement through their lack of French. Drawing together from a number of sources, English as well as French, he produced in *Le Morte D'Arthur*, the classic English Arthuriad, notwithstanding its French title. In Scotland, too, the capacities of the vernacular were being extended by its use in a range of genres: in morality plays, mostly destroyed in the Reformation; in a verse epic like *The Buik of Alexander* (*c.*1438); in the prose writings of Sir Gilbert Hay; and in the political satire of the *Buke of the Howlat*.

Still, the transformation of Scots from an unstable dialect into a literary language was the achievement of three poets active in the reign of James IV, all of whom acknowledged Chaucer's inspiration: Robert Henryson (*c.*1425–*c.*1506), William Dunbar (*c.*1460–*c.*1513), and Gavin Douglas (*c.*1478–1513).

It is hard to measure literacy rates, but all the signs are that the functionally literate were increasing as a proportion of the population. Education was taken seriously, even—in some quarters—for girls. There must certainly have been a broad under-storey of elementary schooling to support the more visible growth of educational provision at the higher level. Since boys had to have acquired some Latin before proceeding to grammar school, the wave of grammar school foundations in later fifteenth-century England would seem to indicate a massive expansion of more basic educational provision. The point can be made too with respect to the universities. Though the number of graduates declined in the early fifteenth century, this decline was increasingly offset by the growing number of laymen who spent time at Oxford and Cambridge without taking degrees, using the universities as finishing schools and preparation for legal studies at the inns of court. At the same time scholars in the higher faculties found better levels of support. Kings, queens, noble widows, and churchmen making provision for their own souls and concerned to counter the drift of clerks to secular employment, endowed university colleges, whose scholarly communities and building programmes created the ambience as well as the skyline of Oxford and Cambridge. The chapel of King's College, Cambridge, conceived and begun in the troubled reign of Henry VI, though not completed until early Tudor times, remains a monument to the aspirations of this age. Meanwhile, north of the border, the Scots proved even more ambitious. In the course of the fifteenth century, universities, or more exactly perhaps university colleges, were founded at St Andrews (1410), Glasgow (1451), and Aberdeen (1494).

For all their fine buildings, Oxford and Cambridge lost much of their intellectual vitality in the fifteenth century. They shared in the general lassitude of scholastic thought in later medieval Europe. Their main business was in training young men for administrative positions in Church and state. The monasteries likewise ceased to play a major role in the transmission of learning and culture. Thomas Walsingham maintained traditions of chronicle-writing at St Albans into the early fifteenth century, but he was very much the last of the line. There were learned monks, some with classicizing interests, like John Wheathamstead at St Albans, but they were few and far between. English monastic libraries were not as rich in classical texts as some of their continental counterparts. When the Italian Poggio Bracciolini was resident in England in the 1420s, he was as disappointed with the lack of interesting books as he was with the lack of educated people with whom to converse. In the decades which followed a number of men began to embrace humanist scholarship. Humphrey, duke of Gloucester, Henry V's youngest brother, was a bibliophile, and at his death in 1447 his collection of classical works passed to Oxford. John Tiptoft, earl of Worcester (d. 1471), was likewise a man of education and intellect. He spent time in Italy, bought classical texts, translated some of them, and patronized English classicists like John Free. All in all, though, England, and Britain generally, was very much a backwater intellectually in the fifteenth century.

Lancastrian and Yorkist England had its share of earnest intelligence, but it lacked the critical mass of nimble minds which made Florence such a vibrant literary and scholarly milieu. Even more obviously, it lacked the large artisan communities and traditions of craftsmanship which formed the seed-bed of high art. In earlier times England had held its own in a number of fields. In the early fourteenth century English embroidery (*opus Anglicanum*) was in demand as far afield as Rome, Spain, and Constantinople. Prior to the Black Death, English traditions of sculpture, stained glass, and manuscript illumination were generally esteemed. The Black Death and subsequent epidemics took a heavy toll of the artisans and the markets that sustained them, and destroyed traditions of craftsmanship. The fifteenth century saw some restructuring. The decline of architectural and figure sculpture was partially offset by a new emphasis on wood-carving, and a new industry centred on alabaster. English alabaster work found a ready market overseas, and fine English pieces survive in churches across north-west Europe. Visitors to London were impressed by the quality of the work of its goldsmiths. Yet it is clear that, even at its best, the artisanal base in England was narrow and lacking in depth. While there is evidence of mounting production and increasing quality of alabaster work through the fifteenth century, it needs to be acknowledged that in this field England had a clear advantage in terms of availability of raw materials.

Of course, it must be recognised that a great deal of the material culture of the time has not survived. Paintings have been effaced, tapestries moth-eaten, wood-carving burned, and glass smashed. Gold and silver plate was readily melted down as bullion or reworked for new purposes. Since much of the best artwork was produced for the Church, and was destroyed in the iconoclasm of the Reformation, it would be unwise to be too dismissive of the standards of later medieval British art. Odd survivals and recoveries give more positive assessments of British craftsmanship and artistry. There survive a number of wholly remarkable examples of wood-carving, like the great oak sculpture of Jesse, once part of a richly carved rood screen, in the priory church at Abergavenny, or the series of confidently designed oak carvings known as the Beaton Panels which seem to have been made at Arbroath Abbey on the eve of the Reformation.

Still, it is hard to escape the conclusion that they represent no more than isolated pockets of creativity. Britain imported rather than exported art in the late fifteenth and early sixteenth centuries. Many of the finest pieces of wood-carving, all the best examples of stained glass, and the only serious portraits from the decades around 1500 are either imports from the Low Countries and the Rhineland or the work of foreign craftsmen working in Britain. Some of the more promising and ambitious local artists sought apprenticeships and employment in continental workshops. Jean Mayelle, a goldsmith of Paris, who produced a ceremonial mace of exquisite beauty and iconographical subtlety for St Salvator's College, St Andrews, signed his work 'John Maiel Gouldsmith' and may have been a native of Scotland. Alexander Bening, a noted Flemish miniaturist of the later fifteenth century, was certainly a Scot. He was an associate of Hugo van der Goes of Bruges, who painted the altarpiece for Trinity College church in Edinburgh. One of the most impressive paintings to survive from later medieval Britain, its extant panels include full-length portraits of James III and his family, their saintly patrons, and the provost of the college, Sir Edward Bonkil, who commissioned the work.

What survives best of all are the buildings themselves. The later Middle Ages was not a period of monumental architecture. There was a scaling down of large building projects, whether ecclesiastical or military, in response to the diminishing income from the land and increasing labour costs. Still, work on the fabric of cathedrals and monasteries, and even some stylistic innovation, continued through into the sixteenth century. In England the Perpendicular style remained dominant. Its austerity was well suited to the times. It was able to take advantage, too, of the increasing availability of glass, opening up the church interiors to light. New foundations were best placed to take full advantage of the new style, but in the more prosperous parts of the countryside many parish churches were enlarged and remodelled. Among the best examples of Perpendicular architecture are the great 'wool churches' of the Cotswolds and East Anglia, like Chipping Norton (Oxfordshire), Steeple Ashton (Wiltshire), and Long Melford (Suffolk). In Scotland some broadly analogous patterns can be discerned. A number of large-scale building projects—for example, the rebuilding of Melrose Abbey, destroyed by the English in 1385—continued through the early fifteenth century. As in England, though, the focus was on enlargement of the main burgh churches, like St Giles, Edinburgh, and on new collegiate foundations like St Salvator at St Andrews. Stylistically, Scottish church architecture remained aloof from English trends: more solid in frame, more rugged in decoration, and less insular. John Morrow, who superintended the work at a number of major churches in the early fifteenth century, had been born and trained in Paris. Local traditions of stone-carving continued to be exploited in architectural schemes. The collegiate church of Roslin (Midlothian), founded and possibly designed by William St Clair, earl of Caithness, exhibits an exoticism of design and exuberance of decoration wholly unparalleled south of the border.

New and old, c.1500

The growth of population and the quickening of economic life in the last quarter of the fifteenth century accelerated the cultural trends. Many of the building programmes of the Middle Ages found completion only in the decades around 1500 with the erection of towers and spires. The building and beautification of parish churches in England is matched by the construction of ampler and more durable houses by the country gentry, the yeomanry and the burgesses. The standards of domestic comfort were increasing, especially in the south and east, with the use of brick as well as timber and stone, the incorporation of more glass, and the installation of chimneys. The better-housed aspired to be better furnished. The ownership of a bed was no longer the preserve of the aristocrat, and the possession of tables, chairs, drapes, pewter, cutlery, and so on may seem to have been becoming far less socially exclusive. This phenomenon is apparent in Scotland as well, where a foreign visitor in the 1490s was surprised to find town houses of the east coast as solidly built and comfortably furnished as in Italy and Spain.

The increasing prosperity and ambition of the middling ranks of society can be seen, too, in the increasing demand for education and books. In the later fifteenth century there is evidence of a marked increase in educational provision. In England hundreds of grammar schools were endowed in the decades around 1500, while in Scotland an Act of Parliament of 1496 required every freeholder to keep his eldest son at school until he had learnt 'perfect Latin'. The establishment of the printing press at Westminster in 1476 served as both a response and a further stimulus to increasing literacy. Books, broadsides, and woodblock prints were put within the reach of householders who could not have afforded manuscripts and paintings. Less is known of conditions in Wales and Ireland, where schools were few and far between, and literacy rates lower. Cultural transmission in Welsh and Gaelic remained traditional in content and form. Precious manuscript anthologies were vulnerable to tempest and fire, and the few survivals from the later Middle Ages may owe something to the increasing use of building in stone. Printing was to play some role in stabilizing the Welsh language. Unlike Catholic Ireland, Protestant Wales was allowed the vernacular Bible in the mid-sixteenth century.

For the most part, though, print technology served as a powerhouse of anglicization. From the outset printers were committed to mass production, and that meant maximizing their market. William Caxton (*c*.1420–*c*.1492) identified the variety of dialects in England as a major obstacle to his business plan, and addressed it by mixing the spelling conventions of a number of regions. His strategy broke the nexus between pronunciation and spelling, leaving the phonetic confusion of words like 'though', 'through', 'bough', and 'cough'. Printing assisted the development of a national culture in other respects. Of course, the processes of homogenization were well under way. The ballads of Robin Hood acquired a national currency long before the age of print. In the fifteenth century they seem to have been as well known in London and the lowlands of Scotland as they were around Sherwood Forest and Barnsdale. Print, though, served to accelerate this process considerably. The Westminster and London printing presses drew on material from regional cultures as well as from overseas, translating and repackaging it for national consumption.

England was becoming increasingly integrated economically and socially. The remarkable growth of London is the most striking manifestation of this process. In the later fifteenth century London began to measure up to other major European cities as a centre of cultural production and consumption. It had a vigorous civic culture, stimulated by the proximity of the English royal court and the seat of government at Westminster, but by no means overshadowed by them. Testimony to its cultural and intellectual maturity can be found in the household of Thomas More (1477–1535), a nursery of 'virtue and learning', likened by Erasmus of Rotterdam to the academy of Plato. Britain had no other truly metropolitan centre. Edinburgh was sometimes styled 'the Paris of Scotland'. The proximity of the Stewart court rescued it from mere provinciality. Yet even the Scots recognized the greater stature of London. It was a Scots poet who penned the most famous eulogy of the southern capital. It is symptomatic that London was the only major publishing centre in Britain. Printing was not introduced into Scotland until the early 1500s, and for a generation remained utterly dependent on royal patronage.

Politics, too, played a role in the increasing integration of English culture. The revival of monarchy counteracted the centripetal tendencies of the Wars of the Roses, and under Edward IV and the Tudors the court became an even more significant centre of cultural patronage. Henry VII's new palace at Richmond, his new chapel at the east end of Westminster Abbey, and his white marble tomb and bronze effigy were regarded by foreign visitors a century later as among the wonders of Christendom. The artist mainly responsible for Henry VII's tomb was a Florentine, Pietro Torrigiano, who brilliantly integrated elements of English tradition in a new humanistic style of effigial sculpture. His revolutionary contribution to English sculpture went beyond the introduction of the first nude *putti* in monumental work. For Sir Thomas Lovell, he produced the first bronze medallion portrait-profile in England, while in the tomb he made for Dr John Yonge (d. 1516) he introduced the use of terracotta to Britain. Henry VII made some use of English craftsmen, but he entrusted his most important projects to foreigners like the king's glazier, Barnard Flower, another import from the Low Countries.

The importance of the royal court is even more strikingly apparent north of the border where, in their various ways, James III (1460–88) and James IV (1488–1513) proved generous, broad-minded, even eccentric patrons of the arts. While in their patronage of the visual arts they tended to look to foreign masters, with respect to music and literature they played an important role in cultivating local talent. The establishment of the chapel royal at Stirling in 1501, and the expansion of the choir at Dunkeld around the same time, held the promise of a revitalization of church music in Scotland. Both James III and James IV loved secular music: the latter played both lute and clavichord. Meanwhile, in the decades around 1500 a number of Scots poets—Henryson, Dunbar, and Douglas—gave Scotland a literature to rival that of its southern neighbour, while the kingdom was able to hold its own against England militarily until the disaster at Flodden (1513). It is instructive that from around this time the term 'Scotis' begins to replace 'Inglis'. Yet this construction of cultural identity excluded more than the English. Just as the Stewart monarchy had brought the semi-independent kingdom of the Isles, with its Gaelic-speaking population, under its control, so the new Scots culture confirmed the subject status of traditional Gaelic culture, and accelerated its decline.

Yet the focus on nation-building should not be too narrow. Both the English and Scottish courts offered generous patronage to foreign craftsmen and scholars in the last quarter of the fifteenth century. Edward IV had strong links with the court of Burgundy, and had a special interest in chivalric pageantry. Henry Tudor came to the throne after spending a formative decade in France and Brittany. The courts of James III and James IV were probably even more open to a range of cultural influences, including, however grudgingly, from its southern neighbour. If Scots poets were more concerned to stress their distinct 'Inglis' identity, it was because of their recognition of the power of English culture. Yet Scotland's distinctness stemmed in some measure from its distinctive relationship with Europe, from cultural links unmediated by England, and perhaps even from its expatriate communities in France, the Low Countries, Germany, and the Baltic. There was no English schoolman at the beginning of the sixteenth century to rank with John Major, a colossus of learning and doyen of the University of Paris. Italian influences were arguably stronger in England. From the 1460s a number of humanist scholars like Pietro Carmeliano and Polydore Vergil found advancement at the English court. The openness of England to the new classicism is seen in the steady growth of humanist scholarship in the decades around 1500. The churchman John Colet (c.1466–1519), the physician William Linacre (c.1460–1524), and the lawyer Thomas More were men well regarded in Christendom's Republic of Letters.

English and Scots consumers, and doubtless the Welsh and Irish who had the means, continued to be drawn to foreign craftsmanship and style. Their passion for portraits, medallions, brasses, tapestries, and even stained glass and wooden sculpture could only really be satisfied by artists from the Low Countries and Germany. The history of English painting began a wholly new chapter with the arrival of Hans Holbein in London in 1526. Scotland at least had the Benings in Bruges: Simon Bening, whose mother was a sister of Hugo Van Der Goes, continued the tradition of service to the Stewart court, and was responsible for the execution of the *Book of Hours of James IV and Margaret Tudor*. Even after the introduction of printing, books remained a major import to Britain. As far as Bibles, the classics and other important texts were concerned, England, and even more Scotland, remained a colony of the great publishing houses of Europe. For all its bombast, English culture in the age of Henry VIII still lacked confidence. In his *The Boke named the Governour* (1531), Sir Thomas Elyot acknowledged that in many of the arts the English were inferior to other people, and 'constrained, if we will have any thinge well painted, carved, or embroidered, to abandon our own countrymen and resort unto strangers'.

Plate 9 Manuscript illumination depicting King David II of Scotland (*left*) and King Edward III of England, clasping each other's hand. Each figure is surmounted by his coat of arms. David was captured by the English at the battle of Neville's Cross (1346); he was later ransomed for 100,000 marks and thereafter adopted a more pacific policy towards England. BL MS Cott Nero DVI. © The British Library.

Kingdoms and dominions at peace and war

Robin Frame

Throughout most of the fourteenth and fifteenth centuries the countries of the British Isles were, formally at least, in a state of war. The Hundred Years War (1337–1453) followed earlier Anglo-French hostilities during the 1290s and 1320s. From 1296 England and Scotland were rarely at peace, and Franco-Scottish alliances meant that the two wars were closely intertwined. The invasion of Ireland by the Scots in 1315 and the landing of French forces at Milford Haven in 1405, though exceptional events, are reminders that these wars affected, directly and indirectly, all the dominions of the English crown. Alongside the two great conflicts, other wars took place. The comparative tranquillity that followed Edward I's conquest of north Wales in 1282–3 was broken by Welsh risings in 1294–5 and again in the first decade of the fifteenth century, under Owain Glyn Dŵr. The government of Ireland, where the English settlements were increasingly on the defensive, was on a permanent war footing; by the later fourteenth century the position seemed sufficiently grave to require intervention from England, culminating in Richard II's expeditions of the 1390s. During all these wars, fighting was spasmodic and often very localized. The major conflicts were punctuated by frequent, and sometimes lengthy, truces. Edward II and Robert Bruce arranged a thirteen-year truce in 1323. Richard II and Charles VI negotiated a marriage alliance and a twenty-five-year truce in 1393. (Typically, both agreements were overtaken by events.) But diplomatic activity, plans, and practical preparations filled the gaps between hostilities; there was no suspension of anxiety and mutual suspicion. Political structures, interregional relations, and attitudes within the British Isles were profoundly affected by war and the expectation of war.

The British Isles at peace, c.1286

It may be helpful, first, to identify some salient features of the various territories during the brief spell of peace that preceded the wars that began in the 1290s. The year 1286 is an arbitrary moment for such a survey, but it has advantages. When it opened, Alexander III was still living, and it seemed likely that his second marriage would supply the heirs he needed. The acceptance in 1266 by Norway of Scottish rule over the Western Isles and the Isle of Man symbolized what has been described as the 'completion' of his kingdom. Alexander's first wife was Edward's sister, and the dealings of the two kings had on the whole been amicable. From an English perspective, there were other reasons for satisfaction. The conquest of north Wales appeared to have been successful. During 1286 Edward was sufficiently confident of his position in Britain to leave for a three-year stay in Gascony. His visit, unlike those made by Henry III, had administrative and diplomatic purposes, and did not take the form of a military campaign. In Ireland, the Dublin government had proved capable of gathering resources across the east and south to support the recent war in Wales. Richard de Burgh, the new earl of Ulster and lord of Connacht, was on the point of leaving England to begin a long career during which he was to dominate the northern and western peripheries of the colonial heartlands. Edward and Alexander between them appeared to exercise a stable hegemony over the entire archipelago. The good relations between the two regimes are apparent in the marriages contracted by the English and Scottish aristocracies which across the thirteenth century had multiplied the number of families who held lands in each kingdom.

Both rulers presided over complex realms, though the complexity is more obvious in the case of the large, dispersed possessions of the English crown than that of the smaller Scottish kingdom, with its single governmental focus. The extent and variety of the English dominions is not fully captured in the titles used by Edward I, who was styled 'king of England, lord of Ireland and duke of Aquitaine'. The kingship of England carried with it the allegiance of marcher lords beyond the boundaries of the kingdom, in eastern and southern Wales. The conquest of north Wales had extinguished the only other surviving princely power within Edward's sphere. Under the Statute of Wales (1284), the new royal lands had been annexed to the crown of England. The lordship of Ireland had its centre of government at Dublin. But while Ireland was in theory a single entity, rule there in practice involved contrasting forms of lordship over the regions controlled in depth by English settlers and those where Gaelic lords—who were no longer usually referred to as 'kings'—held sway. The duchy of Aquitaine (reduced in practice to Gascony) was also a composite region. English power was deeply rooted in and around the towns of Bordeaux and Bayonne, which had become closely tied to England by the wine trade. Beyond that coastal strip lay a patchwork of territories—such as the Agenais, which Philip III had released to Edward only in 1279—where French and English claims to jurisdiction jostled, and lords and communities were not slow to change their allegiance. Edward held other overseas territories. The county of Ponthieu in Picardy had recently come to his wife, Eleanor of Castile, from her mother's family. The Channel Islands, run by a further devolved administration, was a remnant and reminder of the duchy of Normandy, which King John had lost in 1204.

Although England was of course regionalized, by the standards of most sizeable European kingdoms it appears unified and administratively homogeneous. The entire country was divided into shires. Legal cases came to the central courts, of which Parliament was the chief, and revenues flowed to the exchequer, from all parts of the kingdom. Judicial commissions penetrated almost everywhere; where they did not—as in the palatine liberty of the bishops of Durham—the privileges of lords were strictly defined. Above all, a single common law was current; regional custom and seignorial jurisdiction were much less prominent than in contemporary France or Germany. Royal legislation applied across the country: the Statute of Winchester (1285), for instance, had recently updated the obligations incumbent on all able-bodied men to keep arms, armour, and horses according to their wealth, and to participate in watch and ward and in the forcible repression of crime. Unity was also reflected in, and promoted by, the distribution of aristocratic interests. Second-rank lords frequently had a regional focus, and the interests even of leading families tended to be concentrated either north or south of the Trent. But the landed portfolios of magnates were usually scattered across many counties, and those of lesser figures were not always restricted to a single region. That of the de Clare earls of Gloucester, for instance, included extensive estates from East Anglia and the home counties to the Bristol Channel; while the Percy family, not yet established in Northumberland or among the greatest of the kingdom, were Yorkshire barons, but also had important interests in Sussex. Such cross-linkages, which make it impossible to depict England as a collection of magnate supremacies, combined with royal government to ensure cohesion.

The Welsh marcher lordships, which until 1282 formed a chain around native Wales from the hinterland of Chester to Brecon and Pembroke, lay beyond the regular scheme of royal government. Their early formation and frontier position had enabled them to stay outside the developing systems of English law. Each lordship had its own body of custom, amalgamating elements of feudal, Welsh, and (through time) common law. Jurisdictionally each was self-contained; disputes between lordships were regulated through negotiation and occasional violence—for lords claimed the right to make war, not just against the Welsh, but against one another. But any impression that they were independent of crown authority must be heavily qualified. The marchers were not a cohesive group whose horizons were bounded by Wales and the March. Most major lordships were held by men who also had interests in England, and sometimes in Ireland; for many, their marcher holdings were only a subordinate part of a broader inheritance. In Edward I's time the earls of Gloucester were lords of Glamorgan and of Kilkenny, while the earls of Hereford held Brecon. Marcher lordships were pieces on the chessboard of English politics. They were held from the crown, which exercised rights of lordship over them: they came into the king's hand through forfeiture and minorities, and he had influence over the marriages of marcher heiresses and of male heirs who were under age. The March was occasionally troublesome, not because it was separate, but because of its close connection with the wider scene. Its frontier history meant that it could readily lapse into violence at times when national politics were disturbed. This had happened during the Barons' War of Henry III's reign, and was to occur again under Edward II. Jurisdictionally, the March lay beyond England; politically, however, it was an extension of the kingdom.

Upon conquering north Wales, Edward I retained Snowdonia and Anglesey in his own hands, treating them as an administrative unit. The Statute of Wales laid out a legal and governmental structure for north Wales, which was organized into the counties of Caernarfon, Anglesey, Merioneth, and Flint (the last-named administered from Chester rather than Caernarfon). The Statute provided a streamlined version of English law for the settler population. The laws used by the Welsh were radically reformed, sweeping away native criminal codes but preserving much of the existing law of property and inheritance. In practice the higher governmental offices in Wales—justiciars, chamberlains, sheriffs, constables of castles—tended to be held by Englishmen. Lesser positions were, however, open to the Welsh, who continued to manage their own communities. Some indeed, such as Sir Gruffudd ap Rhys (Gruffudd Llwyd) whose career lasted from the 1290s to the 1320s, moved on a wider stage, achieving shrieval office and acting as arrayers and captains of troops raised for the king's wars. The effects of the conquest were paradoxical. Edward insisted that Wales was now inalienably joined to the crown of England, and neither he nor any successor as king used the title 'prince of Wales'. Wales, however, remained administratively separate, and socially and legally distinctive. The habit of conferring the title and its associated revenues on the heir apparent to the English throne neatly encapsulated the situation: on the one hand, it acknowledged the particular history of Wales; on the other, since the principality was bestowed only upon the eldest son or grandson of the sovereign, who could not be displaced in the succession, it emphasized the fact that the principality belonged constitutionally to a larger political whole. The grant to the first English prince, the future Edward II, in 1301, was made 'to Edward and his heirs, *being kings of England*'.

A similar integration was assumed in the case of the lordship of Ireland. When Ireland had been included, along with Gascony and other territories, in an appanage for the future Edward I in 1254, Henry III had stated that all these lands formed an inalienable part of the crown of England. The English king became lord of Ireland by virtue of his accession to the English throne; there was no separate

Irish investiture. By Edward's reign, the whole island had been granted out to settler lords, so that in law his rights over Ireland were sufficiently expressed through the homage and allegiance they owed him. Largely because of the timing of its conquest and settlement, the lordship had received a superstructure of English institutions. The English law that was developing fast in the late twelfth and early thirteenth centuries was formally extended to Ireland in a council held there by King John during his visit in 1210. Dublin emerged as an administrative capital; ministers of a similar stamp operated on both sides of the Irish Sea, working in the Irish chancery, exchequer, and courts of law. By the late thirteenth century a scheme of counties and liberties had become established across the colonized east and south of the island, providing office-holding opportunities, from the posts of sheriff and seneschal downwards, for the settler gentry. A network of towns also existed, from the rich seaports such as Carrickfergus, Drogheda, Dublin, Waterford, Cork, Limerick, and Galway to signifi-cant inland boroughs, of which Kilkenny was the greatest. In these, too, families originally from Britain prospered through a combin-ation of landholding, trade, and magistracy.

This anglicized world was, however, only one aspect of a divided country. Over much of the north and west, settler magnates exercised a shallow lordship over surviving native dynasties, from which they expected to receive tributes and services. In 1286, when the power of Richard de Burgh in Ulster and Connacht was paralleled by that of other barons in the south-west, colonial supremacy was probably at its height. But it remained fragile, and was frequently contested by Gaelic lords such as the O'Neills in west Ulster or the MacCarthys in west Cork. Even in the south and east, there were upland or boggy regions, such as the Wicklow mountains and their fringes, where Irish ruling kins retained power. 'English' Ireland was never a solid terri-torial block; it was broken by zones that were economically marginal and culturally hybrid; often these also formed military frontiers.

Within the colonial districts there remained a Gaelic population, which except in some core settlement areas formed the numerical majority. Whatever may have been the intention in 1210, by Edward's time English legal status was reserved for the settlers; the Irish, unless they purchased charters of 'English law and liberty' from the crown, normally had no direct access to the royal courts and could not aspire to a place in public life. In the legal field at least, English government in Ireland drew firmer lines of demarcation between colonist and native than was the case in Wales either before or after Edward I's conquests. Again, the explanation lies in the chronology of conquest and settlement, together with their incompleteness. Edward's seizure of north Wales occurred at a time of thoroughgoing legal reform in England; its aftermath shows inventive legal minds dealing with a territory that had been finally conquered under royal leadership. Ireland, in contrast, had been partially occupied through spasmodic baronial enterprise. The settler élite carried with them English custom as it had come to exist by the late twelfth century, and legal consciousness was sufficiently developed for John and Henry III to insist that law on the two sides of the Irish Sea should be kept in harmony. But in the early thirteenth century English law was not sophisticated enough to permit adaptation to Irish circumstances; nor was there a definitive royal conquest of Ireland that might have prompted a wholesale fresh design, along the lines of the Statute of Wales.

Viewed from England, Gascony might appear to be another appendage of the English crown. However, its status and political position differed fundamentally from those of Wales and Ireland. Gascony fails to meet several of the criteria that have led historians to apply the epithet 'colonial' to the other two countries. The English king's homage for the duchy confirmed the fact that, willy-nilly, Gascony was within the orbit of the French crown. Nor was England's role as a metropolis fully replicated in the duchy. Some English administrators, soldiers, and merchants acquired property there, but there was no colonization to match that which occurred in Wales and Ireland. The Gascons themselves remained in a full sense Edward's subjects; they did not constitute a 'native' population, subordinate, like the Welsh and Irish, to an intruding élite. The legal position tells a similar story. The English carried their laws wholesale to Ireland and with some adjustments to Wales; in both countries native law was frowned upon as at best eccentric and at worst immoral. Gascon custom, on the other hand, prevailed in Gascony, without English adulteration; this is not surprising, since it was a recognizable mixture of Roman and feudal law. Gascony's integration rested more on economic self-interest and fear of French oppression than on cultural and legal assimilation. To describe it as annexed to the English crown was really a thirteenth-century way of saying that it belonged inalienably to the Plantagenet dynasty, whose centre of political and governmental gravity now lay in England. Such phrases could not conceal the fact that Edward I ruled in Gascony, not as king and sovereign lord as he did in his insular dominions, but as duke and a peer of France.

Unlike Edward I, Alexander III employed just one title—'king of Scots'—to express his authority north of the Tweed and Solway. The regnal status of regions such as Strathclyde, Galloway, Moray, and the Western Isles was now merely a memory. Only the Isle of Man, where the English had strategic interests, offers a possible parallel to the detached parts of Edward I's dominions. Culturally, however, Alexander's kingdom was far from homogeneous; nor did his government operate uniformly throughout it. Across a swathe of territory from the Moray Firth to the Clyde and Solway, taking in all southern Scotland together with the eastern lowlands, he ruled in ways that would have been instantly recognizable in England— though his administration might have struck freemen in the English shires as less elaborate and demanding than the style of government to which they were accustomed. His power was expressed in royal burghs, often the sites of royal castles, from Inverness and Elgin south to Berwick and Roxburgh, and west to Dumfries, Wigtown, and Ayr. There was a common law, owing a good deal to English models, which regulated, among much else, succession to land among the upper classes. Sheriffs and provincial justiciars, many of them descended from Anglo-Normans who had been settled in Scotland by his twelfth-century ancestors, administered justice and generated revenue. On the northern mainland and in the far west, by contrast, he depended upon attracting the allegiance of powerful lords and kins, for some of whom Norwegian lordship had until recently been an option. (Orkney and Shetland were to remain outwith the Scottish kingdom until the later fifteenth century.) These lords presided over regions where Gaelic custom predominated and sea-power mattered. At important moments the unity of the kingdom is visible. In 1275 lords from Argyll and the Western Isles had played a crucial part in subduing a rebellion on the Isle of Man. In 1284, when Alexander provided for the succession after the death of his sons, the document setting forth the arrangement was witnessed by an impressive gathering of magnates, including the lords of Lorn, Islay, and Garmoran. Political coherence was not, however, accompanied by administrative or legal uniformity. As Alexander Grant has pointed out, the apt comparison may be less between the kingdoms of Scotland and England, than between a regionalized and culturally hybrid Scotland and the entirety of the English king's dominions within the British Isles: regal Scotland, too, had its 'Celtic fringe'.

From what has been said already, it will be apparent that by this period England had become the core of the king's dominions, rather than forming one element in a multi-centred Norman or Angevin 'empire'. The loss in 1204 of Normandy and Anjou had severed the Plantagenet house from the areas in which it had its original roots. This had not resulted in any royal disengagement from the continent. Henry III's attachment to his mother's second family, the Lusignans, gave his court a Poitevin flavour; and his wife's connections with Savoy and Provence, together with his anxiety to protect Gascony, had involved him in the politics of the western Mediterranean. Edward I was equally determined to be a major player on the European stage. Nevertheless, the impact of the changed configuration of the royal dominions is unmistakable. In 1259, by the Treaty of Paris, Henry had finally accepted the loss of the bulk of his continental inheritance in return for recognition as duke of Gascony, for which he did homage to Louis IX. Throughout his reign he lavished funds on the rebuilding of Westminster Abbey, where he created a family mausoleum which seems to have been a conscious echo of Louis's Sainte Chapelle in Paris. (Henry II and Richard I had been buried at Fontévrault in Anjou.) He was devoted to the memory of the abbey's founder, Edward the Confessor, after whom Edward I was named. Unlike their predecessors, Henry and Edward spent the bulk of their time in England. The English Parliament, moreover, acquired an 'imperial' dimension, as petitions and appeals flowed to it from Wales, Ireland, the Channel Islands, and the continental lands. With the suppression of the kingdom of Scots in 1296, Scottish business too was handled in English courts and parliaments.

Concentration upon England may have been the product of earlier military failures in France, but the focusing of administration that accompanied it was typical of the late thirteenth century: this was a time when European rulers, with the help of legal experts and increased material resources, were advancing their claims to jurisdiction and their practical control over outlying parts of their dominions. The annexation of north Wales, and the elaboration of English law and government both there and in Ireland, can be viewed in such a context, as can Edward I's assertion of what he saw as his rights as 'lord superior' of Scotland during the 1290s. There is a parallel in the advance of the Scottish kingdom itself in the north and west, though this was less bureaucratic in style and has left fewer traces of legal theorizing. The tendency of the English crown to swallow up other regimes within the British Isles was noticed by contemporaries. In an oft-quoted passage, the chronicler Peter Langtoft, writing after the extinction of the Scottish kingship, celebrated the fact that now only one king—Edward I—reigned within the archipelago.

We should, however, beware of attributing to Edward a conscious project of conquest and assimilation. His first Welsh campaign, in 1277, had been a disciplinary expedition along similar lines to those of his predecessors; he had moved to conquer north Wales only after further disputes with Llywelyn ap Gruffudd proved intractable. There is no sign that the subjugation of Scotland was part of his agenda while Alexander III and his descendants lived. Far from willing a crisis, Edward had his eyes firmly fixed on the consolidation of his rule in Gascony and, after the fall of Acre in 1291, on a crusade. Nor did he set out to obliterate regional diversity. The stage that English government had reached by this period meant that the Plantagenet dominions were tightly managed, through more regular administrative processes, than they had been in earlier generations. Nevertheless, they remained as much a federation as an integrated unit. In 1305, when Edward laid out a scheme for the government of an apparently conquered Scotland, he confirmed the common law of Scotland, described as 'the laws of King David'. His older territories, as we have seen, contained Welsh marcher custom, hybrid customs in the principality of Wales, together with the distinct customs of Gascony and the Channel Islands. In Ireland, minor variants of English law among the colonists were respected, and there was no sustained drive to extirpate the laws of the Gaelic Irish. In some circumstances, indeed, the multiple character of the royal dominions could be regarded as a strength. When Edward II's ministers were planning the recovery of Gascony after its seizure by the French in 1324, they recommended that his army should contain contingents from Wales, Ireland, and Scotland as a way of advertising the English king's power and quasi-imperial status. The inhabitants of the king's dominions might all be regarded as the king's subjects, but this did not mean that they were governed by a single law or that they shared what a later age would have called a common English citizenship.

Interlocking wars

The wars that began between the French and English kings, arising initially from disputes over the status of Gascony, have been described as a collision between two state-building enterprises. The position of the English ruler—sovereign in his variegated insular dominions but a vassal of his French counterpart in his duchy—raised problems that were hard for self-respecting, up-to-date kings to live with. France itself saw an even more striking enlargement of monarchical power, reflected in clashes between the government of Philip IV and regional interests in Flanders, Brittany, and Languedoc. As in Gascony, these often centred on the right of the king's *parlement* at Paris to hear appeals from anywhere in the kingdom. In this climate, Philip could hardly tolerate alliances between the duke of Gascony, whose homage he had received, and those whom he regarded as rebels or enemy powers. Edward I, like other provincial lords in France, resented the growth of royal jurisdiction; nor could he accept that his diplomatic options as king of England should be limited by Philip's veto. The frequency and intensity of Anglo-French friction between the 1290s and the 1370s probably owed more to French monarchical ambitions than to the actions of the English. Edward and his successors represented a major obstruction to the sovereignty of their French counterparts. The Plantagenets in turn felt threatened by a realm far larger, more populous, more urbanized, and more advanced economically and culturally than their own.

In 1293–4 escalating jurisdictional disputes between Edward I and Philip IV produced an outbreak of war. Though there was little military action after 1298, and a partial settlement was reached in 1303, conflict was renewed, and Gascony again seized, during the 1320s. When war flared up yet again in the late 1330s, it proved intractable. Matters were now complicated by Edward III's claim to the French crown through his mother, Isabella, the daughter of Philip IV. Edward delayed assuming the title until 1340, when his proclamation as king of France at Ghent seems to have been prompted by a desire to

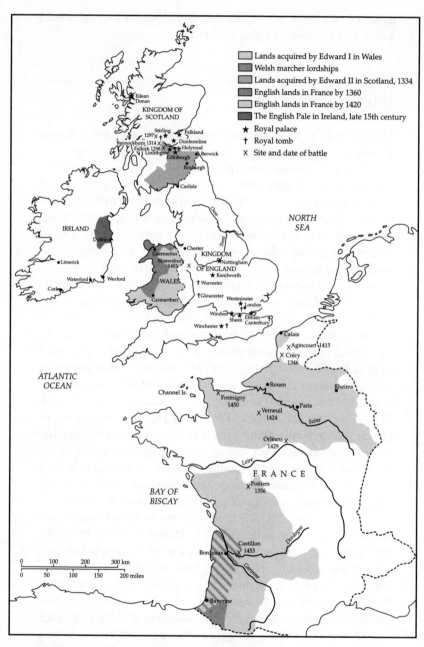

Map 8 England and its dominions in the later Middle Ages.
Source: J. Cannon and R. A. Griffiths, *The Oxford Illustrated History of the British Monarchy* (Oxford, 1985).

provide his allies in Flanders, and eventually (he hoped) in France itself, with legal justification for their actions. Although the claim to the kingship was mostly a diplomatic stratagem, and the French crown only occasionally a goal seriously pursued, the asking price for its abandonment—usually an expanded Gascony and additional territories to be held in full sovereignty—was too massive and humiliating for the French monarchy to contemplate. Such compensation was indeed agreed at the Treaty of Brétigny (1360); but this was when the French cause was at a particularly low ebb, with King John II a prisoner in England after the Black Prince's victory at Poitiers (1356). John's successor, Charles V, seized the opportunity to reclaim sovereignty over the duchy before the end of the decade. So the episodic 'Hundred Years War' resumed, apparently incapable of resolution in a final peace. It is usually regarded as ending in 1453, when Gascony was lost by Henry VI. But no definitive settlement was arrived at, and both Edward IV (in 1475) and Henry VIII campaigned in France.

The wars in France had an additional dimension, which was of profound importance for the British Isles. The 1290s, as well as concluding more than a generation of détente in Anglo-French relations, saw the end of an even longer period of peace between England and Scotland. No Scottish army crossed the English border between 1217 and 1296. The Treaty of York (1237) had seen the surrender of the claims of the Scottish royal house to Cumbria and Northumberland, which had been the main source of disputes during the twelfth century. Henry III and Edward I had thereafter been content to remind the Scots now and then of the English claim to their homage for the kingdom, without pressing the point. Dynastic mishaps, however, introduced new tensions. An acute succession problem arose from the deaths of the two sons of Alexander III in 1281 and 1284, of Alexander himself in 1286, and of his only surviving descendant, his granddaughter, Margaret, the 'Maid of Norway', in 1290. Edward I was invited to arbitrate among the claimants, who were distant kinsmen of the late king. Edward, however, insisted upon acting as judge, and went on to behave as the domineering feudal superior of John Balliol, to whom the kingship was awarded in 1292. In these circumstances, the French option, which had periodically been explored by the Scots at least from the 1160s, again beckoned. A Franco-Scottish treaty—traditionally regarded as the start of the

'Auld Alliance'—was concluded in 1295. In 1296 a disastrous invasion by the Scots led to John's deposition and the forfeiture (as Edward saw it) of Scotland to its English overlord.

The French commitment to the Scots remained limited and self-serving, but from this point onwards the two wars overlapped, producing in the English a persistent fear of encirclement. Without the Scottish complication, it is likely that Anglo-French relations, both in the 1290s and in the 1330s, while no doubt stormy, would have taken a different course. When England, weakened by the political troubles surrounding the deposition of Edward II, at last recognized Robert Bruce's kingship in the Treaty of Edinburgh (1328), the Franco-Scottish alliance, which had been renewed at Corbeil two years earlier, remained in place. When Edward III reopened the war in 1333, forcing the young David II into exile, David received the protection of Philip VI. Philip's backing for the Bruce cause proved to be one of the most important triggers of the Hundred Years War. Edward's absence on the Crécy-Calais campaign of 1346–7 saw David, who had returned to Scotland in 1341, invade northern England, only to be captured at the Battle of Neville's Cross. Edward's decision not to campaign in person in France in 1355–6 was motivated by the danger which the Franco-Scottish alliance posed to Berwick; Scottish acceptance of the ransom treaty that eventually freed King David in 1357 was directly related to the defeat of the French at Poitiers. Richard II's campaign against the Scots in 1385 was provoked by the arrival of French troops in Scotland. The Dauphinist armies opposing Henry V and Henry VI were augmented by Scottish troops, some 6,000 serving in the army defeated by the duke of Bedford at Verneuil in 1424. The Scots had an obvious interest in the continuation of the French war, and the triangular relationship between England, France, and Scotland long outlasted the collapse of the English position in France. But after 1453 other options could at times be explored: in 1474 Edward IV and James III were able to reach an accommodation that endured to 1485.

Throughout most of the Hundred Years War the English kings, while aiming to maximize their frontiers and rights in Gascony, were not engaged in territorial conquest. Edward III, for all his continental military successes during the 1340s and 1350s, occupied nothing save Calais. During the 1370s and 1380s, it is true, Cherbourg and Brest were added. But the ports of northern and western France were regarded more as 'barbicans', necessary for the defence of England itself and the sea routes to Bordeaux and Bayonne, than as steps towards conquest. The permanent garrisoning of such centres was inordinately expensive, and Cherbourg and Brest were given up during peace negotations by Richard II. There was, however, one exception to this pattern of limited commitment. After the capture of Harfleur and the victory at Agincourt (1415), Henry V embarked on a systematic conquest of Normandy, taking and garrisoning towns and granting to English settlers lands forfeited by those who continued to oppose him. This policy was maintained for a generation after his death, creating in Normandy an additional English dominion, which at its height extended into Maine. Henry's reign was exceptional in a further sense. It coincided with feuding between the various branches of the Valois dynasty under the mentally unstable Charles VI. Pre-eminent among the contending parties were the dukes of Burgundy, who since their acquisition of Flanders in 1384 had been constructing a powerful state in the frontier zone between France and the German Empire. These circumstances provided Henry with the levers to gain, through the Treaty of Troyes (1420), recognition as heir to Charles, whose daughter he married. The boy king Henry VI was actually crowned at Paris in 1431 as successor to his French grandfather. These events were shot through with ambiguities. Did Henry VI rule Normandy as its duke, or was the duchy to be regarded as part of France, of which he was titular—and for a time partially also in practice—king? Did his status as king of France mean that the burden of sustaining the war should now fall on his French (and Norman) subjects rather than his English ones? Did the Treaty of Troyes, which had involved Henry V in recognizing Charles VI's sovereignty in order to inherit it, supersede the old claim to France based on Edward III's descent from Philip IV? Such questions were never resolved. The English were happy to accumulate justifications of their position, no matter that some of these might contradict others.

The effect of Henry V's startling successes was to impose additional obligations upon those who followed him, making it even harder to withdraw from positions that had been taken up. English nobles—among them Henry VI's uncle, Duke Humphrey of Gloucester, and his most famous commander, John Talbot, earl of Shrewsbury—had a stake in conquered French lordships. More important, there was a substantial group of settler gentry, merchants,

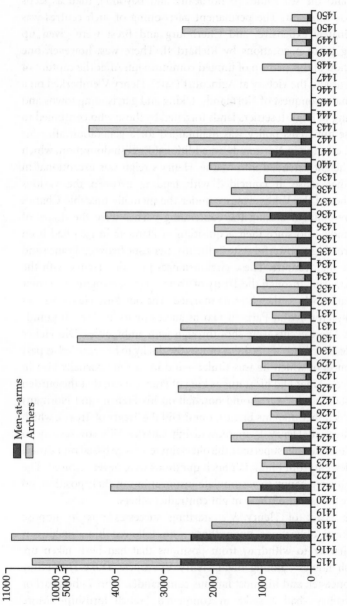

Figure 3 Numbers and ratios of archers and men-at arms in English expeditionary armies to northern France, 1415–50. Source: A. Curry, 'English Armies in the Fifteenth Century', in A. Curry and M. Hughes eds., *Arms, Armies, and Fortifications in the Hundred Years War* (Woodbridge, 1994).

and churchmen in Normandy who expected their interests to be pro-tected; or, failing that, at least to receive compensation for what they lost. The collapse of the Anglo-Burgundian alliance in 1435, followed by the fall of Paris in 1436, led to a progressive waning of enthusiasm in England for funding an increasingly unsuccessful war. Sharp dif-ferences emerged about the strategies to be pursued. Nevertheless, there was an underlying consensus that the work of Henry V should be defended and maintained. Henry VI's policy of pursuing an accommodation with the French, exemplified by his cession of Maine in 1445, aroused deep suspicions. After the collapse of Normandy in 1450–1 and the final defeat in Gascony in 1453, the English might hold nothing in France save Calais; but the title 'king of France' had become inseparable from the English kingship itself. Rival Lancas-trian and Yorkist claimants to the throne could not afford to seem to take it other than seriously.

The impact of war on political geography

When evaluating the effects of war on the British Isles, it is important to remember that the 'Anglo-French' conflict was not a matter simply for England. Wales was throughout the war an important recruiting ground for infantry: in that sense, Shakespeare's Fluellen embodies a historical reality. On the other side, 'Owen of Wales'—Owain ap Thomas ap Rhodri (d. 1378), the last significant survivor of the dis-inherited princely house of Gwynedd—could find military employ-ment under the Valois kings. But for most of the period English power was sufficiently secure for Wales not to attract the attention of the French. The rebellion of Owain Glyn Dŵr in Henry IV's reign briefly altered these circumstances; it was all the more threatening because there were men around Owain who were themselves veterans of English campaigns in France and Scotland. In Ireland, there were occasional rumours of contacts between disaffected elements and the continental enemies of England. Now and then Anglo-Irish lords served abroad, as in Flanders in 1297 or at the sieges of Calais in 1347 and Rouen in 1418. But Ireland was too distant and disturbed to play a major role in the calculations of either side. Only in Henry VII's time, when the Pale and the southern ports became a springboard and

refuge for the Yorkist pretenders Lambert Simnel and Perkin Warbeck, did it begin to attract sustained continental attention as a possible 'backdoor to England'. In theory, however, the king's lordship of
Ireland was as much at war with France as were England and Wales.
Irish merchants were forbidden to trade at enemy ports. Irish as
well as English shipping might be threatened by Scottish, Breton, or
Castilian pirates. Lands held in Ireland by French religious houses
or secular lords, such as the Norman count of Eu, were subject
to forfeiture.

The chief significance of the war for Ireland was, however, rather
different. Security within the English colony deteriorated during the
fourteenth century, as economic conditions worsened, population
levels fell, and tillage contracted. The more marginal areas of the
original settlement passed into the control of Gaelic and 'Gaelicized'
lords; they and their adherents competed, often violently, for grazing
in what was largely a cattle economy. By the 1350s the settler communities of eastern and southern Ireland increasingly looked to the
crown for financial assistance and military intervention. In 1361
Edward III sent his son, Lionel of Clarence, across the Irish Sea
in command of the first of a series of expeditionary forces. From
this point on, an inverse relationship is apparent between activity on
the continent and military commitment to Ireland. The armies of the
1360s were sent during the long hiatus in the French war that followed
the Treaty of Brétigny. Richard II's Irish expeditions of 1394–5
and 1399 likewise took place while the continental war was in abeyance. By contrast, the 1370s and early 1380s, when Anglo-French hostilities entered a particularly intensive phase, saw English governors
stranded in Ireland without the funds they had been promised. It is
entirely in keeping with this pattern that it was Henry V who took the
decision to reduce expenditure on Ireland and rely upon his subjects
there to provide for their defence as best they could.

It is, of course, improbable that the lordship's complex problems
would have proved amenable to the sort of military solutions that
were within the resources of the English crown. Nevertheless, the
king's subjects in Ireland were convinced that the problems could be
solved in this way; and it certainly did not help that English involvement proved fitful and half-hearted. A contemporary view from
Ireland is contained in part of the tract known as *The Libelle of
Englyshe Polycye*, which was composed in the late 1430s, probably to

support a strategy against the French that would forward Humphrey of Gloucester's ambitions in the Low Countries. The author stressed the king's title to Ireland, the potential wealth of the country, its importance to England's security, and the desirability of a military initiative that would bring the entire island under effective royal control. The case is thought to have been inspired by James Butler, fourth earl of Ormond (d. 1452), the most powerful Anglo-Irish lord of the day:

> I herde a man speke unto me full late,
> Whyche was a lorde and of ful grete astate,
> That exspenses of one yere don in Fraunce,
> Werred on men well wylled of puissaunce
> Thys seyde grounde of Yrelonde to conquere . . .
> Myght wynne Yrelonde to a fynall conquest
> In one soole yere, to sett us all in reste.

The argument was in fact more subtle than this. It did not present war in France and war in Ireland as stark alternatives; rather, it sought to promote a full conquest of Ireland by claiming that this would strengthen England's position in the wider contest.

The full implications of the Anglo-French conflict become apparent, however, only when it is considered together with the Anglo-Scottish war, which had a major impact on the distribution of power and shape of interregional relations across the entire archipelago. Northern England and southern Scotland became frontier zones, in a way they had ceased to be during the thirteenth century. Until the 1290s the far north of England had relatively few castles; its aristocracy was not heavily militarized; the normal operations of sheriffs and itinerant judges embraced Cumberland, Westmorland, and Northumberland. Across the border, Lothian and eastern Strathclyde formed a core area of Scottish royal power, with numerous royal burghs, a tight network of sheriffdoms, and few large, compact lordships. Decades of war profoundly altered these conditions. By 1400 the entire region, on both sides of the border, was dotted with small castles and pele towers. Berwick, once the richest trading town of the Scottish kingdom, was now a heavily defended English advance post. The power of regional magnates—notably the Percys and Nevilles on the English side and the Douglases and Dunbars on the Scottish— had grown, nourished by the possession of wardenships and captaincies, and the manpower and funds associated with them. Nobles such as Henry Percy, first earl of Northumberland (d. 1408) and William, eighth earl of Douglas (killed by James II with his own hand in 1452) were, as a result, significant in politics at national level.

The make-up of the Scottish kingdom was affected in another way. The thirteenth century had seen the lords of the western highlands and islands increasingly drawn within the orbit of the crown. From the 1290s the Balliol–Bruce competition, together with English diplomatic and naval intervention, gave western magnates and kin-heads alternative focuses for their allegiance. For a time, Robert Bruce, who had himself been earl of Carrick, was able to prevent the unravelling of royal power through military campaigns and a personal network of support in the west. But the weakness of his successors allowed the MacDonalds to construct a hegemony that stretched from the Hebrides into Argyll and Ross. The Lordship of the Isles came to have an ambiguous relationship with the Scottish kingdom: while not repudiating their allegiance to the king, John of the Isles (d. 1387) and his successors did not hesitate to enter into diplomatic relations and alliances with the English. It retained its semi-detached position until the 1490s, when Scottish royal authority advanced again, largely by exploiting disputes within the MacDonald kin.

These changes had important consequences for Ireland. In the thirteenth century, English power in the north and west of the island—which had seen only very patchy settlement from Britain and southern Ireland, mostly in fertile coastal areas such as those around Belfast Lough, Coleraine, and Galway—had depended crucially on individual magnates: from 1286 to 1315 Richard de Burgh ran Ulster and Connacht virtually as a personal fiefdom. His necessary involvement with the Gaelic Irish was counterbalanced by his continued membership—evidenced by the marriages of his son and daughter into the family of the earls of Gloucester—of English court and aristocratic society. Initially, he held the north of Ireland steady against Scottish intrusion, participating in English campaigns against the Scots, and playing an important role in Anglo-Scottish diplomacy. But in 1315 Edward Bruce, King Robert's brother, invaded Ulster and began a series of campaigns deep into midland and southern Ireland. For three years Bruce occupied the main centres of the earldom and presented himself to the Gaelic Irish as 'king of Ireland'. His activities began the process by which the de Burgh supremacy

Plate 10 Bunratty Castle, County Clare. This large tower house was built in the mid-fifteenth century for the Gaelic McNamara lords of the Clan of Cullein. It passed to the Anglo-Irish earls of Thomond in the sixteenth century. Photo J. Allan Cash.

was undermined; the murder in 1333 of Earl Richard's grandson and successor advanced it markedly. His inheritance passed to an infant heiress, and through her to absentees. By the later fourteenth century English power in the north of Ireland had shrunk to the coastal enclaves. Bands of galloglasses (mercenary foot soldiers) flowed without hindrance from Argyll and the Isles into the employ of Gaelic lords in northern Ireland, where they established their own chieftaincies. Around 1400 a branch of the MacDonalds expanded into the Glens of Antrim, turning the north-east corner of Ireland into a virtual extension of the Lordship of the Isles. By the 1430s the settler communities of north Leinster, Meath, and Louth were subject to attack from the O'Neills and O'Donnells from Ulster. The Dublin government portrayed itself as menaced by a combined Irish and Scottish threat emanating from what now seemed a wholly alien region.

Despite the power of lords such as the MacDonalds and the O'Neills, the Gaelic world that stretched from Argyll and Ross to Sligo and Armagh lacked cohesion. There was little likelihood that anglophone Scotland or the anglicized areas of southern Ireland would be overrun. Nevertheless, the outskirts of English and Scottish royal power, which in the 1280s appeared to be coming increasingly within the field of dominance of two centralizing monarchies, now formed a threatening penumbra for both. These shifts cannot be attributed solely to the wider wars of the period. But war, by focusing the attention of the English and Scottish monarchies on each other, and on France, played a significant part in altering regional relationships and political balances within the British Isles.

War and national identities

The protracted experience of war had a significant impact, not just on political structures but also on perceptions. Many—perhaps most—of the familiar ingredients of national identities were already present in the 1280s. Two centuries later, however, identities were more sharply etched and allegiances less complicated by alternative ties. There were, of course, many reasons for this, among them a rise in lay literacy and the increased use of the written vernacular. But war was undoubtedly important. It swept populations into 'national' enterprises, spawned royal propaganda and patriotic prose and verse, and encouraged collective anxieties and xenophobia.

Scotland provides an appropriate starting point, for there has been considerable debate over the extent to which it already possessed a national identity before 1286, and how far that identity was a product of the Wars of Independence. The most satisfactory answer may be that, while key elements of Scottish identity were present in the time of Alexander III, the following century gave them a clearer focus, while removing certain ambiguities. In the thirteenth century Scotland had a single king, whose court and patronage were import-ant for the élites, not just of the closely governed core of the kingdom, but also of its fringes. There was a Scottish Church whose bishops had fought a successful battle against any suggestion that they were subordinate to the archbishop of York. Despite the lack of an arch-bishopric, since the late twelfth century the papacy had placed it beyond doubt that the Church in Scotland answered directly to Rome, without any English intermediary. The importance of such markers was evident in events during the decade 1286–96. Even without a king, the kingdom continued to exist, and was governed successfully by panels of Guardians, made up of lay nobles and ecclesiastical leaders. During the period when a marriage was being negotiated between the Maid of Norway and the future Edward II, the Guardians formulated positions, accepted in the Treaty of Birgham (1290), which conceptualized the kingdom's rights: to its proper territorial and jurisdictional boundaries, to its own laws, and to its established traditions of government.

There were, however, some potential stumbling blocks. The existence of complexes of 'cross-border' property—the Scottish royal house itself had English estates—had served to reinforce the thirteenth-century peace. But when conflict did come, Anglo-Scottish proprietors faced awkward choices, not least since the war against the English was complicated by the existence of pro-Balliol and pro-Bruce parties. Those who made the wrong choices formed a group of disinherited, who were likely to align themselves with the English. Though the process took several decades after 1296, the wars ulti-mately removed this complication, producing a more clearly Scottish nobility. In 1313, the year before his victory at Bannockburn, Robert Bruce had declared that all those who did not join him would be subject to forfeiture; this was confirmed in the Cambuskenneth Parliament held shortly after the battle. Edward III's occupation of parts of southern Scotland during the 1330s gave temporary hope to the losers. By the later fourteenth century, however, a firm line had been drawn between the English and Scottish aristocracies, which was to last until 1603 or even 1707. Scottish earls and barons no longer possessed English property; for all but the occasional renegade, the political focus was the Scottish court, councils and parliaments, together with the French connection. There was now a neater match between the kingdom itself and the horizons of its nobility.

The protracted wars also affected the way that Scots thought about their past. An existing body of historical matter told the story of the *Gaedhil* (Gaels). While its original relevance was to the regions north of the Forth, there are signs that during the thirteenth century it had come to be regarded as belonging to the kingdom as a whole. The material, however, was common to Ireland and Scotland, and stressed the Irish origins of the Scots. This proved useful to the Bruces when they sought support in Ireland, but it had the capacity to complicate the vision of a national past. Three generations of war helped to give the story a more distinctive character, and to make it unambiguously relevant to the southern parts of the kingdom, where Scots or lallans (that is, English) was becoming the accepted language. (The Gaelic tradition continued to be developed in the north and west, where the Lordship of the Isles offered ready patronage to a learned class for whom the narrow seas between Scotland and Ireland were a highway, not a barrier.) Between the 1370s and the 1440s a series of prose and verse histories by John Barbour, John Fordun, Andrew of Wyntoun, and Walter Bower reworked the remoter past, adding to it the story of heroic resistance to the English from 1290 onwards. Barbour, writing a celebratory metrical biography of Robert Bruce in Scots, was more barefaced than Fordun in the way he highlighted the Bruces and Stewarts and edited out or blackened the reputations of Scots who had opposed them. But, whatever their political emphasis, together these works served to purvey the same patriotic message.

There can be little doubt, too, that they found a broad and receptive audience. It was, after all, in the lowlands that the experience of war was most intense. It is striking that during periods—such as the kingless years 1296–1304 or David II's exile of 1334–41—when magnate leadership was weak and divided, English garrisons in southern Scotland suffered constant harassment, and the occupation failed to attract durable support at local level. In 1296 Edward I's government demanded fealties from a wide spectrum of society: the so-called 'ragman rolls' in which these are recorded contain more than 1,500 names, which must represent a substantial proportion of the lesser landholding class between the Tweed and the Forth. Edward III's occupation of the same area a generation later came in the wake of extensive ravaging and involved numerous forfeitures. Alongside such intrusion and oppression, there was the experience of mobilization by Scottish leaders against the English, and of profitable raids south of the border. Scottish armies were recruited on the basis of a general levy, which meant that the population at large participated from time to time in hostings under the command of the local and regional élites. This system meant that Scotland did not suffer the heavy war taxation that shaped the English polity at the same period. Even so, taxation became more frequent, notably during the decade after 1357 when David II's ransom was being raised. The royal need to tap the wealth of the towns led to the appearance of representatives of the burghs in Parliament. In all these ways, the war loomed large in the consciousness of the inhabitants of the kingdom. It was the work of Barbour and the others to make sense of this common experience.

Such reinforcement of national identity in Scotland finds some parallels in Ireland, though the position there was more complex. The shrinkage during the fourteenth century of securely settled 'English' territory, and with it the extent of the directly governed lordship, led to a reduction, particularly apparent from the 1360s, in the number of magnate interests that spanned the sea. Numerous English families liquidated their Irish properties, selling the portions that retained value to men who were resident in Ireland. For example, important properties in the region between Dublin and Dundalk fell into the hands of the Prestons and the Bellews, who were to be leading families of the Tudor Pale; and in 1392 the Butler earls of Ormond acquired Kilkenny from the Despensers. There remained important exceptions to the rule, above all the Mortimers, lords of Trim in Meath and titular earls of Ulster (whose eventual heir was Richard, duke of York), and the Talbots, lords of Wexford. Members of these families served as governors of Ireland between 1379 and 1460. Nevertheless, the late medieval period saw a geographically reduced English

Ireland increasingly dominated by a group of resident lords who by the fifteenth century were forming a parliamentary peerage.

Within the contracting lordship of Ireland, there was an intensified sense of Englishness. The inheritance of English law and government, together with an awareness that their titles to property and expectations of patronage tied them to the crown, had nurtured the English identity of the settlers in the thirteenth century. This was enhanced by their participation in the Scottish wars, and even more by their increasing embattlement within Ireland itself. Fourteenth-century legislation, notably the Statutes of Kilkenny (1366), outlawed unlicensed marriages and negotiations between English and Irish, together with the use among the settlers of the Irish language, dress, and customs. It betrays deep-rooted worries about Gaelic cultural influences, which in earlier, confidently expansionist days passed with little remark. Anxiety is the keynote of much of the surviving evidence. When around 1420 James Young of Dublin wrote, in English, a book of guidance for James Butler, fourth earl of Ormond, he included elaborate justifications of the English title to Ireland, adding extra points to those listed by Gerald of Wales more than two centuries earlier. He also regaled Ormond with stories of his ancestors' military achievements against the Irish. Instances when Henry VI's government casually lumped all those born in Ireland together as 'aliens' within England—for fiscal purposes or admission to the inns of court—fuelled feelings close to paranoia on the part of the 'English of Ireland'. The Irish portion of the *The Libelle of Englyshe Polycye* betrays these sentiments. It tries on the one hand to raise the profile of the lordship in English eyes, and to counter any suspicion that royal rights to the entire island were weak; and on the other, through scathing remarks about the primitive character of the native Irish, to promote the idea that the crown should identify itself with the Anglo-Irish, and sponsor a final conquest that would spread civilization and prosperity.

These developments were matched by—and were partly a response to—a revival of the Gaelic culture, in which, ironically, elements of the settler nobility, including junior members of the Butler family, participated. In the thirteenth century, literary production along traditional Gaelic lines had languished. By contrast, the late fourteenth and fifteenth centuries saw the compilation of impressive compendia such as the *Book of Lecan* and the *Book of Uí Mhaine*, written in

Gaelic and employing an Irish script. Among their contents were genealogies of ruling families and topographical lore that might express the territorial rights of dynasties. There was also a flowering of bardic poetry, often extolling the stylized attributes and military exploits of Irish lords. Behind all this lay, not merely renewed confidence in the native culture, but also the availability of patronage from Gaelic-speaking lords, many of whom were of mixed descent. Among the courts where Irish men of learning gained employment was that of the MacMurroughs of south Leinster, where in the thirteenth century the Gaelic traditions appeared to have been virtually obliterated. It is not surprising that, in the eyes of the Anglo-Irish, the military threat to their position in Ireland had come to seem inseparable from a challenge to their English identity.

Late medieval Wales has some similarities to Scotland and Ireland, but it reveals important differences. Save during the crisis of the Glyn Dŵr rising, the country remained firmly under English control. The ties of the marcher lords with England did not weaken, let alone snap. Accidents and strategies of marriage and inheritance concentrated holdings in the March in the hands of progressively fewer families, some of whom were major players on the English political stage. For instance, the marriage of the future Henry IV to an heiress of the Bohun earls of Hereford brought additional Welsh interests to the Lancastrian dynasty; while Richard, duke of York, as heir of the Mortimers, gained another complex of marcher property. At the same time, royal ministers, acting in the name of the king himself or of an assertive heir to the throne such as the Black Prince, who held the principality from 1343 to 1376, kept a firm and exploitative grip on the royal territories. Under Richard II, Chester and north Wales together formed a redoubt of manpower and political support.

Despite the political integration, the opportunities of officeholding available to members of the Welsh squirearchy, and intermarriage and cultural exchange between English and Welsh, barriers and differences persisted. Legal processes could work against those of Welsh status. While many boroughs had substantial Welsh populations, the families who controlled economic and political life were usually English, and self-consciously so. In the March, aspects of Welsh custom were kept alive by English lords who found them financially lucrative. English domination of the higher offices in both zones of Wales was a perpetual reminder that this was a conquered country. English administrative documents were peppered with stereotyped references to the unreliability and moral shortcomings of the Welsh. In return, the Welsh squirearchy patronized—and in some cases, such as that of the fourteenth-century poets Dafydd ap Gwilym and Iolo Goch, themselves composed—works that synthesized native and foreign traditions. One strand in Welsh literature commemorated ancient glories, lamented the oppressive present, and took comfort in a future when Wales would come into its own again. Such ideas were widely propagated during the Glyn Dŵr rising. Owain was deeply aware of his royal descent, and portrayed himself as successor to the dispossessed native princes. On the English side, the sense of insecurity resulting from the rebellion led to attempts to reinforce the walls of exclusion. Legislation of 1401 sought to prohibit the Welsh from holding office and from acquiring property in the boroughs. It seems to have been little enforced. English domination of Wales was sufficiently secure to continue to allow intermarriage, cultural exchange, and the advancement of reliable native families, such as the Herberts of Raglan, in the service of the crown and of marcher lords. The emergence of the partly Welsh Tudors as heirs of the House of Lancaster added a fresh dimension to the long story of accommodation.

As this sketch suggests, the various peoples within the archipelago had come to be defined in relation to England and Englishness. The Scots had validated their political separateness. The native Irish and Welsh had asserted their distinctiveness, in the former case with some success in the military as well as the cultural sphere. Except in the region where Gaelic Ireland and Gaelic Scotland flowed into one another, links between the peoples who resented English claims were transient and more often a matter of propaganda and wishful thinking than of practical cooperation. Nevertheless, sources from the various countries exhibited fellow-feeling. Irish annalists recorded Edward I's oppression of the Welsh and Scots. A Scottish cleric in the 1360s opposed a scheme to recognize one of Edward III's sons as heir to the childless David II with arguments that included the maltreatment that the Welsh and Irish had already received at the hands of the English. Such ideas were sufficiently familiar for Edward Bruce and Owain Glyn Dŵr to float schemes for a grand alliance among the non-English peoples of the British Isles. Over against such fantasies lay a state defined by an Englishness that was not confined within the borders of England itself: in Ireland, in Wales, and briefly in Normandy, there were substantial settler groups which saw themselves as sharing an English identity, with its accompanying rights—which included entitlement to protection by the English crown.

The force of such ideas owed not a little to the intensification of national feeling in later medieval England itself. Nowadays no historian is likely to argue that English national identity was a new phenomenon in the age of the Anglo-Scottish and Anglo-French wars. Anglo-Saxonists have explored the construction of identity during the centuries between the conversion of the English and the defeat at Hastings. A strong case has been made for the speed with which the Normans inherited and remodelled the English past, so that by the time of the first conquests in Ireland most contemporary observers referred to the invaders as 'English', not as 'Normans' or 'French'. Further signs appeared in the thirteenth century: from the explicit references to the common law as 'English', to the insistence by English barons and chroniclers alike that Henry III should be advised by 'native-born' counsellors, rather than by foreign relatives and administrators.

Persistent and burdensome wars contributed to a heightened sense of Englishness during the fourteenth and fifteenth centuries. The crown constantly taxed and mobilized its subjects: between 1336 and 1453 around three-quarters of the royal income came from taxation, which was justified by military necessities. It spread information and justifications of its policies, through addresses in parliaments and great councils, proclamations in county courts, and the preambles of thousands of individual orders relating to military service, the raising of supplies, coastal defence, and the requisitioning of ships. The official view of war was also inculcated through sermons, and by the circulation of newsletters—the equivalent of dispatches from the front—which found their way into chronicles from Westminster to York and Dublin. It was in the king's interests to stress the threat enemy action posed to the kingdom. In 1344 Edward III's ministers told the Commons in Parliament that the king had received clear intelligence that Philip VI intended to occupy England and 'destroy the English language [nation]'. The naval victory at Sluys in 1340 was followed by the striking of a gold noble with an enduring design: it showed the king standing in a ship, with the resonant legend *Jesus autem transiens per medium illorum ibat,* a reference to Christ walking on the water. But fear of invasion or encirclement was not merely a neurosis played upon by the crown. The movement of Philip's fleet from Marseilles to the Channel ports in 1336 was a major contribution to the outbreak of war in the first place. The south coast was raided in 1338–9. In the late fourteenth and early fifteenth centuries, Breton, Castilian, and Scottish pirates, allied with the French, preyed upon English and Irish shipping. The late fourteenth-century 'barbican' policy symbolizes the sense of English interests and need for defence. Henry V's conquest of Normandy reduced the fear of attack for a generation; the loss of the continental lands was followed by renewed investment by Edward IV in a fleet of royal ships.

Wars that may strike the modern observer as essentially dynastic thus acquired a national and patriotic character. It is not, of course, surprising that influential individuals and particular groups should have associated themselves with the war effort. During the fourteenth century in particular, France offered wealth in the form of plunder and ransoms. According to Jean Froissart, Richard II's bellicose uncle, Thomas of Woodstock, duke of Gloucester, was scathing about the comparative poverty of the rewards from campaigning in Ireland. For the gentry of Cheshire and Lancashire, a region exploited as a recruiting ground by the Black Prince, John of Gaunt and others, war was a profession offering wages and other rewards. The prosperity of the merchants of Bristol was founded partly on the Gascon wine trade. Henry V's conquests added French lands and titles to the inducements. But there was undoubtedly an identification of wider public opinion with Plantagenet goals. This is apparent in attitudes towards Gascony. The claim that the duchy was an integral part of the 'crown of England' became an article of faith. Edward III's successes had enabled him in the Treaty of Brétigny to extort from the French an acceptance that he held the duchy in full sovereignty. When this arrangement broke down, the status of Gascony was once more at the centre of the conflict. In the 1390s, Richard II toyed with the idea of passing the duchy to John of Gaunt, who might have reached an accommodation with the French over the question of homage. It is not surprising that this inflamed opinion among the powerful Gascon interests who feared a sell-out; but it also seems to have aroused hostility in the English Parliament, where magnates and gentry alike saw it as dismemberment of the crown and as the surrender of the very point that Edward III, with their help, had campaigned long and hard to establish. It was only with the military, political, and financial catastrophes of the later 1440s that the consensus finally unravelled. The English who were clinging on in Normandy were left to lobby desperately for support at home, while Gascon lords made what terms they could with the advancing power of France.

At the end of the fifteenth century

In the later fifteenth century political relationships and perceptions within the British Isles were markedly different from those in the time of Edward I. Scotland had established its independence, and the networks of landholding that once tied its élites to England had been broken. Its separateness was expressed in the maintenance of a characteristic diplomatic orbit, involving Burgundy, the Hanse towns, the Scandinavian kingdoms, and, above all, France. From the Scottish monarchy's standpoint, these successes had exacted their price. Relations with England were complicated by the existence of powerful border families, whose interests—like those of their counterparts on the other side of the frontier—were not always congruent with those of the crown. More seriously, perhaps, royal control over the *Gaeltacht*, which had been advancing in the thirteenth century, had loosened, not least through the revival of the ancient ties between western Scotland and the north of Ireland. This was only the most dramatic sign of change within Ireland itself. There too central power had ebbed, more quickly than might have been the case had the English crown not been so absorbed with France. Edward I had taken for granted the ability of his ministers to hold courts and gather revenues across most of the area south and east of a line drawn roughly from Dundalk to Limerick and Cork; he could also be confident that powerful magnates would dominate what lay beyond. The Yorkist kings, by contrast, contemplated an English land limited to the counties around Dublin, the ports of the south coast, and (more doubtfully) some southern lordships, whose social complexion was at best hybrid. Only in Wales were structures of power relatively unchanged across the fourteenth and fifteenth centuries.

These shifts were important for the way that England perceived itself in relation to its neighbours. In the late thirteenth century it had been the focus of a collection of dominions that were regarded as pertaining to the crown, and whose inhabitants, whether English or not, were regarded as the king's subjects. In the late fifteenth century it was still the centre of dispersed territories. However, the position differed in several ways. The outlying lands were much smaller in relation to the whole. Gascony, together with Henry V's acquisitions, had been lost, reducing the continental possessions to the single foothold of Calais with its hinterland or 'pale'. Likewise, the heavily fortified 'land of Berwick-upon-Tweed' was the sole remnant of Edwardian expansion into southern Scotland. Despite the continued claim to lordship over Ireland, the emergence under the early Tudors of the concept of a pale around Dublin also suggests the image of an embattled bridgehead. Within these contracted frontiers there was a more insistent sense of Englishness, reflected, for instance, in Irish legislation—echoed in the by-laws of towns such as Waterford—which equated the English language, law, and social customs with political loyalty. During Henry VI's reign, the status within England of persons born in overseas territories had become a problematical question, as we saw in relation to the English of Ireland. By the 1480s the issue had been resolved through the acceptance that the (loyal) inhabitants of all the king's lands—including Calais and the Channel Islands—not merely were his subjects, but enjoyed English status. As in the 1280s, Britain contained two kingdoms; but it was now clearer that each contained a distinct national community, which in the case of England included those who lived in what might be described as English dependent territories. Not all the inhabitants of Wales, and only a minority in Ireland, fitted into this desirable category. It was left to sixteenth-century rulers to develop strategies—which in Ireland proved disastrous—for incorporating them.

Plate 11 The Court of King's Bench in session at the Great Hall at Westminster. The picture illustrates the rituals and procedures of English justice in the fifteenth century. Beneath the royal arms, five justices are shown presiding. Below them, around the green cloth-covered table, are officers of the court including clerks writing the rolls; of the two ushers with staves, one is administering the oath. The prisoners are marshalled in chains, to appear in turn at the bar of the court. Courtesy the Masters of the Bench of the Inner Temple.

Kingship and government

Anthony Goodman

The environmental foundations of government

Environmental factors influenced the efficacy of governments and the character of political cultures. The power structures which existed in 1300 were shaken up by the economic and social effects of climatic deterioration, the pandemics of 1348–9, 1361, and 1379, and the persisting low levels of population in the fifteenth century until its last decades. The medieval English polity had assumed its impressive and strategically dominant profile because of the proximity of a large number of rich agrarian and pastoral tracts, with few daunting physical barriers, though the Lakeland fells and the forest of the Weald in Sussex and Kent could deter travellers. By 1300 forested areas had largely been cleared. The nearness of much of England to the sea facilitated movement by coastal shipping, which in many regions linked with riverine transport. For instance, in the early fifteenth century boats regularly plied between the leading port of King's Lynn (Norfolk) and Cambridge. The Roman network of roads, radiating from London, had been greatly expanded by the making of ways to markets. By the early fourteenth century over 1,000 places had market rights. The Gough Map of about 1360 depicts about 2,940 miles of roads and ways, covering most of England. They seem to have been generally passable in good weather. Edward I, a king who spent much of his life in the saddle, rode 360 miles in January 1300, averaging about twenty miles a day. In July 1482 the chancellor of the realm, then at Westminster, acknowledged receipt of a report dated at Newcastle (285 miles away) six days earlier. Although from the later fourteenth century onwards the number of functioning markets declined and the carting of grain diminished, movements of wool, cloth, and luxury goods increased. It remained the case that in few other parts of the British Isles were there comparable densities of traffic, a stimulus to people to move around, fleeing the burdens of serfdom, hiring out their labour, giving professional entertainment, and visiting shrines.

Travellers do not seem to have been generally impeded by threats of robbery or local mayhem. The rioters who broke the king's peace with force and arms, about whom there were often complaints in petitions to the crown, sensibly left travellers alone, unless incensed by the high price of victuals. The occasional movement of soldiers could be a menace. Highwaymen were not high on the list of those frequently denounced—in fact one of them, Robin Hood, became a folk hero. According to some legends, he operated along a stretch of the Great North Road north of Doncaster, Yorkshire, a haunt of future generations of highwaymen. A number of factors combined to minimize such threats to travellers. Edward I's Statute of Winchester (1285) enacted that undergrowth and ditches were to be destroyed for 200 feet on either side of roads, so that there should be no cover for malefactors. Male travellers were well equipped to defend themselves, since skill with the longbow was a common accomplishment. On market routes there were companies of traders to provide security. Sir John Fortescue, a former chief justice of King's Bench, writing in the 1460s, implied that a solitary highwayman often had to hold up groups. In this environment, the king's proclamations and writs circulated easily, many of them carried by the corps of royal messengers. Royal sergeants-at-arms attached to the king's household could be speedily dispatched to arrest those trying to defraud the king, or disobeying the tenor of his writs. Political gossip and rumours spread with ease too—as the widespread provincial risings and disturbances in reaction to the rebel commons' admission to London during the Great Revolt of 1381 demonstrated. Ease of travel thus fostered the continuity of effective royal government and the development of common political attitudes. It had repercussions too on other parts of the British Isles, for it facilitated the array of naval and land forces both to defend England and to invade its neighbours.

The widespread sense of a north/south divide, whose notional boundary was often considered to to be the River Trent, reflected the growth of common political attitudes. It was fostered by the relative poverty of most northern regions, and the outstanding wealth of some in the south, such as East Anglia and parts of the West Country, where rural cloth production burgeoned in the fourteenth century. Southern resentment or suspicion was sometimes directed at career-ist or impoverished northern immigrants. The recurrent inability of northerners to defend the frontier regions, which became perman-ently under threat as a consequence of Edward I's and Edward III's aggressive Scottish policies, and more vulnerable through depopula-tion, produced new tensions. Although Border balladry implied that the warlike men of Northumberland were heroically capable of defending the realm on their own, its defence in fact required injections of subsidies, supplies, and manpower from richer regions, especially during intense bouts of campaigning such as in the 1380s. In 1497 Cornishmen rose in rebellion against the imposition of a parliamentary subsidy to fund war against the Scots, and gained sympathies elsewhere in southern England. However, there was probably a widespread appreciation that the vulnerability of the north was a matter of common concern, especially when England was often at the same time confronting the superior might of the French crown. Although Geoffrey Chaucer professed a dismissive ignorance of the geography of Northumberland, it is likely that warfare, com-merce, itinerant labouring, pilgrimage, and competitions (such as in minstrelsy, pugilism, and archery) gave men and women—including humble ones—an extensive mental map of their native land and wide political horizons.

In other parts of the British Isles, the environment was less propitious for the development of universally strong central institu-tions to which a common sense of identity became linked. In Wales the central upland mass impeded communications, and so did great estuaries, like that of the River Conwy, which in 1399 was a barrier to the seizure of Richard II by Henry of Bolingbroke's forces. Richard was holed up in the great fortress which Edward I had built at Conwy: it had taken him about nine or ten days, travelling in haste, to cover the 200 or so miles from Carmarthen. Rivers flowing into the more fertile eastern plains, which the Anglo-Normans had colonized, mainly aided trafficking with the west. In Wales, as in other mountainous parts of the British Isles, local people might travel nimbly through harsh environments. Owain Glyn Dŵr, after his proclamation as prince of Wales in 1400, over the next few years bemused his English and Welsh opponents by his ability to strike swiftly in different parts of Wales.

The individual administrations of the multiplicity of marcher lordships, and the porous nature of their borders, reflecting the imperatives of an upland country, facilitated cross-border raiding, especially into lush nearby English shires in search of booty (notably cattle and sheep), legal redress for which was cumbersome and uncertain. More coordinated governance might ensue when adjacent lordships came into the hands of one family. The greatest agglomeration in this period belonged to the Mortimer earls of March, and descended from them to Edward IV through his father, Richard, duke of York (d. 1460). In Edward's reign the crown, now the greatest of marcher lords, was well placed to develop institutional mechanisms to discipline all such lordships, especially in their external relations. Edward IV and Henry VII used the councils of their respective eldest sons Edward (who was briefly king in 1483) and Arthur (d. 1501), in their capacity as princes of Wales, to govern the principality's shires and the crown's marcher lordships, and to supervise the administration of justice throughout the March and even in neighbouring English shires. It reflected geographical convenience that this seat of government for the whole of Wales was in a centrally placed English border town, Ludlow in Shropshire. However, the first attempt to provide Wales with a single authority had been a Welsh one. Remarkably, Glyn Dŵr had succeeded in 1403–4 in setting up a principality which fleetingly secured the allegiance of many Welsh folk—a unique appearance of a state based on a unifying sense of nationhood and mirroring features of the English realm, with which many Welshmen were acquainted. Glyn Dŵr's achievement was fuelled by long-felt discontents concerning racially discriminatory ordinances, harsh English financial exploitation, and the carpet-bagging tendencies of the English élites, eager to absorb the profits of office in the principality and marcher lordships. A revival of verse-making in the Welsh vernacular, recalling ancient British glories, provided a national ideology. Yet the attempt failed, because of the strength of age-old, kin-based localism, the devastation of the fragile Welsh economy by the conflict, and superior English resources. English élites remained more resolved to maintain rule over the Welsh than over the Scots or Irish, partly because of the menacing proximity of the Welsh, but also because the English shared a prophetic tradition with them, one interpretation of which was that the Britons might one day wrest empire over Britain from the Saxons. Indeed, ecclesiastical as well as secular blueprints which Owain produced for his Welsh principality included large parts of England.

Scotland had even greater contrasts and challenges in terrain than Wales. However, later English visitors recounted how easy it was to reach the central Lowlands and the eastern seaboard, by land as well as by sea. These regions sustained the greatest concentration of towns and villages in the British Isles outside England. Since royal charters to burghs gave merchants monopolies in trading wool, there were well-frequented tracks over large hinterlands. The mercat cross helped to form common opinions in the sheriffdoms. Edinburgh played an increasing role in their wider formulation, as the export of wool, hides, and cloth from Lothian, the Borders, and Fife became increasingly channelled through Leith. Difficulties of communication did not hinder contingents from much of Scotland, including the Highlands, from joining royal armies mustered in the south against the English, nor English armies (which were often reliant on naval supply) from operating in the Borders, the central Lowlands, and eastern coastlands. The Englishman John Hardyng advised Edward IV in the 1460s that the regions south of 'the Scottish Sea' (that is, the Forth and Clyde estuaries) could easily be ravaged by English forces in a month; even the woods and mosses of the Lammermuir Hills would present no obstacle to a force of footmen. The southern regions, and some others (including eastern parts of the Highlands) had long been embraced by an evolving royal government which, as in England, stimulated the sense of belonging to a 'community of the realm'. The vulnerability of southern and eastern parts to English incursions in and after the Wars of Independence, and after the decline in population, encouraged the formation of settled opinions that kings and magnates had a supreme duty to work together to frustrate mischievous schemes like Hardyng's. The problem of the geographical integrity of the realm remained unresolved since, down to 1461, and from 1482, the English occupied Scottish soil.

Although much of Highland terrain was daunting to Lowlanders, leading to lurid speculations about this *terra incognita*, it did not

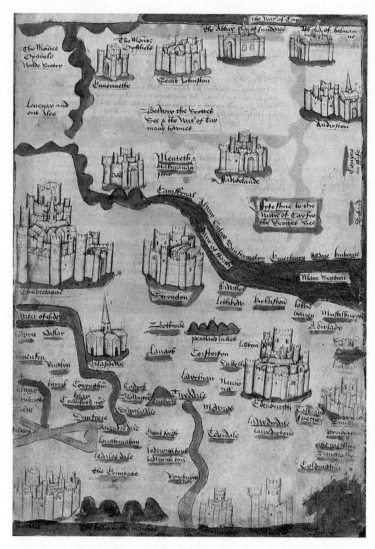

Map 9 A traveller's map of the Scottish Lowlands, from John Hardyng's *Chronicle*, *c*.1464. It illustrates castles and religious houses, and also the main rivers and dales. Source: MS Selden B.10, fol.184 (Bodleian Library, Oxford).

isolate Highlanders, who had the skills to reach burgh markets by land and sea. The holders of Highland earldoms and their entourages were customarily integrated into Scottish noble society. This was true of the independent-minded Lords of the Isles, whose ambitious embroilment in Scottish politics often set them at odds with crown or magnate. What made John, son of Angus Óg of Islay (d. 1387) and his successors formidable players was their success in imposing their rule over the septs of Clan Donald and other clans on the western seaboard and in the Hebrides. To maintain this, they needed to demand naval and military support from their vassals; they could field powerful armies. The militarized clansmen, the caterans, whom magnates led on the march or on campaign through lowland regions, probably helped to create the image of the alien Highlander. However, the ability of the Lords of the Isles to take the offensive did not guarantee the security of their fastnesses: determined royal expeditions to strategic fortresses and burghs, like James I's to Inverness in 1428, procured submissions. James IV's expeditions of 1495 and 1498 demonstrated how superior naval power could be used to subdue recalcitrant chiefs in the lordship.

In much of Ireland communications were patchy and difficult. In the thirteenth century the development of agrarian and pastoral resources by settlers from England, particularly in Leinster, had stimulated the use of trackways to Dublin and the ports of the south and east; external demand for hides and wool continued to engage the ports in trade with Gaelic lordships too in the later Middle Ages. However, agrarian decline in the fourteenth century left the Galls (the Anglo-Irish) poorer and fewer in number, and so less able to resist the raids of neighbouring Gaels on the stock on which they increasingly relied. On his expedition to Ireland in 1394 Richard II tried to reverse the decay of the colony. The English army passed through regions which were heavily wooded and where cultivation had declined; the nobles disliked campaigning in this menacing environment and were reluctant to invest in property there.

The general agrarian decline consequent on depopulation had serious effects on the ambitions of English kings to rule the British Isles—which had seemed attainable at the end of the thirteenth century. In the rich parts of England diet generally had higher calorific value than in Celtic lands, where the kinds of crop that could be grown were often restricted, and the yields often poorer. English soldiers, unlike most of their British and Irish opponents, expected to be fed with large quantities of ale and superior bread and meat, especially since many of them wore heavy harness. As English expeditions were generally mounted, fodder was required for their typically large horses—which contrasted, for instance, with the nimble ponies on which the Gaels of Ireland launched lightning attacks on them from bogs and down precipitous hills. The expense of mounting large-scale or prolonged campaigns into England's bleak and rainy hinterlands, without the prospect of commensurate gain, was unappealing. The wisdom of Edward III's reorientation of military ambitions in the 1340s to the continent was shown by the effects on the British Isles of the great economic downturns. It was more rewarding and easier to ride in arms along river valleys deep in France, with better expectations of good victuals, wine, fodder, fair weather—and material gain.

The English disengagement from the rest of the British Isles and concomitant continental assertiveness had social as well as political and military implications. English settlement petered out in Ireland in the thirteenth century, and was revived only briefly in Wales when Edward I founded boroughs supporting his new castles in Gwynedd. On the other hand, Calais became an English town, which briefly sent burgesses to Henry VIII's parliaments, and Normandy, conquered by Henry V in 1417–19, by the 1430s had a wide sprinkling of English and Welsh settlers. Relatively few English folk visited other parts of the British Isles, except as traders, diplomats, soldiers, and 'colonial' administrators. Some northerners were drawn to the shrine of St Ninian at Whithorn (in Galloway), but the galaxies of Celtic saints held little attraction for English pilgrims, compared with the great religious sites south of the Pyrenees and the Alps. Although Welsh and Irish traders and immigrants were familiar in Chester and Bristol, and Scottish chaplains and labourers north of the River Tees, the lands they came from were often considered marginal in England, *terrae incognitae*, where there were reputedly disorders, barbarities, magicians, wonders. In a period when the English crown struggled to maintain a semblance of hegemony over the British Isles, projecting it more by symbolism than in reality, such myths sustained the English belief that their nation inhabited the part of the British Isles which had been home to superior civilizations since the Trojans had founded Britain and built a network of great cities and castles mainly

in what was to be England, in whose origins the English were showing an antiquarian pride. God had favoured the English, as He had
the people of Israel. Their land, with which their blood was mingled,
was specially blest, and their tenure of it gave them the right to
mastery of the British Isles.

Princely authority

In 1403 a traveller from Cardiff, a certain John Sperhauke, lodged
with a tailor who lived near Baldock in Hertfordshire. The tailor's
wife, he alleged, remarked on how much it had rained, and how many
thunderstorms there had been during the reign of the present king,
Henry IV; he had no right to the throne, his rule was evil, and thunderstorms had occurred because of his failure to obey the pope. The
tale illustrates how the people's faith in the right to rule was funda-
mental to the acceptance of princely authority. Firm acceptance in
England and Scotland of the feudal custom of primogeniture had for
long helped to ensure regal stability. However, when Alexander III of
Scotland died in 1286, his recognized heir was his granddaughter,
Margaret. In 1289 noble 'guardians of the realm' agreed that she
should marry Edward I's son and heir, the future Edward II. Margaret's death on her way from her native Norway to Scotland put the
right to succeed in turmoil. The chosen arbitrator, Edward I, in 1292
awarded the throne according to feudal rules to John Balliol, the
senior direct descendant of the royal line—in preference to Robert
Bruce, earl of Carrick, the next such descendant (but by one fewer
generation). This might not have been a recipe for civil war if Edward
had not deposed Balliol in 1296, on the grounds that he was a con-
tumacious vassal—like the other claimants, he had perforce acknowledged Edward's right to the overlordship of Scotland. Since Balliol's
partisans (notably Sir William Wallace) were eventually unable to
resist English might, and Edward was now inclined to treat Scotland
as a lordship attached to the English crown, Carrick's grandson
Robert Bruce had himself inaugurated as king in 1306. As Robert I, he
faced a long struggle not only with the English crown but also against
adherents of the Balliol cause. Within three years of King Robert's
death in 1329 and the succession of his infant son, David II, John

Balliol's son Edward invaded the realm and enjoyed some spectacular if ephemeral success. He was mainly sustained by Edward III, to whom he angrily resigned his shadowy crown in 1356. That ended the civil war.

Despite the fact that David II had been captured on a disastrous invasion of England in 1346, and remained a prisoner for eleven years, his subjects and generations of their descendants gave firm faith to the line of Robert I. David himself was childless; his feudal heir was the nephew he hated, Robert the Steward, son of Robert I's daughter Marjorie. David's attempts to divert the succession to a son of Edward III were strongly resisted by the political community. The Steward succeeded him as Robert II in 1371, the first of the Stewart line, which was blessed with a father-to-son succession down to 1513. Despite frequent minorities, and predatory royal kinsmen, some of whom aspired to the throne, the Stewart line of succession survived intact. Popular attachment to it explains how David, duke of Rothesay, son and heir of Robert III, was accounted a martyr; he had died in 1402 after his arrest, in which his brother the duke of Albany was involved, and was rumoured to have been starved to death.

England had had a father-to-son succession from 1216, apart from Richard II succeeding his grandfather, Edward III, in 1377. This clear line was broken by Henry IV's usurpation in 1399, which introduced a recurrent element of instability into English regal politics. Five of the next six kings had their right to the throne challenged on the grounds of the dynastic issue (the remaining king, Edward V, had his right overturned on related grounds). Richard II's most plausible heir, descended through the senior line from Edward III, had been Edmund Mortimer, earl of March, a boy in 1399. In 1460 Mortimer's heir, Richard, duke of York, a long-time critic and rebellious protester against the policies of Henry IV's grandson Henry VI, forced Parliament into recognizing his superior right to the throne. Soon afterwards, York was killed in battle by Henry's supporters. His son had himself proclaimed as Edward IV in 1461. The dynastic issue was to give repeated impetus to savage bouts of fighting over the next quarter of a century (the 'Wars of the Roses'), involving the ambitions of noble factions, popular grievances, and the machinations of foreign princes. A white rose was a badge of the House of York, and Henry Tudor, who claimed the throne as the nephew of the Lancastrian Henry VI, adopted the emblem of a mixed red and white rose in order to project his propaganda that, by marrying Edward IV's daughter Elizabeth, after usurping Richard III's throne as Henry VII in 1485, he had ended the strife of the two royal stems.

There were notable contrasts between the ways in which royal and noble authority was transmitted in England and the feudalized parts of Scotland and Ireland on the one hand, and on the other in Celtic societies which maintained that rights to succession—and to have a say in succession—might embrace a wide kin group—notions which also still had currency among leading Welsh landowners (or *uchelwyr*). This system was 'tanistry': the tanist ('second in place') was chosen in the lifetime of a ruler (*taoiseach*), either by his overlord or at an assembly of the gentlefolk of the territory. Those eligible as tanist were males, descendants of a common ancestor in four generations. In practice the tanist often did not succeed smoothly, for clans might be riven by rival candidates, and their power or independence consequently undermined. Chieftains were inclined to promote eldest sons as tanists: father-to-son successions were common. In Ireland the Mac Carthaig Mor (MacCarthy) of Munster had such a succession from 1359 to 1508, and three successive Lords of the Isles were able to get their eldest sons accepted. So, in fact, the traditional system of succession maintained vigour in large parts of Ireland and Scotland, and was capable of delivering a stable result.

How was princely authority conferred, and how was its continued validity restated and reaffirmed? A Czech visitor to England in 1466 noted that Edward IV's subjects knelt at the mention of his name, and kissed his letters. English kings were exalted in the ancient liturgy of the coronation, receiving divine sanction to rule through unction. It was popularly believed that they pulsed with sacred energy, manifest in the public rituals when they healed skin disease and rheumatism. They maintained a high-profile image of Christian kingship through their solemn celebration of the principal feast-days (when they appeared crowned), their maintenance of chapels royal, patronage of cults, and ritualized charity. When Richard II ceremonially entered London in 1392, and Henry V did so after his victory at Agincourt in 1415, religious tableaux made analogies between them and Christ entering Jerusalem. People claimed that miracles were performed by some kings who had been deposed and allegedly murdered—notably Edward II and Henry VI—and their tombs were treated as shrines. Care was taken to avoid this in the like cases of

Richard II and Edward V by their respective usurpers, Henry IV and Richard III: Richard II was originally buried inaccessibly, Edward in lasting obscurity.

Scottish kings came to receive divine authority in ways similar to English ones. They had been traditionally inaugurated at Scone, in a ceremony which had pre-Christian elements: they sat on a sacred stone at a pagan site. These features were similar to ceremonies conferring lordship in Celtic societies. The Lords of the Isles put their foot in a footprint in a stone at their residence, Finlaggan on Islay; clothed in a white habit, they received a white rod, a symbol of rulership, and a sword. They did not receive authority in a dedicated liturgy, hearing mass only after the ceremony. Conveniently forgetting their allegiance to the Scottish crown, they claimed to rule 'by the grace of God'. Irish chiefs, who occasionally acknowledged their fealty to the 'Saxain' (English) king likewise had authority conferred on them at sacred sites, sometimes standing on a stone, sometimes receiving a white rod. Edward I appropriated the prehistoric magic of Scottish kingship by having the Stone of Scone taken to Westminster in 1296. Scottish kings continued to be inaugurated at Scone, but in a liturgical ceremony more like that of France or England. The infant David II was the first to be crowned and to receive unction, in 1331. Scottish kings had a less awesome religious aura than English ones: they lacked miraculous medical expertise, and kings killed by their subjects—James I in 1437 and James III in 1488—attracted no cults.

The practice of magnificence was generally thought to be appropriate for princes, and was often indulged by them on an increasingly grand scale, as a means of projecting majesty and winning the support of fellow princes and subjects. The number of court officials and hangers-on tended to grow, and the life-style of kings and courtiers became more elaborate and expensive. By 1467 the number of servants of all kinds in Edward IV's household (excluding the queen's separately organized establishment) had risen to over 630. Early in January 1508, during the Christmas festivities, more than 260 servants and nobles attended James IV's household. From the second half of the fourteenth century onwards, English kings in peaceful times usually moved with the court, or a select retinue, between palaces and secluded lodges in the vicinity or within easy reach of London, when not being entertained by noble families or monasteries. The merchants of London were best able to supply the unequalled demands of the royal household, both for luxury items and for basic goods. Kings concentrated on rebuilding and extending a few palaces, thereby creating more impressive settings for their private living and court entertainment. The poorer Scottish kings were for a long time more traditional in their living arrangements. The organization of their households was, indeed, similar to that of other European courts, but they tended to journey further than the larger English court, relying for consumption on the resources which royal estates and abbeys could provide. In the later fifteenth century, Scottish kings had more restricted itineraries, with normal circuits in Lothian and Fife and extending to Perth and Stirling. They built palaces on a scale to rival those of the kings of France and England. James IV's great hall at Stirling Castle (built about 1498–1503) was slightly bigger than that of Edward IV at Eltham Palace, Kent, and the setting for dazzling entertainments, sometimes accompanying tournaments staged in the elaborate manner made fashionable by the Valois dukes of Burgundy—as in 1507, when James participated as 'the wild knycht', accepting challenges from all comers. Kings could best afford to stage these supreme representations of the chivalrous values of nobility. In stylized play, royal tournaments projected the propositions to participants and spectators (including numerous groundlings) that the king was the fount of honour, and that nobles might best augment their honour as adornments and faithful servants of the crown.

The claims of English kings to have a unique eminence as chivalrous patrons in the British Isles (supposedly emulating King Arthur) were embodied in the Order of the Garter, one of the first secular orders of chivalry, founded by Edward III in honour of the Blessed Virgin Mary and her knight St George in 1348. Most of the knights of the Garter were Englishmen in royal service and a growing number of foreign princes. There were Welsh and Anglo-Irish members, but no Scots, since membership would have conflicted with their native allegiance. The English court only rarely appeared a British court like the legendary Arthur's: Scottish lords occasionally attended, to win honour in chivalrous challenges, or in the entourages of David II and James I during their captivities (the latter from 1403 to 1424). The Scottish court was the only other one in the British Isles which had similar prestige and political significance, though there the crown had no permanently instituted chivalrous order. In Wales, English and Welsh lords and, in Ireland, Anglo-Irish and Gaelic ones made traditional use of hospitality to cement regional loyalties: its abundance at Glyn Dŵr's residence, Sycharth, was immortalized in verse. In Ireland there were only briefly princely courts whose patronage was a general focus—notably when Richard II held court at Dublin Castle in 1394–5, and Irish chiefs apparently made strenuous efforts to master an alien court culture.

What authority was exercised by princes? They, like leading nobles, received an education in Latin grammar which familiarized them with Biblical and classical precepts, and examples of both good rule and tyranny. More specifically, they often possessed copies of treatises known as 'mirrors for princes', which reflected the adaptation to Christian society of Aristotelian politics by thirteenth-century schoolmen, notably Thomas Aquinas. The works of authors such as Aegidius Colonna (Giles of Rome), who wrote *De Regimine Principum* (Concerning the Rule of Princes), were popular in England and Scotland. They insisted that kingship and other forms of rule were offices, whose purpose was to promote the common good of a community divided into a hierarchy of 'estates': churchmen, nobles, and commons. Kings ought to defend and provide justice for all, respecting the privileges of the estates, and ruling with the advice of mature and disinterested counsellors.

The estate of the king was the most exalted: he had, in accordance with precepts of Roman law, sovereign jurisdiction over his subjects (though that sat uneasily with recognition of papal jurisdiction). Sovereignty was underlined by the ferocious penalties for treason, a theatre of cruelty, dishonour, and family ruin. Though the king's prerogative to take decisions affecting his estate and the realm's was nationally sacrosanct, there was a consensus that he should act within the law, an expectation in England embodied in Magna Carta and reaffirmed by kings at their coronation. What was to be done if a king came to be widely perceived as a failure in office, incompetent and/or tyrannical? In Celtic societies, rival claims facilitated replacement with the approval of kindred. In Scotland, Robert II and Robert III acquiesced in the appointment, by the three estates or a council general, of a son or brother as lieutenant of the realm (as in 1388, January 1399, and 1402). The 'scotophile' Henry of Bolingbroke, after he had captured Richard II in 1399, may have toyed with these precedents, fleetingly considering a lieutenancy based on his office of steward of the realm. Such expedients worked only with elderly and infirm kings; confronted with a vigorous and ruthless king—James I—dissident nobles revenged themselves for family grievances by assassinating him. Regicide earned them general execration. Classical discourse advocating the death of tyrants was not widely approved, though assassination had also been attempted against Henry IV. In Scotland, blatantly tyrannical and arbitrary behaviour may perhaps have been more readily tolerated, because political discourse emphasized the need for strong rule to defend the realm and impose order. James II got away with killing his most powerful subject, the earl of Douglas, without much of a stain on his reputation. In 1452, at a supper party in Stirling Castle, after a heated argument, the king stabbed the earl and courtiers finished him off.

In England a 'constitutional' process had been devised which provided a semblance of legality and broad consent for the deposition of arbitrarily-minded kings. Edward II alienated opinion by his addiction to favourites, his failures to observe the reforming ordinances of 1311 and to defend the North against incursions by the Scots in the years after his defeat at Bannockburn (1314), and by his harsh punishment of rebellious nobles in 1322. In 1327, at the behest of rebels including his queen, Isabella, the estates of Parliament declared him deposed, following the recital of articles demonstrating his unfitness to govern. In the late 1390s Richard II alienated opinions by his criminalization of opposition in 1387–8 to his youthful rule, and his harsh and drastic reordering of magnate families' fortunes. The estates in 1399 withdrew their allegiances after the recitation of his supposed act of resignation and articles rehearsing his 'many crimes and defects'. These precedents may have encouraged depositions (though on more clear-cut dynastic grounds) in the fifteenth century—a proclivity condemned as a sign of faithless English blood by hostile foreigners. This tendency helps to account for the countervailing reverence claimed by, and shown to, monarchy and avoidance of the dubious constitutional processes of 1327 and 1399. The febrile kneeling and kissing observed by the Czech visitor of 1466 was a corollary of the sad deaths of kings.

Princely government

Kings were expected to rule in person from their early or mid-teens onwards. Some of those habitually in their company played leading roles in government: the royal household was the customary seat of rule. This remained the norm, except during royal minorities, even in England, where some key governing departments—the chancery, exchequer, and privy seal office—and common-law courts (King's Bench and Common Pleas) had discrete personnel and premises 'out of court'. An English king frequently consulted his leading officials, such as the chancellor, and his nobles when they were resident at court, and some of the officers of the household who attended on him, especially knights and esquires attached to the chamber (or suites of royal apartments). Access to the king gave them prime opportunities to petition for offices, wardships, forfeitures, pardons, protection from lawsuits and appointments to commissions. The chamberlain at their head (or his deputy) was especially well placed to influence and profit from the flow of patronage, as he controlled access to the chamber. The queen, served by ladies and officers of a separately organized and accommodated chamber, was expected to use her unique access to the king to win favours for the deserving, and in particular—taking as a pattern the Blessed Virgin Mary's intercessions with her Son—mercy and pardon for penitent offenders. Such were the burgesses of Calais condemned to death in 1347 by Edward III for resisting his siege, yet who were granted their lives on Queen Philippa's well-choreographed public pleading as they stood before him vilely arrayed in shirts and halters. In 1429, in similar vein, James I's queen, Joan Beaufort, pleaded with him on behalf of the rebel Alexander, Lord of the Isles, as he knelt garbed as a penitent before the high altar of Holyrood Abbey.

It was, indeed, generally accepted that able household servants whom the king took to his bosom would act as his prime confidential agents, not only giving counsel (and sometimes being formally appointed as councillors) but also despatched to fulfil special commissions, either to ensure that his commands were obeyed in town and shire or to convey the secrets of his heart to fellow princes. Knights and esquires retained by the king, some of them 'household men', formed the backbone of companies in his military retinue, the main component and core of an 'army royal'. Some died for their lord like chivalrous heroes, fighting alongside Richard III at Bosworth in 1485, and with James IV at Flodden in 1513.

Particularly in England, the influence that could be gained at court by up-and-coming laymen, especially if young or of undistinguished social origins, was a matter of concern; there were fears that they might ignore the interests of magnates or of the wider political community of gentlefolk and urban élites. Secular magnates—dukes (a title first conferred in England in 1337 and in Scotland in 1398) and earls—were regarded as among the king's 'natural' councillors, in their feudal capacity as leading tenants-in-chief, and were frequently royal kinsmen. Most of them regarded continual involvement in the minutiae of conciliar work as drudgery. So their opportunities to impress their views in person tended to be occasional: on social visits to court, during royal progresses, and when sitting as peers of Parliament or in 'great councils' (weighty, enlarged meetings of the king's council). When there was widespread disillusion with royal policies, opinion in England inclined to support disgruntled magnates, even to the point of condoning or joining in rebellion, as in the crisis of 1387–8. Five rebellious lords, headed by Richard II's uncle Thomas of Woodstock, duke of Gloucester, procured condemnations for treason of some of the king's confidants, including his former tutor, Sir Simon Burley, the vice-chamberlain; they had enthusiastic backing from the Commons in the 'Merciless Parliament' of 1388. The court of Henry VI (who came of age in 1437, when he was fifteen) soon gained a sleazy reputation, since, absorbed in his religious studies, he put his trust in leading officials and courtiers too intent on monopolizing royal patronage in ways which alienated some noble families and other important elements in regional societies.

Courtiers were sometimes blamed too for the high costs of running the English royal household (the most expensive item in royal expenditure). The king, it was generally agreed, ought to 'live of his own', that is, fund his living costs from his customary revenues, without calling on the resources of his subjects. However, the great royal demesne which the crown had possessed after the Norman Conquest had been largely dissipated. Customs revenues were a major but variable resource, particularly the high tariffs on wool exports in the fourteenth century, and those on the growing volume of cloth exports in the fifteenth. However, the exchequer system of leasing resources failed to produce an adequate cash income. The Commons in Parliament petitioned Henry IV and Henry VI for Acts of Resumption to divert annuities granted by the crown to the payment of royal debts and living expenses. A major achievement of Edward IV was the introduction of changes in financial administration which, when applied generally, obviated political tensions over household costs. Whereas under Henry VI some magnates seemed to overshadow the crown in the extent of their patronage, the position was decisively reversed under his successor. The estates of Edward's brother George, duke of Clarence, forfeited in 1478, instead of being leased at the exchequer, were put in the charge of receivers, who accounted to officers of the chamber, and paid income into its treasury, where the king kept his jewels and cash. By the last years of Henry VII, the treasurer of the chamber was acting as receiver-general of all crown lands and most other revenues. Whereas it had been estimated in 1433 that cash received centrally from customary revenues (excluding direct taxation) would amount to £33,000 per annum, by 1483 it may have amounted to between £90,000 and £93,000, and for the years 1502–5 it averaged about £104,860.

Sound counsel was considered essential to good government. We have more certain information about decision-making out of court than about when the king was closeted in secret or 'privy' counsel. Parliaments had evolved from formal meetings between the king and his leading officials (the chancellor, treasurer of the exchequer, and justices), and tenants-in-chief, lay and ecclesiastical. Parliaments were the highest courts of appeal and legislative bodies; in them royal authority was awesomely projected, especially through the judicial and legislative roles of the House of Lords, whose historic institutional profile emerged in the fourteenth century. During the 1320s it became the norm to summon knights of the shire, citizens, and burgesses to Parliaments. Writs dispatched from the chancery to sheriffs ordered the election of two representatives from each of thirty-seven English shires and from cities and boroughs, London uniquely returning four. They were to attend with full and sufficient powers to give assent on behalf of their communities to what was ordained. By the end of Edward III's reign the representatives sat together as a group—the Commons (seventy-four knights of the shire and about 200 urban representatives). In theory they were there to present petitions for redress, and to assent to the decisions of king and Lords. However, our knowledge of their conduct in the 'Good Parliament' of 1376, when the declining Edward III had lost his grip on affairs, shows that shire representatives sometimes debated the state of the realm in a lively and disrespectful way. By the fifteenth century, bills for legislation came to be habitually framed in the form of petitions from the Commons.

During the Hundred Years War (1337–1453), frequent summonses of Parliament resulted from the crown's need for the cooperation of the estates, not only to pay for armies and navies, but to meet the continuous costs of maintaining garrisons, mainly abroad, notably in the March of Calais and the king's vestigial lordship of Scotland. Edward III and his successors were unwilling to relinquish the exaction of financial aid and material levies (or purveyance), but they found that the surest way to raise large sums was through the grant of subsidies in Parliament. Multiples of the basic assessment (fixed at £37,000 in 1334, and later reduced) were granted with extreme reluctance; parliamentary experimentation with new taxes was unpopular, such as the notorious ungraded poll tax granted in 1380, a prelude to the Great Revolt.

The Commons became adept at bargaining over fractions and multiples of subsidy. Their concerns about value for money, failures to win an honourable peace, enemy attacks on shipping, and threatened invasions—even of England itself—were among causes of discontent which their speaker (an office which appeared in 1376, and was thereafter occupied by a royal retainer) perforce relayed to the king and his ministers. The Commons even adapted the common-law device of impeachment to make communal accusations of peculation or even treason against royal ministers and favourites— in the Good Parliament of 1376, in 1386, 1388, and 1449.

Another Commons panacea for poor government was reform of the king's council. On occasion in the later fourteenth and early fifteenth centuries, they petitioned for nominations to principal royal offices and the council to be made subject to parliamentary approval, and for the council to deal with certain categories of business, notably the making of grants. With its fixed membership, businesslike habits, and frequent sessions, it seemed to some an ideal vehicle for good government. However, parliamentary initiatives of this sort helped to convince Richard II that some of his subjects were incorrigibly inclined to make treasonable inroads on his 'estate'. Henry IV was more circumspect. In 1406, when it seemed he was becoming an invalid, the Commons produced a blueprint for putting government into the hands of the council. King and Lords accepted this, but it was soon put in abeyance, without recriminations, because Henry's health improved. Under Edward IV and his immediate successors, the crown's financial basis strengthened, kings became more concerned to make their authority effective in England and Wales, and committees of the council were set hard to work to provide remedies for complaint where the common law was unable to do so. The Commons, in more rarely summoned Parliaments, were not minded to interfere with the conduct and personnel of government.

Parliaments might meet in different places (though at the king's convenience), and the council in his household, but for both the best venues were in the public chambers in Westminster Palace, within easy reach of a choice of lodgings, record repositories, and the advice of 'civil servants'. Their working day was regulated by the great bell and clock of the clock tower built opposite Westminster Hall in 1365–6. At dawn and dusk a stream of royal officials (the majority, 100 or so, attached to the chancery) commuted between the palace and London and the suburbs. Westminster Hall housed the courts of King's Bench, Common Pleas, and Chancery (which had an appellate jurisdiction). Twice a year, after Easter and at Michaelmas, sheriffs and others submitted their accounts at the exchequer. Suitors from all parts of the realm and beyond congregated to answer summonses from the council and the courts. In other parts of the British Isles there was no equivalent administrative and judicial powerhouse: other fixed centres had, in comparison, a limited geographical range. London already had generally known landmarks. Llywelyn ap Gruffudd, prince of Gwynedd (d. 1282), allegedly believed that he would be crowned in East Cheap: his garlanded head was paraded there. In the 1340s David II was rumoured to have boasted that he would stable his horses in Westminster Hall.

In Scotland, royal government had developed along similar lines to England's, but presented a distinct model. Government remained more focused in the royal household. Edinburgh only developed as the administrative capital by the sixteenth century. In the royal household, clerks of the chapel, under the chancellor's direction,

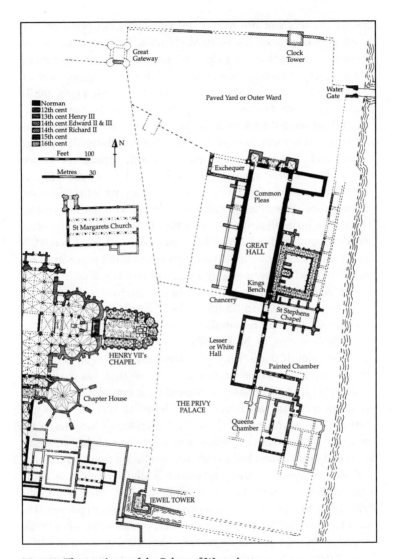

Map 10 The precincts of the Palace of Westminster.
Source: J. Steane, *The Archaeology of the Medieval English Monarchy*
(London, 1993).

drafted charters and brieves (or orders to justices); other officials based there controlled and received revenues. There were no professional corps of auditors or judges; *ad hoc* appointments were made. The king, or the justiciar whom he appointed for a region, travelled to hold justice ayres (Latin *iter*, 'journey'). Scottish kings, unlike English ones, were expected to deal personally with criminals: in 1504 James IV arrested thieves in Teviotdale at night, and without benefit of trial escorted them, noosed, for execution at Jedburgh. The king's council and Parliaments were inundated with appeals for justice: commissioners were appointed to deal with them in the fifteenth century, anticipating the civil jurisdiction of the later court of session. However, society was less regulated by the crown than in England. There were no equivalents to the justices of the peace, whose office was developed under Edward III: commissions of local gentlefolk appointed for a shire with individual powers to arrest peace-breakers, and with judicial powers as a quorum. The crown loaded increasing responsibility on them to enforce statutes concerned with economic and social regulation. In Scotland, sheriff courts exercised criminal jurisdiction and were responsible for such statutory regulation, but sheriffships tended to be hereditary—which was not the case in nearly all English shires, where the crown exercised tight control of appointments. By 1400 about one-tenth of Scotland was outside the normal jurisdiction of sheriffs, consisting of heritable regalities in which an ecclesiastical or secular lord heard all types of pleas and enforced statutes. Moreover, elsewhere the holders of baronies (often no larger than an English manor) had their courts baron, which arbitrated disputes and had a criminal jurisdiction over theft.

Royal revenue in fourteenth-century Scotland rarely rose above £10,000 per annum[1]: the royal demesne had been drastically depleted as a result of Robert I's need to reward his supporters. The main resource was customs revenue on exports of wool, whose yield dipped in the later fourteenth century, but picked up a century later. In the fifteenth century crown revenue was boosted by forfeitures of earldoms. Scottish kings were parsimonious in their military provisions; they maintained few garrisons, and for warfare they relied

---

[1] Until 1367 English currency weighed about the same as Scots, but thereafter the latter was devalued at a faster rate.

generally on the unpaid obligations of nobles and other able-bodied lieges. Consequently most kings did not press Parliaments hard for grants of subsidies (which were at lower levels than in England). Sitting as one chamber, Parliaments came to be constituted as the three estates—two composed of tenants-in-chief, ecclesiastical and secular, the latter comprising earls, barons (later commonly known as 'lairds'), and freeholders. From 1363 onwards, representatives of burghs were summoned, an index of their financial worth. Members of the estates were on occasion forceful in their criticisms of royal financial exploitation and default of justice. However, the personnel and costs of the royal household rarely became political issues. In the fifteenth century, service in the household became a ladder to landed wealth for many well-educated lairds from Lothian and Fife, and, as the factional strife during the minority of James II showed, some of them became powerful enough to contest control of the crown with magnates. Yet there was only one notable occasion when nobles targeted royal servants: in 1482 some were hanged from Lauder Bridge. In the words of a contemporary chronicler, James III 'wrought more the counsel of his household that were but simple than he did of them that were lords'. There was probably a broader expectation of access to the king than in England. James IV's chaplain, William Dunbar, in his poem on the 'Solistaris (or solicitors for favours) in Court', reflected on the king's availability for importuning:

> Sum hes thair advocattis in chalmir [the king's chamber] . . .
> Sum singis, sum dances, sum tellis storys,
> Sum lait at evin bringis in the moryis [Morris dancing].

Popular ballads credited his son James V (who took the splendour of royal living to new heights in his Renaissance palaces) with moving at ease—disguised—among humble folk. The institutional bases of monarchy were in some respects sketchy compared to England's, but kings' personal contact with the people (contact ritualized in England in the miracle-working ceremonies) facilitated the strengthening of their loyalties and the ability of kings to gauge a broad spectrum of opinion.

In Ireland, where a 'Westminster' model of government operated from Dublin, the evolution of Parliament had strong English parallels. By the later fourteenth century, besides a similar House of Lords, there were two representative houses: the Commons, similarly constituted as in England, and the clerical proctors. Gaels, who were mostly excluded from access to common law, did not attend Parliaments, and attendance shrank with the declining reach of the Dublin government. Nevertheless, its persistent financial demands invigorated the Commons, who consolidated their right to negotiate subsidies. In the eastern shires where Anglo-Irish government still exercised some control, justices from Dublin itinerated, and sheriffs performed functions like those in England, but these more vulnerable societies elected their own sheriffs, and raised and spent defence subsidies. Anglo-Irish lords increasingly displaced the influence of Dublin in the affairs of their lordships, though they did not cease to cooperate in defence and attend Parliaments when it suited them, and sometimes valued appointment to the lieutenancy of Ireland as an adjunct to their power. One must not assume that the government of Gaelic lordships, because it appears institutionally less elaborate and comprehensive than English and Scottish royal models (for instance, in lacking full control of the administration of justice), was less effective. In Scotland, the Lordship of the Isles, the traditional administration of which had parallels with that of Gaelic lordships in Ireland, had a council composed of clan chiefs which often met at Finlaggan. It was consulted by the lord on a wide variety of matters, and acted as a supreme court of appeal for the lordship.

What characteristic experiences of government did common folk have? Looming probably largest in the lives of many was government emanating from a manorial (in Scotland, baronial) court or an urban court, in which the inheritances and tenurial obligations of tenants were recorded, and the conduct of men and women regulated. The requirements of princely government were largely imposed, and the tenor of its legislation implemented, by courts owned or controlled by landlords and urban élites. The minor officials whom husband-men and artificers mostly encountered were drawn from the higher ranks of their own communities, men who spoke the same tongue and knew their ways. In England, the constable of the vill was the agent of the crown as well as of the manor court presided over by the lord's steward, enforcing customary obligations to both. In the many parts of the British Isles where great landowners exercised semi-regal powers, as in the March of Wales, they had more freedom to make demands on their subjects' possessions and labour. In Celtic societies, the hereditary character of many financial offices may have eased relations between lords and tenants, but the demands of constant warfare were an incentive to maximize obligations to provide food, rents, hospitality, and labour services, or payment in lieu in kine or coin. Moreover, Anglo-Irish lords in their lordships, and gentry in the shires, were often eager to copy these Gaelic devices, imposing cuddies (*cuid oidhche*, hospitality for a night for the lord and his men) and coyne and livery (*coinnmheadh*, billeting or quartering). In England in the fourteenth century, great landowners often recruited hard-nosed lawyers as councillors and estate officers, to attempt to reverse their generally declining incomes by researching and enforcing their tenurial rights. Tenants retaliated, by violence, by resort to the common law, or by abandoning their tenements to earn good wages as casual labourers or soldiers. Symptomatically, in the Great Revolt of 1381 rebels often burnt manor court rolls and lynched lawyers. In the fifteenth century 'village Hampdens' went on bickering with manorial stewards and, on occasion, making their opinions known about princely misgovernment—popular political stances which were uniquely well-articulated traditions in a much-governed England.

Political cultures

Throughout the British Isles political power remained closely connected with noble birth and the inheritance of property. However, in cities and towns the key to entry into governing élites was acquisition of a mastery in a guild merchant or craft guild. Leading merchants were eager to become connected socially, as well as in business, with the nobility. Urban communities were equally eager to become enfolded within the structures of noble power. Some Scottish burghs sought stable noble patronage: Peebles customarily elected one of the knightly Hays of Yester as provost, with the expectation that he would defend the burgh's privileges, oppose encroachments on its common lands, and win favours for it at court. In the 1470s and early 1480s the city of York looked to Edward IV's younger brother, Richard, duke of Gloucester, as its protector and advocate. Cities and towns were cornerstones of noble power, augmenting the wealth and influence of landowners through marketing the produce of their estates, supplying them with luxury status symbols, keeping them financially afloat with loans, and supporting them with men and materials for their retinues. A testimony to urban–rural symbiosis was the building of fine tower houses by fifteenth-century lairds in the hinterland of Aberdeen.

How were noble élites constituted? Recognition of noble descent was important everywhere, but especially in Celtic societies, where poets recited and embellished genealogies. Glyn Dŵr's claim to be prince of Wales was widely accepted, for his extolled descent from two princely lines made him pre-eminent among the *uchelwyr*. In Celtic societies, extended kinship led to the recognition by nobles of blood ties with those considered inferior in feudal society; such bonds of 'kindness' promoted loyalties between masters and men that were essential to the maintenance of chieftaincy and the structure of clans. When Irish chiefs mingled with Richard II's courtiers in Dublin in 1395, the English were scandalized that they had their minstrels and principal servants seated with them, sharing their plates and goblets at table. Protocol in Gaelic society was equally intricate, but reflected a different social structure.

In England and societies like it in the British Isles, lifestyle was a general test of nobility, though there was a world of difference in the levels of consumption of Chaucer's franklins and 'bonnet lairds', equally claimants to gentility. Where there were ministerial opportunities for upward mobility, acceptance depended on ability to conform in demeanour, culture, and living standards. Forms of officeholding in Gaelic societies remained strongly traditional. In Ireland, hereditary succession often applied to offices such as that of brehon (*breitheamh, brithem*), the lord's collector of customary dues (*maor*) and his marshal (*marasgal*), responsible for billeting and exacting costs for soldiers. Indeed, as the advancement of galloglasses (*gallóglach*) to clan status showed, professional soldiering could elevate socially. Elsewhere in Britain, the Hundred Years War expanded opportunities. One example was Sir Robert Salle, lynched by the Commons in the rising of 1381 because he haughtily rejected their appeal to his lowly origins—his father was a serf of the manor of Salle in Norfolk.

In England, and to some extent in Wales and lowland Scotland, lords recruited administrative and legal services promiscuously. Particularly in England, the exaltation of the linear feudal family had loosened bonds with wider kin groups. The spread there in the four-teenth century of legal devices circumventing a feudal heir's right to inherit, either temporarily or permanently, encouraged lawsuits over property, and, in such cases, pressure for the exercise of 'affection' by the crown, and resort to violence. Substantial landowners needed to retain as watchdogs both sergeants-at-law at Westminster and coun-try solicitors. Moreover, the decline in grain markets in England, the agrarian heartland of Britain, in the wake of depopulation made such landowners peculiarly dependent on stewards and receivers to maintain precarious rent rolls. These needs for technical services (as well as the crown's special and voracious needs) were met by the sons of gentlefolk and commoners (including a new class of 'super-rich' peasants) who wanted to found a family fortune, or augment an ailing one, and who exploited more accessible educational opportunities for laymen.

The landed aspirations of successful careerists were sometimes a disruptive force in local politics, as the roles of the Paston family in fifteenth-century Norfolk demonstrate. The competing needs of crown and nobles to cultivate the goodwill and gain the services of established gentlefolk might be too. In England feudal loyalties had often become attenuated, as a result of the fragmentation of fiefs, and the inability to create new ones resulting from Edward I's Statute *Quia Emptores* (1290). Great landowners with clusters of properties scattered in different shires and often in the March of Wales needed the goodwill of influential neighbours. The threat of rival claimants seizing them, or winning the 'affection' of juries, had to be countered. As landowners emparked and stocked game in the wake of depopula-tion, they needed to minimize the risk of trespass in a society eager for the chase. The political standing of magnates in 'court' and 'coun-try' depended heavily on their success in commanding the goodwill and services of local power-brokers, who sat as justices of the peace or as knights of the shire in Parliament. The richest nobles could afford to retain knights and esquires for life, contracting with them for readiness to give service in war and peace, in return for large annuities. More commonly, nobles sought to extend a network of influence by granting fees, robes, livery badges, and promises to maintain the interests of their clients, commoners as well as gentle-folk. In the later fourteenth century the Commons protested on occasion about the failures of lords to restrain intimidation and corruption of justice by livery-holders exploiting their protection. In Henry IV's first Parliament (1399), a statute was enacted forbidding the distribution of any livery except the king's (a collar of linked S's), and that was not to be worn out of court. The ills associated with livery and illegal maintenance were not easily curbed, as later statutes bore witness: they were inherent in the structure of landholding power. However, there was concern to observe the letter of the law: Henry VI's esquire, Edward Grimston, had his portrait painted holding, not wearing, the collar of S's. It does not seem to have been a matter of complaint when, under Henry VII, the statutes were harshly enforced in some high-profile cases. For it was generally accepted that magnates (who, like kings, were brought up on the precepts of good government found in 'mirrors for princes') should use their 'affinities' on behalf of the crown to promote good order and effective justice in the localities, not instigating or tolerating their behaviour as disruptive factions. Such affinities, linking *uchelwyr* to magnates and office-holders, developed in Wales too in the fifteenth century.

In England, and in Henry VI's Wales, regions might be disrupted for years when a great family's interest in their 'country' was challenged by the crown, by an ambitious rival family, or by both acting together. In his early years Henry IV was anxious to assert his control over relations with Scotland by reducing the role in border affairs of Henry Percy, first earl of Northumberland (d. 1408) and his son Sir Henry ('Hotspur'). His policies weakened the ties between the family and their knightly neighbours in the East Riding of Yorkshire who were accustomed to seek honour and profit through military service in the retinues of the Percys as wardens of the Marches and captains of the garrison at Berwick-upon-Tweed. The Percys led a series of revolts, in 1403, 1405 and 1408. In the 1440s there were clashes in Yorkshire between the kinsmen and affinities of Hotspur's son, the second earl of Northumberland, and the adherents of Richard Neville, earl of Salisbury. These foreshadowed alignments in the Wars of the Roses, in which Northumberland was killed in the first battle, at St Albans in 1455, defending Henry VI against a coalition of the duke of York, his brother-in-law Salisbury, and the latter's son Richard, earl of Warwick ('the Kingmaker'). Salisbury was executed by the Lancastrians in 1460 after the battle of Wakefield, Yorkshire. Edward IV relied on the earl's sons, Warwick, John Neville, earl of Northumberland, and George, archbishop of York, to rule much of the north—though Percy adherents remained fractious. After Warwick and his brother John died fighting Edward IV at Barnet in 1471, having changed allegiance to Henry VI, Edward built up an impressive hegemony in the north for his brother Richard of Gloucester, whom he allowed to inherit Neville lordships there from his late father-in-law, Warwick. The Battle of Bosworth can be seen as the last act of Percy/Neville rivalry. As Richard III charged to his death, Henry Percy, fourth earl of Northumberland, and his retinue remained spectators.

In Scotland and Ireland there were similarities and contrasts with England in the ways in which the politics of clientage worked. Scottish earls such as the Douglases built up similar affinities, in which ties of kinship and vassalage were important. As in England, concerns about abuses associated with retinues were reflected in parliamentary legislation. Although royal support was generally essential to the maintenance of magnates' interests, the degree of local institutional control at their disposal made them less dependent on the vagaries of court favour than their English counterparts, and so, perhaps, inclined to express grievances against king or rival by a burst of mayhem rather than the grave panoply of English-style rebellion. However, the loyalty of client families could be equally brittle. They acquiesced after James I seized the Dunbars' long-held earldom of March (1434–5), and after James II destroyed the impressively sustained Douglas hegemony (1455). By contrast, after James IV declared the Lordship of the Isles forfeited in 1493, some of Clan Donald plotted and agitated for several generations for the restoration of the lordship to one of their clan chiefs. Indeed, Gaelic clans might be unstable too. Clansmen might pay for protection (*slainte*) from lords outside the clan. Clans were sometimes recent amalgams of different kin groups. Chiefs of septs and of subordinated clans might attend the lord's court, foster their children there, and lead retinues in his army only out of necessity, nursing historic grudges about raids and seizures endemic in a society where resources were limited, and where the boundaries of cattle pastures and shielings were difficult to define and defend. The pressure on chiefs from their kin to displace or subordinate neighbouring septs and clans could destabilize society. However, shared pastoral necessities sustained clan mentalities with a lasting vigour rare in lowland affinities.

It is difficult to compare habitual levels of disorder in the various societies of the British Isles. There were certainly notable continuities in the stability of political cultures, though those in Wales and Ireland were most affected by institutional change—the former by the imposition of English 'colonial' administration, the latter by its failure. Order depended a good deal on 'hands-on' rule by a vigorous and politic lord. The Lords of the Isles were remembered—probably too rosily—as having maintained peace in their domains. In contrast to Gaelic chiefs, marcher lords in Wales were usually absentees, especially in the fifteenth century. English and lowland Scottish magnates improved favourite residences, neglecting to visit lordships elsewhere. John of Gaunt, duke of Lancaster (d. 1399), seems to have spent only a few days in his castle and borough of Lancaster, but built fine apartments at Kenilworth Castle, in Warwickshire, where he had few properties. The sophistication of the English system of estate administration facilitated such absenteeism, but did not always promote the exercise of good lordship. Complaints about disorder and misgovernance were litanies in many parts of the British Isles. Above all, the Anglo-Irish and the English viewed Gaelic Ireland as a 'land of war'. Writers of Gaelic annals considered this state of affairs natural, whereas in England, nobles leading rebellions and their royal opponents (for example, in the Wars of the Roses) were sensitive about alienating general opinion by plundering. Feud between kin groups was generally practised outside England and Wales, though it lingered in parts of Wales and the northernmost English shires. Indeed, the conventions of feud, and its systems of compensation, were deterrents to violence. Feud was a necessary institution where the royal systems of justice were weakly applied, or, as in Gaelic Ireland, had never penetrated. A rough indication of the prevalence of violence between gentlefolk is provided by the distribution of tower houses. They were common in lowland Scotland and in Ireland: in England the only clusters are found in Northumberland, Cumberland, and Westmorland. Generally, the defences of English castles were neglected. In the fifteenth century, what were essentially country houses started to be built with flimsy or ornamental defences. One of the few genuine, newly built castles, at Caister in Norfolk, had its walls easily breached by artillery fire in 1469.

Most of those who participated in war and disorder, armed with war axe, bill, or longbow, can be bracketed together as 'commons'. They were shepherds, tillers, artisans, and labourers. What were their

Map 11 The distribution of tower houses in the British Isles from the fourteenth to the seventeenth century, showing concentrations in Ireland, southern Scotland, and northern England.
Source: RCAHMW (Crown copyright).

political outlooks and why did they take up arms? Gaelic annalists in Ireland equated clan with 'nation'. The political horizons of clansmen and their tenants were presumably filled by this sense of nationality and its ramifications—their genealogical relationships, fulfilment of the demands of superiors, exterior threats to kine, and quality of protection. This seems to have been a static sense of popular nationality, contrasting notably with an evolving English sense. Royal propaganda for war, heavy taxation for it, and recruitment for service in it, legislation about apparel, wage norms, and (in 1401) heresy, all affected husbandmen, labourers, and artificers; women, too, were to experience government interference with their earning power and religious beliefs. In 1381 the commons of Kent and Essex, under the leadership of Wat Tyler and John Ball, an unbeneficed priest, occupied London for a few days. They aspired to reform the government of the realm, punishing leading ministers whom they held responsible for the poll tax, and abolishing hated aspects of economic and social regulation. The speedy collapse of the Great Revolt did not school future generations of the commons to restrict their politics to outsmarting the steward in the manor court or rioting against élitist regulation by oligarchically minded mayors and aldermen. There were long-standing popular traditions denigrating royal 'tyranny', embodied in the cults of St Thomas of Canterbury and of rebel leaders such as Thomas, earl of Lancaster, executed in 1322 after rebelling against Edward II. Henry IV's execution in 1405 of Richard Scrope, archbishop of York, who had taken control of a protest movement against the government, made his tomb in York Minster a pilgrimage centre for Yorkshire folk. Future noble rebels tapped into popular sentiment, as when the allies of Richard, duke of York, who landed in Kent in 1460 had their manifesto against Henry VI's government put on the gates of Canterbury. The élites no longer feared political interventions by the commons in the ways they had in the later fourteenth century. Tensions had eased because landlords and employers, faced with a chronic shortage of manpower, had to be more amenable to their demands. In 1429 a statute had fixed the franchise for freeholders in parliamentary elections at possession of property or rent yielding 40s. per annum in the shire (archers on war service then received a standard rate of 6d. a day from the crown).

In these circumstances, a uniform sense of nationality connected with the concept of the 'community of the realm' spread in the fifteenth century. Richard II in 1385 and Henry V in 1417 promoted the royal cult of St George by decreeing that soldiers in their 'army royal' should wear his cross. He was regarded as a warrior saint defending the realm on behalf of its owner, the Blessed Virgin Mary. By the end of the century, his vanquishing of the dragon was enacted on his feast-day in many rural parishes and in urban pageantry, and was commonly depicted in parish churches. In Scotland the cult of St Andrew as protector of the realm received royal patronage and attracted widespread devotion. However, the sense of English nationality carried uniquely hegemonic baggage in and over the British Isles. An English sense of racial superiority is reflected in denigration of England's neighbours. For the Welsh, restricted by statues enacted in reaction to Glyn Dŵr's rebellion, for the Gaelic Irish, stigmatized as barbarous, for the Anglo-Irish, accused of degeneracy, and for the Scots, some regarded as savage and others as generally inferior and faithless simulacra of the English, the rise of English national sentiment strengthened their own varied senses of nationality.

Plate 12 Stained glass panel representing Sir Robert Wingfield (d. 1481), from the east window of the church of SS Peter and Paul, East Harling, Norfolk. The second husband of Anne, daughter of Sir Robert Harling, he is shown as a knight, bare-headed and kneeling in contemplation; he is wearing the collar of suns and roses of Edward IV, of whose household he was controller, and also sports a pilgrim's scallop shell. Parish church of St Peter and St Paul, East Harling.

Epilogue

Ralph Griffiths

The historian is able to discern elements of tradition and continuity, change and innovation, and portents of future developments, in varying measure, in practically every generation of the past. As we have seen, this may certainly be said of the generation alive in 1300, when Edward I seemed about to exert his superior lordship over the entire British Isles. Something similar might be said of the plague- and war-ridden generation around 1350, whilst the aftermath of the political revolution in England in 1399 had significant consequences in Wales, Ireland, and Scotland as well as a profound impact on the English realm. If these generations may arguably be judged turning points in some significant respects, so too might the continuities, discontinuities, and novelties of life around 1500 be regarded as marking another watershed in the history of the British Isles.

The two realms in 1500

At the end of the fifteenth century, the English and Scottish realms were at different stages of development. The two monarchies had distinctive approaches to rulership as well as some resemblances; and as kings, Henry VII in England (victorious at the battle of Bosworth in 1485) and James IV in Scotland (who inherited the crown after his father was killed at Sauchieburn in 1488) shared certain attitudes with continental rulers. It was the English realm which had the greater adjustment to make as it emerged from the French war and its ancillary Scottish theatre, and sought to retain the allegiance of Wales and Ireland during dynastic strife and the Wars of the Roses. Decisive military defeats in France in 1449–53 led to English withdrawal from both Gascony and Normandy, leaving only Calais to be defended and administered. Occasional English expeditions across the channel from then until the loss of Calais in 1558 had limited, short-term objectives. It may have been a sign of the times—and of a more relaxed atmosphere in England's only remaining continental foot-hold—that three years after Edward IV's expedition of 1475 returned to England without engaging the enemy, the menfolk of Calais's wool staple turned from defence 'to disport and pleasure', arranging a chivalric archery contest between the bachelors and the married men, for the prize of a good meal.

The dynastic question raised by the death of the Black Prince in 1376, and the accession in 1377 of a boy king, Richard II, whose rule ended in deposition in 1399, had spawned bitter political rivalries that overwhelmed Henry VI in the Wars of the Roses. Composing the divisions of civil war is never easy, and compromise over the dynastic issue between Lancaster and York proved difficult to achieve in 1460 and 1470–1, and made further violence inevitable after the usurpation of Richard III in 1483. Even the marriage propaganda of Henry Tudor and Elizabeth of York from 1486 was not an instant panacea, to judge by the appearance of royal impostors and their acknowledgement as the true king in Ireland in the case of Lambert Simnel, and in both Scotland and Ireland in the case of Perkyn Warbeck. Towards the end of the century, French statesmen (admittedly a biased breed) took to noting with disapproval what seemed the English habit of deposing and murdering their kings and the children of kings with a regularity unmatched anywhere else in western Europe. It was the fresh face and more authoritarian regime of Henry VII which had the best chance of laying these ghosts to rest, less by new departures in rulership than by exploiting the king's powers more effectively. In England and its dominions the legacy of political events since the 1390s hung heavily over the Tudor age: it was an obsession with Tudor writers, culminat-ing in Shakespeare and his contemporaries, who taught the lessons of enfeebled monarchy right down to the death of Queen Elizabeth in 1603.

What seemed by 1500 to be a state of equilibrium in the lordship of Ireland between the English enclave (or Pale) around Dublin, the Anglo-Irish earldoms and the Gaelic lordships to the north and west was an illusion, and the situation satisfied no one. The English regime was on the defensive. The Anglo-Irish lords enjoyed considerable power, which was entrenched during the Wars of the Roses by successful claims to even greater autonomy: from the 1470s the dominant earls of Kildare even made advances against the Gaelic lords. Henry VII saw the dangers and tried (in 1494–5) to reassert royal control, but the English government's practical authority continued to be weak. By 1500 much of Ireland was more peaceful and prosperous than at any time in the previous two centuries, but the situation remained uneasy.

In Wales the balance of authority between the crown, the marcher lords, and leading Welsh landowners and townsmen made for greater stability than in Ireland, although Wales was often the scene of military operations in the Wars of the Roses. The fighting, however, did not prejudice the recovery of population and prosperity from the 1460s, or prevent the local landowning élites of Wales from advancing their own fortunes and enhancing their lifestyles. The concentration of lordship in both the principality counties and the March in the hands of Yorkist kings enabled a measure of devolved and unified royal supervision which the accession of Henry Tudor confirmed, at the same time laying foundations for a legislative union between England and Wales in 1536 that few in either country seem to have opposed. To the Venetian observer in 1498 it seemed as if Welsh dreams had come true, not least because the king himself was a Welshman!

Although Scotland's development was intimately connected with England's fortunes, the northern kingdom seems to have emerged by 1500 with greater assurance as a united realm. Although all of its fifteenth-century kings had been minors when they succeeded to the throne, and had sometimes been plagued by dissident relatives, the Scottish monarchy had not faced a crippling dynastic dispute since the return of David II from exile in 1341. Moreover, beyond defending themselves against the English, the Scots had no ambitions to go conquering beyond their borders and thereby placing greater strain upon the resources of their kings. More straightforwardly, the situation in England was 'the touchstone of Scottish unity and independence', and England's difficulties were usually Scotland's opportunity. Under James III and especially James IV, the monarchy was able to portray itself as self-confident and pragmatic, albeit with resources more limited than those at Henry VII's disposal. The

Scottish Parliament had declared in 1469 that James III had 'full jurisdiction and full empire' within his kingdom, just as English kings claimed in theirs; and from about 1470 Edinburgh was acknowledged to be a capital city, like London. James IV wore an imperial crown, like Henry VII's, portraying visually the self-contained sovereignty that both monarchs enjoyed in their respective kingdoms. When James named one of his sons Arthur in 1509, he was staking a claim to a heritage that rivalled that of Henry Tudor, whose own son Arthur had been born twenty years earlier. The cult of kingship was not new; however, in the second half of the fifteenth century it extended in both realms to building works and literary and artistic patronage, as well as to ceremony and ritual, aping what could be observed on the continent. Although the Scots king's position in relation to his nobility (even the Lords of the Isles), and his government's control of the localities seemed more stable than at any time in the past, they could not compare with the regional influence and sophisticated administrative structures at the disposal of the English monarch. Both Henry VII and James IV appreciated the potential benefits of a more secure peace between the two kingdoms, though this was a difficult and crooked path to follow—indeed, James fell at Flodden in 1513 fighting Henry VIII's army.

By 1500, much of the British Isles—except perhaps for the turbulent Anglo-Scottish borderland and parts of Ireland—was more peaceful, following the political uncertainties, protests, and uprisings of the past two centuries.

Social changes

Conditions of life had undergone major changes during the fourteenth and fifteenth centuries, not always for the better in all sectors of society. In 1500 the population was smaller than it had been in 1300, perhaps by as much as a half, though there were signs of recovery from about 1470. Life expectancy had not noticeably improved and may have been rather worse than before the era of famine and plagues, which could still strike with alarming effect. Chroniclers noted attacks of plague in 1500 in places as far apart as London, Edinburgh, and towns in the Scottish Lowlands; a year earlier it had struck in Oxford and parts of Ireland. In Wales the unholy trinity of famine, disease and war, which had unnerved entire communities in town and countryside over the past 150 years, could still stir the poet Dafydd Nanmor. New diseases had recently appeared, ostensibly from the continent: people were just as incapable of combating them as they had been in confronting the earlier plagues. The sweating sickness carried off a number of prominent Londoners in 1485 'for lack of good guiding, for they were kept so hot and close that many were smothered that might have been saved with moderate keeping'. It was blamed by some on Henry VII's French mercenaries; a few years later it struck in Meath and Ulster. The nationality of disease extended to the Spanish pox which, in 1498, 'reigned in this Land [and] continued upon men's bodies two years before they were fully healed'.

At the same time, the British Isles were not necessarily or generally a land of poverty. The smaller population was associated with the growth of pasturelands and the spread of enclosures for sheep rearing and the developing domestic cloth industry in lowlands and hill country. There was no great economic change in prospect in 1500, but some communities would enjoy greater prosperity as peace and overseas contacts flourished. Many towns were admittedly smaller than they had been, with more open spaces where burgages had once been occupied; some villages had disappeared completely since the mid-fourteenth century. Yet other towns like Bristol, Haverfordwest, Edinburgh, and Waterford were growing, and especially London, 'so famous throughout the world', declared the Italian visitor Dominic Mancini in 1483. London impressed foreign visitors not simply as the governmental capital of the English realm but even more as the metropolis for people from all the other countries of these islands.

Society was less hidebound and more mobile, and social relationships less constrained than they had once been, with opportunities for advancement in many walks of life. The Palmers' Guild of Ludlow was of such reputation that by the end of the century it was recruiting members from as far afield as western Wales and southern England, and from London and the court at Westminster. The road to gentility could be taken by lawyers, merchants, townsmen, and officials employed in Church and state; the successful among them could acquire property, build country and town houses, and support churches and religious and charitable foundations in their adopted villages and towns. Popular, peripatetic Welsh poets were keen to be rewarded with clothing and the paraphernalia of gentility by patrons who were often Welsh- and English-speaking by turns. Yet the differences among the ranks of society were being accentuated by marks of status and position: by titles from dukes to yeomen, by dress and its conventions, by lifestyles and housing. Individuals encountered hurdles in their social progress—poverty, birth and, most notably, opportunity—but many were able to vault them and move from one class to another. As Sir Thomas More reflected in 1515, by the beginning of the sixteenth century England, with its social hierarchies and social exploitation, was no utopian society. But this was 'an age of ambition' for individuals from newly and well-established families in all the counties of England and Wales at least.

European horizons

Older certainties and conventions were crumbling even in relation to religious belief and practice, though this did not presage Henry VIII's breach with Rome or the later Reformations in England and its dominions and in Scotland. Without compromising their control over their respective churches, both Henry VII and James IV in fact forged close ties with the papacy, and only partly for diplomatic reasons; Scotland indeed was known as 'its special daughter'. And whilst there may have been weakening respect for ecclesiastical hierarchies in the British Isles, in the later fifteenth century popular devotion and lay piety flourished, and the mendicant orders were welcomed in England, Ireland, and Scotland.

The relationship of both kingdoms with continental Europe was changing. The English and the Scots were increasingly proud of their independent and autonomous realms, and directed their propaganda, policies, and administrative practices to proclaim their pride—the English to sustain their position in the British Isles and in relation to the continent, the Scots to assert their hard-won independence from their neighbour to the south, each focusing attention less exclusively on relations with France after the emergence of a united kingdom of Spain (1479) and the dynastic realignment of the Low Countries and Burgundy (after 1477). English kings retained their claim to the French crown (and continued to do so until the Treaty of Amiens in 1802) and Yorkist and early Tudor monarchs occasionally led armies across the Channel, but they scaled back past ambitions in favour of regarding themselves as the equals of French kings—as Henry VIII demonstrated at the sumptuous Field of the Cloth of Gold in 1521. Scotland, too, which had relied on the 'Auld Alliance' to buttress resistance to English threats, now also looked to Spain and the Baltic for royal marriage alliances and commercial partners. After France, the largest source of foreign burgesses in fifteenth-century Bruges was Scotland.

Cultural novelties

Innovative intellectual and artistic developments in the Low Countries, as well as in Italy, influenced Henry VII's England and James IV's Scotland. Occasional contacts with Italian humanistic learning during the fifteenth century multiplied in the century's latter decades. The humanist scholar Erasmus of Rotterdam had an entrée to both the English and Scottish courts, and visiting Italian and French humanists fitted easily into the London-based circle of humanist lawyers, writers, and teachers in the 1490s. The invention of the moveable-type printing press was bound to have consequences in many walks of life, even if not immediately following the establishment of William Caxton's press at Westminster in 1476 and the authorization given to two burghers of Edinburgh to set up their press in 1507–8. Caxton printed almost 100 titles in little more than a decade, three-quarters of them in English. These first books to be printed in the British Isles were mostly traditional in subject matter—popular romances, history, handbooks, religious tomes, and translations—yet they proved a major force in encouraging literacy and advancing education, helping to revive Oxford and Cambridge universities and supporting a new university college in Aberdeen (1495). Other printed books had been imported from Germany, France, and the Low Countries since the 1460s, alongside more traditional illuminated manuscripts.

England had long produced illuminated manuscripts and books.

The exuberances of fourteenth-century illustrations, accompanying texts in Latin and French, had given way to more mature and controlled styles in the fifteenth century. Workshops in several urban centres, especially in London, now produced mostly English illuminated works for buyers royal and mercantile, and for gentry as well as churchmen and monasteries. Artists from France and the Low Countries, who brought greater realism to their work, were more easily recruited after the ending of the Hundred Years War. Pictures (including portrait painting) in the new Netherlandish style were admired in the British Isles as elsewhere during the second half of the fifteenth century, though the passage of time and changes of fashion have meant that few commissions seem to have survived. The occasional English and Scottish visitor to Bruges ordered pictures from these painters which, when they were brought home, doubtless attracted admirers. In the 1470s the Anglo-Welsh knight Sir John Don (d. 1502), friend and diplomat of Edward IV, commissioned a triptych with family portraits from Hans Memling (d. 1494) to serve as a portable altar; when he or his family took it to his Kidwelly home in south Wales or to his new Buckinghamshire house near Aylesbury, a wide circle of acquaintances could have seen it. About the same time, Edward Bonkil, provost of the new Trinity College chapel in Edinburgh, commissioned a triptych with his own and royal Scottish portraits from the equally notable Hugo van der Goes (d. 1482); in the college chapel it would have been seen by even larger numbers in Scotland's leading city.

Enterprises at sea

People's horizons were about to be extended even further afield. From 1480, seafarers and merchants from Bristol were regularly venturing beyond Ireland and Iceland in search of fish stocks and the fabled Isle of Brazil. Welsh captains were among them, and their little fleets sometimes called at Irish ports; when they made a landfall to the west during the following decade, the discovery aroused widespread interest in these islands and among continental map-makers. John Cabot, the Genoese who was also a citizen of Venice, returned to Bristol after locating an island in 1497; the momentous news created a stir in London and at the court, as the Great Chronicle of London reported:

The king, by means of a Venetian which made himself very expert and cunning in knowledge of the circuit of the world and isle lands of the same, as by a chart and other demonstrations reasonable he showed, caused the king to man and victual a ship at Bristol to search for an isle land which he said he knew well was rich and replenished with rich commodities, which ship was manned and victualled at the king's cost divers merchants of London adventured in her small stocks being in her as chief patron the said Venetian, and in the company of the said ship sailed also out of Bristol three or four small ships fraught with slight and gross merchandise as course cloth, caps, lace points and other trifles. And so departed from Bristol in the beginning of May . . .

On Cabot's return from what seems to have been a more ambitious voyage of discovery in 1503, the same chronicler was quite startled:

This year also were brought unto the king three men taken in the New Found Isle land, that before I spoke of . . . These were clothed in beasts' skins and ate raw flesh and spoke such speech that no man could understand them, and in their demeanour like to brute beasts whom the king kept a time after, of the which upon two years passed after I saw two of them apparelled after English men in Westminster palace, which at that time I could not discern from English men till I was learned what men they were, but as for speech I heard none of them utter one word.

For people in the British Isles, the world was literally changing.

These developments reflected the importance of the overseas interests of both realms; their inhabitants were largely maritime peoples, trading within the British Isles and with foreign ports from the Baltic to the Mediterranean. England especially had a defining relationship with the sea, which served both 'in the office of a wall' (as Shakespeare would put it in the 1590s) and as an avenue for the attempted domination of other lands. It helped, too, to fortify the English spirit of independence and mistrust of others. Edward III had gloried in his description as 'King of the Sea', and his new gold coinage in 1348 depicted him as commander of the ship of state; Henry V was remembered in the *Libelle of Englysche Polycye* as 'Lorde round about environ of the sea'. To supplement their merchant marine, they and their successors built 'king's ships'—albeit irregularly—and developed a rudimentary naval organization for war and defence, for the protection of merchant shipping, and to impress. Scotland's links with France and northern European countries were an antidote to pressures from the south across the land border, and most of its relatively modest overseas trade was plied from royal burghs. From the mid-fifteenth century Scots kings too invested in a royal navy, which in particular assisted them to cut an international dash. Mastery of the seas was a touchstone of nationhood for the generation of 1500. It also helped to emphasise, to continental Europeans, the separateness and distinctiveness of the peoples of the British Isles.

Further reading

Each of the countries of the British Isles in these two centuries is well served by writers of general histories: M. H. Keen, *England in the later Middle Ages* (London, 1973), and A. J. Pollard, *Later Medieval England, 1399–1509* (London, 2000); R. R. Davies, *Conquest, Coexistence and Change: Wales, 1063–1415* (Oxford, 1987), and G. Williams, *Recovery, Reorientation and Reformation: Wales, c.1415–1642* (Oxford, 1987); A. Cosgrove (ed.), *A New History of Ireland, ii: Medieval Ireland, 1169–1534* (Oxford, 1987), and S. Duffy, *Ireland in the Middle Ages* (Dublin, 1997); R. Nicholson, *Scotland: The Later Middle Ages* (Edinburgh, 1974), and A. D. M. Barrell, *Medieval Scotland* (Cambridge, 2000). More integrated studies are few, and rarely address the fourteenth and fifteenth centuries as a whole; but see R. R. Davies, 'The Peoples of Britain and Ireland, 1100–1400 [i–iv]', *Transactions of the Royal Historical Society*, 6th series, 4–7 (1994–7); R. R. Davies, *The First English Empire: Power and Identities in the British Isles, 1093–1343* (Oxford, 2000); R. Frame, *The Political Development of the British Isles, 1100–1400*, rev. edn. (Oxford, 1995); and J. Cannon and R. Griffiths, *The Oxford Illustrated History of the British Monarchy* (Oxford, 1988), ch. 3 (pp. 176–298).

Introduction

Bower, W., *A History Book for Scots*, ed. D. E. R. Watt (Edinburgh, 1998).

Brown, J. M. (ed.), *Scottish Society in the Fifteenth Century* (London, 1977).

Davis, N. (ed.), *Paston Letters and Papers of the Fifteenth Century* (2 vols., Oxford, 1971, 1976).

Dodgshon, R. A., and Butlin, R. A. (eds.), *An Historical Geography of England and Wales*, 2nd edn. (London, 1990).

Ellis, H. (ed.), *The Chronicle of John Hardyng* (London, 1812).

Falkus, M., and Gillingham, J. (eds.), *Historical Atlas of Britain* (London, 1981).

Froissart, J., *Chronicles*, ed. G. Brereton (London, 1968).

Given-Wilson, C. (ed.), *The Chronicle of Adam Usk, 1377–1421* (Oxford, 1997).

Griffiths, R. A., *King and Country: England and Wales in the Fifteenth Century* (London, 1991).

Harvey, J. H. (ed.), *Itineraries of William Worcester* (Oxford, 1969).

Letts, M. H. I. (ed.), *Travels of Leo von Rozmital* (Cambridge, 1957).

McNeill, P. G. B., and McQueen, H. L. (eds.), *Atlas of Scottish History to 1707* (Edinburgh, 1996).

Newton, S. M., *Fashion in the Age of the Black Prince* (Woodbridge, 1980).

Parsons, E. J. S., and Stenton, F. M. (eds.), *The Map of Great Britain circa A.D. 1360 known as the Gough Map* (Oxford, 1958).

Sneyd, C. A. (ed.), *A Relation, or rather a true Account, of the Island of England* (London, Camden Society, 1847).

Wallace, D., *The Cambridge History of Medieval English Literature* (Cambridge, 1999).

Warner, G. (ed.), *The Libelle of Englyshe Polycye* (Oxford, 1926).

Chapter 1

Aston, T. H., and Philpin, C. H. E. (eds.), *The Brenner Debate: Agrarian Class Structure and Economic Development in Pre-Industrial Europe* (Cambridge, 1985).

Beresford, M. W., *New Towns of the Middle Ages: Town Plantations in England, Wales and Gascony* (London, 1967).

Bolton, J. L., *The Medieval English Economy, 1100–1500* (London, 1980).

Britnell, R. H., *The Commercialisation of English Society, 1100–1500* (Cambridge, 1993).

Campbell, B. M. S. (ed.), *Before the Black Death: Studies in the 'Crisis' of the Early Fourteenth Century* (Manchester, 1991).

—— *English Seigniorial Agriculture, 1250–1450* (Cambridge, 2000).

Carus-Wilson, E. M., and Coleman, O., *England's Overseas Trade, 1275–1547* (Oxford, 1963).

Chaucer, G., *The Canterbury Tales*, trans. N. Coghill, rev. edn. (London, 1977).

Davies, R. R., *Lordship and Society in the March of Wales, 1282–1400* (Oxford, 1978).

Dyer, C., *Standards of Living in the Later Middle Ages: Social Change in England, c.1200–1520*, rev. edn. (Cambridge, 1998).

—— *Everyday Life in Medieval England* (London, 1994).

—— *Making a Living in the Middle Ages: The People of Britain, 850–1520* (New Haven, Conn., 2002).

Grant, A., *Independence and Nationhood: Scotland, 1306–1469* (London, 1984).

Griffiths, R. A. (ed.), *Boroughs of Medieval Wales* (Cardiff, 1978).

Harvey, B., *Living and Dying in England, 1100–1540: The Monastic Experience* (Oxford, 1993).

Hatcher, J., *Plague, Population and the English Economy, 1348–1530* (London, 1977).

Horrox, R. (ed.), *The Black Death* (Manchester, 1994).

Lloyd, T. H., *The English Wool Trade in the Middle Ages* (Cambridge, 1977).

Lynch, M., Spearman, M., and Stell, G. (eds.), *The Scottish Medieval Town* (Edinburgh, 1988).

Miller, E., and Hatcher, J., *Medieval England: Rural Society and Economic Change, 1086–1348* (London, 1978).

—— *Medieval England: Towns, Commerce and Crafts* (London, 1995).

Palliser, D. (ed.), *The Cambridge Urban History of Britain, i: 600–1540* (Cambridge, 2000).

Platt, C., *King Death: The Black Death and its Aftermath in Late-Medieval England* (London, 1996).

Postan, M. M., *The Medieval Economy and Society: An Economic History of Britain in the Middle Ages* (London, 1972).

Whyte, I., *Scotland before the Industrial Revolution: An Economic and Social History, c.1050–c.1750* (London, 1995).

Chapter 2

Brown, J. M. (ed.), *Scottish Society in the Fifteenth Century* (Edinburgh, 1977).

Carpenter, C., *Locality and Polity: A Study of Warwickshire Landed Society, 1401–1499* (Cambridge, 1992).

Coss, P. R., *The Knight in Medieval England, 1000–1400* (Stroud, 1993).

—— *The Lady in Medieval England, 1000–1400* (Stroud, 1998).

Davies, R. R., *Lordship and Society in the March of Wales, 1282–1400* (Oxford, 1978).

—— *The Revolt of Owain Glyn Dŵr* (Oxford, 1997).

Denholm-Young, N., *The Country Gentry in the Fourteenth Century* (Oxford, 1969).

Dobson, R. B. (ed.), *The Peasants Revolt of 1381*, 2nd edn. (1983).

Dyer, C., *Making a Living in the Middle Ages: The People of Britain, 850–1520* (New Haven, Conn., 2002).

Fleming, P., *Family and Household in Medieval England* (London, 2001).

Given-Wilson, C., *The English Nobility in the Later Middle Ages* (London, 1987).

Grant, A., *Independence and Nationhood: Scotland, 1306–1469* (London, 1984).

Hilton, R. H., *Bond Men Made Free: Medieval Peasant Movements and the English Rising of 1381* (London, 1973).

—— *The English Peasantry in the Later Middle Ages* (Oxford, 1975).

Horrox, R. (ed.), *Fifteenth-Century Attitudes: Perceptions of Society in Late Medieval England* (Cambridge, 1994).

Keen, M., *English Society in the Later Middle Ages* (Harmondsworth, 1990).

—— *Origins of the English Gentleman* (Stroud, 2002).

Leyser, H., *Medieval Women: A Social History of Women in England, 450–1500* (London, 1995).

McFarlane, K. B., *The Nobility of Later Medieval England* (Oxford, 1973).

Mate, M. E., *Women in Medieval English Society* (Cambridge, 1999).

Nicholls, K., *Gaelic and Gaelicised Ireland in the Middle Ages* (Dublin, 1972).

Richmond, C., *The Paston Family in the Fifteenth Century* (3 vols.: vols. i and ii, Cambridge, 1990, 1996; vol. iii, Manchester, 2000).

Rigby, S., *English Society in the Later Middle Ages: Class, Status and Gender* (Basingstoke, 1995).

Thrupp, S., *The Merchant Class of Medieval London* (Chicago, 1948).

Woolgar, C. M., *The Great Household in Medieval England* (New Haven, Conn., 1999).

Chapter 3

Cowan, I. B., *The Medieval Church in Scotland*, ed. J. Kirk (Edinburgh, 1995).

Dobson, R. B. (ed.), *The Church, Politics and Patronage in the Fifteenth Century* (Gloucester, 1984).

Duffy, E., *The Stripping of the Altars* (New Haven, Conn., 1992).

Ellis, S. G., *Tudor Ireland: Crown, Community and the Conflict of Cultures, 1470–1603* (Harlow, 1985).

Grant, A., *Independence and Nationhood: Scotland, 1306–1469* (London, 1984).

Gwynn, A., *Anglo-Irish Church Life in the Fourteenth and Fifteenth Centuries* (Dublin, 1968).

Heath, P., *Church and Realm, 1272–1461* (London, 1988).

Macdougall, N. (ed.), *Church, Politics and Society: Scotland, 1408–1929* (Edinburgh, 1983).

Mooney, C., *The Church in Gaelic Ireland: Thirteenth to Fifteenth Centuries* (Dublin, 1969).

Rex, R., *The Lollards* (Basingstoke, 2002).

Richter, M., *Medieval Ireland* (Basingstoke, 1988).

Swanson, R. N., *Church and Society in Late Medieval England* (Oxford, 1989).

—— *Catholic England: Faith, Religion and Observance before the Reformation* (Manchester, 1993).

Thomson, J. A. F., *The Early Tudor Church and Society, 1485–1529* (Harlow, 1993).

Watt, J., *The Church and the Two Nations in Medieval Ireland* (Cambridge, 1970).

Williams, G., *The Welsh Church from Conquest to Reformation*, rev. edn., (Cardiff, 1976).

—— *Recovery, Reorientation and Reformation: Wales, c.1415–1642* (Oxford, 1987).

Wormald, J., *Court, Kirk and Community: Scotland, 1470–1625* (London, 1981).

Chapter 4

Abraham, G., *The Concise Oxford History of Music* (Oxford, 1979).

Alexander, J., and Binski, P., *Age of Chivalry: Art in Plantagenet England, 1200–1400* (London, 1987).

Brewer, D. (ed.), *A Companion to the Gawain-Poet* (Cambridge, 1997).

Bromwich, R. (ed.), *Dafydd ap Gwilym: A Selection of Poems*, rev. edn., (Llandysul, 1993).

Brown, J. M. (ed.), *Scottish Society in the Fifteenth Century* (London, 1977).

Caldwell, J., *The Oxford History of English Music, i: From the Beginnings to c.1715* (Oxford, 1991).

Cobban, A. B., *English University Life in the Middle Ages* (London, 1999).

Coldstream, N., *The Decorated Style: Architecture and Ornament, 1240–1360* (London, 1994).

Cosgrove, A. (ed.), *A New History of Ireland, ii: Medieval Ireland, 1169–1534* (Oxford, 1987).

Cottle, B., *The Triumph of English, 1350–1400* (London, 1969).

Davies, R. R., *Conquest, Coexistence and Change: Wales, 1063–1415* (Oxford, 1987).

Evans, J., *English Art, 1307–1461* (Oxford, 1949).

Ford, B. (ed.), *The Cambridge Guide to the Arts in Britain, ii: The Middle Ages* (Cambridge, 1988).

Given-Wilson, C. (ed.), *An Illustrated History of Late Medieval England* (Manchester, 1996).

Graham-Dixon, A., *A History of British Art* (London, 2000).

Grant, A., *Independence and Nationhood: Scotland, 1306–1469* (London, 1984).

Hellinga, L., and Trapp, J. B. (eds.), *The Cambridge History of the Book in Britain, iii: 1400–1557* (Cambridge, 1999).

Horrox, R. (ed.), *The Black Death* (Manchester, 1994).

Lindley, P. G., *Gothic to Renaissance: Essays on Sculpture in England* (Stamford, 1995).

—— (ed.), *The Black Death in England* (Stamford, 1996).

—— 'The Black Death and English Art: A Debate and some Assumptions', in W. M. Ormrod and P. G. Lindley (eds.), *The Black Death in England* (Stamford, 1996), 125–46 (quoting J. M. Maddison).

Macmillan, D., *Scottish Art: 1460–1990* (Edinburgh, 1990).

Marks, R., *Stained Glass in England during the Middle Ages* (London, 1993).

Pearsall, D., *Old English and Middle English Poetry* (London, 1977).

—— *Gothic Europe, 1200–1450* (London, 2001).

Platt, C., *The Architecture of Medieval England* (New Haven, Conn., 1990).

Salter, E., *Fourteenth Century English Poetry: Contexts and Readings* (Oxford, 1983).

Saul, N. (ed.), *Age of Chivalry: Art and Society in Late Medieval England* (London, 1992).

Wallace, D. (ed.), *The Cambridge History of Medieval English Literature* (Cambridge, 1999).

Wilkins, N., *Music in the Age of Chaucer* (Cambridge, 1979).

Chapter 5

Allmand, C. T., *Lancastrian Normandy, 1415–1450: The History of a Medieval Occupation* (Oxford, 1983).

—— *The Hundred Years War: England and France at War, c.1300–c.1450* (Cambridge, 1988).

Barnie, J., *War in Medieval Society: Social Values and the Hundred Years War, 1337–99* (London, 1974).

Barrow, G. W. S., *Robert Bruce and the Community of the Realm of Scotland,* 3rd edn. (Edinburgh, 1988).

Bartlett, R., and McKay, A. (eds.), *Medieval Frontier Societies* (Oxford, 1989).

Cosgrove, A. (ed.), *A New History of Ireland, ii: Medieval Ireland, 1169–1534* (Oxford, 1987).

Davies, R. R., *Lordship and Society in the March of Wales, 1282–1400* (Oxford 1978).

—— *Conquest, Coexistence and Change: Wales, 1063–1415* (Oxford, 1987).

—— 'The Peoples of Britain and Ireland, 1100–1400 [i–iv]', *Transactions of the Royal Historical Society*, 6th series, 4–7 (1994–7).

—— *The Revolt of Owain Glyn Dŵr* (Oxford, 1995).

—— *The First English Empire: Power and Identities in the British Isles, 1093–1343* (Oxford, 2000).

Ellis, S., *Ireland in the Age of the Tudors, 1447–1603: English Expansion and the End of Gaelic Rule* (London, 1998).

Fowler, K. (ed.), *The Hundred Years War* (New York, 1971).

Frame, R., *The Political Development of the British Isles, 1100–1400* (Oxford, 1990).

—— *Ireland and Britain, 1170–1450* (London, 1998).

Grant, A., *Independence and Nationhood: Scotland, 1306–1469* (London, 1984).

Griffiths, R. A., *King and Country: England and Wales in the Fifteenth Century* (London, 1991).

—— *Conquerors and Conquered in Medieval Wales* (Stroud, 1994).

Jones, M., and Vale, M. (eds.), *England and her Neighbours, 1066–1453: Essays in Honour of Pierre Chaplais* (Oxford, 1989).

Macdonald, A. J., *Border Bloodshed: Scotland and England at War, 1369–1403* (East Linton, 2000).

McNamee, C., *The Wars of the Bruces: Scotland, England and Ireland, 1306–1328* (East Linton, 1997).

Otway-Ruthven, A. J., *A History of Medieval Ireland* (London, 1967).

Prestwich, M., *Armies and Warfare in the Middle Ages* (London, 1996).

Simms, K., *From Kings to Warlords: The Changing Political Structure of Gaelic Ireland in the later Middle Ages* (Woodbridge, 1987).

Tuck, A., and Goodman, A. (eds.), *War and Border Societies in the Middle Ages* (London, 1992).

Vale, M. G. A., *English Gascony, 1399–1453* (Oxford, 1970).

—— *The Angevin Legacy and the Hundred Years War, 1250–1340* (Oxford, 1990).

Watson, F., *Under the Hammer: Edward I and Scotland, 1286–1307* (East Linton, 1998).

Webster, B., *Medieval Scotland: The Making of an Identity* (Basingstoke, 1997).

Chapter 6

Allmand, C. T., *Henry V*, new edn. (New Haven, Conn., 1997).

Barrow, G. W. S., *Robert Bruce and the Community of the Realm of Scotland*, 3rd edn. (Edinburgh, 1988).

Boardman, S., *The Early Stewart Kings: Robert II and Robert III, 1371–1406* (East Linton, 1996).

Brown, A. L., *The Governance of Late Medieval England, 1272–1461* (London, 1989).

Brown, M., *James I* (Edinburgh, 1994).

Chrimes, S. B., *Henry VII*, new edn. (New Haven, Conn., 1999).

Cosgrove, A. (ed.), *A New History of Ireland, ii: Medieval Ireland, 1169–1534* (Oxford, 1987).

Davies, R. R., *Conquest, Coexistence and Change: Wales, 1063–1415* (Oxford, 1987).

—— *The Revolt of Owain Glyn Dŵr* (Oxford, 1995).

Dickinson, W. C., *Scotland from the Earliest Times to 1603*, rev. and ed. A. A. M. Duncan (Oxford, 1977).

Frame, R., *English Lordship in Ireland, 1318–1361* (Oxford, 1982).

Grant, A., *Independence and Nationhood: Scotland, 1306–1469* (London, 1984).

Griffiths, R. A., *The Reign of King Henry VI: The Exercise of Royal Authority, 1422–1461*, new edn. (Stroud, 1998).

—— and Thomas, R. S., *The Making of the Tudor Dynasty* (Stroud, 1985).

Harding, A., *The Law Courts of Medieval England* (London, 1973).

Lydon, J., *Ireland in the Later Middle Ages* (Dublin, 1973).

Macdougall, N., *James III: A Political Study* (Edinburgh, 1982).

—— *James IV* (Edinburgh, 1989).

McGladdery, C., *James II* (Edinburgh, 1990).

Nicholls, K., *Gaelic and Gaelicised Ireland in the Middle Ages* (Dublin, 1972).

Nicholson, R., *Scotland: The Later Middle Ages* (Edinburgh, 1974).

Ormrod, W. M., *The Reign of Edward III: Crown and Political Society in England, 1327–1377* (New Haven, Conn., 1990).

Pollard, A. J., *Late Medieval England, 1399–1509* (Harlow, 2000).

Prestwich, M., *The Three Edwards: War and State in England, 1272–1377* (London, 1980).

—— *Edward I*, new edn. (New Haven, Conn., 1997).

Ross, C., *Edward IV*, new edn. (New Haven, Conn., 1997).

—— *Richard III*, new edn. (New Haven, Conn., 1999).

Saul, N., *Richard II* (New Haven, Conn., 1997).

Thomson, J. A. F., *The Transformation of Medieval England, 1370–1529* (London, 1983).

Tuck, A., *Crown and Nobility, 1272–1461: Political Conflict in Late Medieval England* (London, 1985).

Waugh, S. L., *England in the Reign of Edward III* (Cambridge, 1991).

Williams, G., *Renewal, Reorientation and Reformation: Wales, c.1415–1642* (Oxford, 1987).

Epilogue

Barrell, A. D. M., *Medieval Scotland* (Cambridge, 2000).

Blake, N. F., *Caxton and his World* (London, 1969).

Bradshaw, B., *The Irish Constitutional Revolution of the Sixteenth Century* (Cambridge, 1979).

Briggs, A., and Snowman, D. (eds.), *Fins de Siécle: How Centuries End, 1400–2000* (New Haven, Conn., 2000).

Britnell, R., *The Closing of the Middle Ages: England, 1471–1529* (London, 1997).

Calendar of State Papers, Spanish (London, 1862–).

Chrimes, S. B., *Henry VII*, new edn. (New Haven, Conn., 1999).

Duffy, S., *Ireland in the Middle Ages* (Dublin, 1997).

Griffiths, R. A., 'After Glyn Dŵr: An Age of Reconciliation?', *Proceedings of the British Academy* (2002).

Macdougall, N., *James IV* (Edinburgh, 1989).

—— *James III* (Edinburgh, 1982).

Mancini, D., *The Usurpation of Richard III*, ed. C. A. J. Armstrong (Oxford, 1936).

Quinn, D. B., *England and the Discovery of America, 1481–1620* (London, 1974).

Smith, P., *Houses of the Welsh Countryside*, 2nd edn. (London, 1988).

Sneyd, C. A. (ed.), *A Relation, or rather a true Account, of the Island of England* (London, Camden Society, 1847).

Thomas, A. H., and Thornley, I. D. (eds.), *The Great Chronicle of London* (London, 1938).

Webster, B., *Medieval Scotland: The Making of an Identity* (Basingstoke, 1997).

Williams, G., *Recovery, Reorientation and Reformation: Wales, c.1415–1642* (Oxford, 1987).

Wormald, J., *Court, Kirk and Community: Scotland, 1470–1625* (London, 1981).

Chronology

Norway should marry Edward, son of Edward I; Margaret dies two months later

Statutes *Quia Emptores* and *Quo Warranto* define English law of landholding

Jews are expelled from England

1291 At Norham, Scottish lords acknowledge Edward I as overlord and his right to adjudicate on the Scottish succession ('the Great Cause')

New assessment of English benefices for papal taxation (*Taxatio* of Pope Nicholas IV)

Building of the nave of York Minster begins

Ten stone crosses erected (1291–4) to mark the stages of bringing Queen Eleanor of Castile's body to London

1292 Edward I awards the Scottish crown to John Balliol

English judges to provide training for lawyers in inns of court

1294 Philip IV of France seizes Gascony and precipitates war with England

Treaty of Nuremberg between England and Germany

Widespread revolt in Wales

1295 Edward I defeats the Welsh at Maes Moydog

Scotland and France conclude the 'Auld Alliance'

Edward I summons knights and burgesses to his 'Model Parliament'

1296 Pope Boniface VIII's bull, *Clericis Laicos*, forbids kings from taxing the clergy

Edward I captures Berwick and defeats the Scots at Dunbar; John Balliol abdicates and Edward takes the 'Stone of Scone' to Westminster

1297 Edward I outlaws English and Welsh clergy for refusing to pay taxes

William Wallace leads risings in Scotland; defeats the English at Stirling Bridge and ravages northern England

A representative Irish Parliament is summoned

1298 William Wallace appointed guardian of Scotland

Edward I defeats the Scots at Falkirk

1299 English nobles force Edward I to reissue Magna Carta and Charter of the Forest

Pope Boniface VIII upholds Scottish claims to independence

The Scots capture Stirling Castle

1300 Edward I issues the Charters again

1301 Edward I creates his eldest son prince of Wales
Edward I reissues the Charters once again

1303 Edward I embarks on a fourth campaign in Scotland
England and France conclude the Treaty of Paris

1304 Scots leaders submit to Edward I at St Andrews in Parliament

1305 William Wallace tried and executed in London for treason
Edward I issues ordinances for Scotland's government

1306 Robert Bruce crowned king of Scots; he murders John Comyn at Dumfries
The English defeat the Scots at Methven

1307 Edward I dies and is succeeded by his son, Edward II

1308 Edward II crowned king of England; he marries Isabella of France
Robert Bruce invades northern England
The Order of Knights Templar suppressed in the British Isles

1310 Edward II is forced to appoint a commission of governmental reform (the Lords Ordainer)

1311 Edward II forced to banish Peter Gaveston, and the Lords Ordainer limit the king's power

1312 Peter Gaveston murdered by rebellious earls

1313 The Scots recover the Isle of Man

1314 Robert Bruce defeats Edward II at Bannockburn
Thomas, earl of Lancaster, takes charge of English government
Foundation of Exeter College, Oxford

1315 Edward Bruce invades Ireland and is proclaimed king
The great famine begins in England

1316 Edward Bruce crowned high king of Ireland
Revolt led by Llywelyn Bren in Glamorgan

1317 Robert Bruce joins his brother Edward in Ireland

1318 Robert Bruce captures Berwick
Edward II confirms the Ordinances at the Treaty of Leake
Edward Bruce killed by English forces at Faughart
The Pope acknowledges the foundation of a *studium generale* at Cambridge

1319 The Scots defeat the English at Myton-on-Swale (Yorkshire)

1320   Declaration of Arbroath

1321   Marcher lords and English nobles seize Hugh Despenser's Welsh lordships

      Edward II forced to banish Hugh Despenser and his son

1322   The crossing-tower of Ely Cathedral collapses; a new octagonal stone and wood tower is begun

      Edward II defeats Thomas, earl of Lancaster, at Boroughbridge and executes him

      Edward II's Parliament at York repeals the Ordinances and the marcher lords submit

1323   Edward II concludes a truce with Robert Bruce

1324   Treaty of Corbeil between Scotland and France

1325   Queen Isabella visits France

1326   Representatives of Scottish burghs first attend a Scottish Parliament

      Queen Isabella and Roger Mortimer land in England

      Hugh Despenser, father and son, are executed and Prince Edward is made keeper of the realm

      Edward II captured by Queen Isabella's forces near Neath Abbey

1327   Edward II deposed; his son, Edward, succeeds him

      Edward II murdered

      The Scots invade England

1328   Edward III marries Philippa of Hainault

      Edward III concludes peace with the Scots by the Treaty of Edinburgh

      The Treaty of Northampton acknowledges Scottish independence and Robert Bruce as king

1329   Robert Bruce dies and is succeeded by David II

1330   Edward III arrests and executes Roger Mortimer and puts his mother, Queen Isabella, in custody

1331   Rebuilding at Gloucester Abbey begins in Perpendicular style

1332   Edward Balliol crowned king of Scotland; he is forced to flee to England

1333   The earl of Ulster's murder undermines crown control in north and west Ireland

      Edward III seizes the Isle of Man from Scotland

      Edward III defeats the Scots at Halidon Hill and captures Berwick

1334   David II seeks refuge in France

1335   Edward Balliol's authority in Scotland disintegrates

1337   Edward III seeks allies in the Low Countries
Philip IV of France confiscates Gascony: the Hundred Years War begins
Edward III claims the French crown through his mother, Queen Isabella

1338   Edward III appointed imperial vicar in the Low Countries

1340   Edward III takes the title of king of England and France
English naval victory at Sluys over a French fleet
Truce of Esplechin between Edward III and Philip VI

1341   David II returns to Scotland from France

1342   The Scots capture Roxburgh castle
Edward III leads a campaign to Brittany against the French

1344   The gold noble, worth 6s. 8d., is first coined in England
Edward III holds a chivalric 'round table' at Windsor Castle

1345   Edward III causes Italian bankers to go bankrupt

1346   Edward III lands in Normandy and is victorious at Crécy
David II defeated and captured by the English at Neville's Cross
The Book of the Anchorite, the largest and earliest collection of Middle Welsh religious texts, is written in Carmarthenshire

1347   Edward III captures Calais after a long siege

1348   Edward III founds the Order of the Garter at Windsor
The Black Death arrives in southern England and eastern Ireland

1349   The Black Death spreads to northern England, Wales, Scotland, and Ireland
Death of Richard Rolle, writer of scriptural commentaries

1351   The Statute of Labourers seeks to control wages and labourers' movements
The Statute of Provisors limits papal appointments in England

1352   The Statute of Treasons specifies treasonable offences

1353   Edward III transfers the English wool staple from Bruges to England and extends it to Ireland
The Statute of *Praemunire* prohibits unauthorized appeals to Rome

1354   The Statute of the Staple confirms the ordinance of 1353
The devotional work of Henry, duke of Lancaster, *Livre des Seyntz Medecines*, is written

1355   Edward III leads an expedition to Picardy while the Black Prince
        conducts a raid across southern France

1356   Edward III captures Berwick

        Edward Balliol transfers his claim as king of Scotland to
        Edward III

        The Black Prince defeats the French at Poitiers and captures
        John II

1357   The Treaty of Berwick arranges peace between England and
        Scotland, and the ransom of David II

1359   The Treaty of London cedes French territory to Edward III

        Edward III begins the siege of Rheims

1360   Edward III besieges Paris

        The Treaties of Brétigny–Calais cede sovereignty over French
        territory to Edward III and arrange the release of John II

1361   The Statute of Westminster creates JPs in English shires

        The second outbreak of plague

        Jean Froissart arrives in England

        Lionel, duke of Clarence, leads an English expedition to
        Ireland

1362   The English wool staple established at Calais

        Aquitaine given to the Black Prince

1365   The second Statute of *Praemunire* is enacted

1366   The Statutes of Kilkenny seek to insulate Anglo-Irish colonial
        society from Irish practices

1367   The Black Prince's victory over Henry of Castile at Najera

1368   Edward III reassumes the title of king of France and war
        resumes

1369   Further outbreaks of the Black Death

1370   The Black Prince sacks Limoges in France

1371   David II of Scotland dies and is succeeded by Robert II
        Stewart

1372   John of Gaunt, duke of Lancaster, claims the throne of Castile

        Owain ap Thomas ap Rhydderch, descendant of Llywelyn ap
        Gruffydd, prince of Wales, tries to invade Wales

1373   Treaty of London between England and Portugal

1375   Treaty of Bruges between England and France

1376   The 'Good Parliament' meets; first speaker of the Commons
        elected

Death of Edward the Black Prince
Earliest known record of Corpus Christi plays at York

1377 Edward III dies and is succeeded by Richard II
The French attack the Isle of Wight
The first poll tax granted in Parliament
The Pope condemns John Wycliffe's writings

1378 Foundation of Winchester College by William of Wykeham

1379 William of Wykeham founds New College, Oxford
A further outbreak of plague occurs

1380 The English Parliament grants a second poll tax

1381 The Peasants' Revolt in eastern England
John Wycliffe's *On the Eucharist* denies transubstantiation

1382 Richard II marries Anne of Bohemia
John Wycliffe condemned at Blackfriars and expelled from
Oxford University

1384 The English invade Scotland
John Wycliffe dies

1385 Richard II sacks Edinburgh

1386 Treaty of Windsor between England and Portugal
The 'Wonderful Parliament' impeaches the chancellor, Michael
de la Pole, earl of Suffolk

1387 Richard II's opponents—the Lords Appellant—defeat Robert de
Vere, earl of Oxford, at Radcot Bridge

1388 At the 'Merciless Parliament', the Lords Appellant accuse Richard
II's confidants of treason
Scottish victory over the English at Otterburn ('Chevy Chase')

1389 Richard II takes control of government

1390 Robert II dies and is succeeded by Robert III
Richard II's ordinance allows only lords to give livery to their
retainers
Second Statute of Provisors enacted

1393 Third Statute of *Praemunire* enacted

1394 Anne of Bohemia, queen of England, dies
Westminster Hall rebuilt under Henry Yevele's direction
Richard II visits Ireland and receives the submission of Irish
kings

1396 Treaty of Paris between England and France; Richard II marries
Charles VI's daughter, Isabella

1397   Richard II destroys the Lords Appellant in Parliament
Thomas, earl of Gloucester, is mysteriously murdered

1398   Richard II banishes Henry Bolingbroke, duke of Hereford, and
Thomas, duke of Norfolk

1399   John of Gaunt dies and Richard II seizes the Lancastrian
inheritance
Richard II's second campaign in Leinster
Henry Bolingbroke returns from France and deposes Richard II;
he claims the crown as Henry IV

1400   Conspiracy against Henry IV suppressed at Cirencester
Richard II dies in mysterious circumstances
Owain Glyn Dŵr's revolt begins in Wales
Geoffrey Chaucer dies

1401   The Statute *De Heretico Comburendo* against heretics is
enacted
Henry IV leads a second army against Welsh rebels
Penal laws enacted against the Welsh

1402   Glyn Dŵr defeats and captures Sir Edmund Mortimer at Pilleth
in the Welsh March
The earl of Northumberland and his son, Hotspur, defeat the
Scots at Homildon Hill
Henry IV leads a further army into Wales

1403   The Percy revolt shattered by Henry IV's victory at Shrewsbury,
where Hotspur is killed

1404   Glyn Dŵr holds a 'parliament' at Machynlleth and concludes an
alliance with France

1405   A tripartite agreement is made between Glyn Dŵr,
Northumberland, and Mortimer
Henry IV suppresses the revolt of Archbishop Scrope, who is
executed
French troops land in south Wales

1406   The Scottish heir, James, captured by the English
Robert III dies and is succeeded by James I
The duke of Albany becomes guardian of Scotland
Glyn Dŵr's policy for an independent Wales is formulated
Henry IV forced to make concessions to his longest Parliament

1408   Defeat and death of the earl of Northumberland at Bramham
Moor
John Gower dies

1409   Harlech castle, Glyn Dŵr's last stronghold, surrenders

1411   The Guildhall in London is founded

Donald, Lord of the Isles, invades north-east Scotland and is defeated by the earl of Mar at Harlaw

1412   Treaty of Elmham between Henry IV and the Armagnacs against the duke of Burgundy

1413   Henry IV dies and is succeeded by Henry V

St Andrews University founded

1414   The Lollard rising of Sir John Oldcastle is dispersed

Henry V negotiates an alliance with Burgundy

1415   Leaders of the earl of Cambridge's plot against Henry V executed

Henry V invades France, captures Harfleur, and wins at Agincourt

Henry V founds a Brigittine monastery at Twickenham

1416   Emperor Sigismund visits England and concludes the Treaty of Canterbury with Henry V

1417   Henry V begins the conquest of Normandy

Sir John Oldcastle executed as a traitor and heretic

1418   English forces capture Falaise

1419   English forces capture Rouen

1420   By the Treaty of Troyes with Charles VI, Henry V is acknowledged as heir to the French throne; he marries Catherine of Valois

The duke of Albany, governor of Scotland, dies

1421   The English defeated at Baugé; Thomas, duke of Clarence, is killed

1422   Henry V dies and is succeeded by the baby Henry VI

Charles VI dies and is succeeded, according to the Treaty of Troyes, by Henry VI

John, duke of Bedford, nominated regent of English France, and Humphrey, duke of Gloucester, becomes protector and chief councillor in England

Thomas Walsingham's Chronicle, written at St Albans, comes to an end

1423   The first Observant Franciscan priory in Ireland is established

1424   By the Treaty of Durham, James I is released; he marries Joan Beaufort

The English defeat a Franco-Scottish force at Verneuil

1425   James I executes the duke of Albany

1426   Treaty between Scotland and Denmark
       The English enclave in eastern Ireland raided by Gaelic forces

1429   Joan of Arc relieves Orléans and arranges the coronation of
       Charles VII
       French victory over the English at Patay
       Alexander, Lord of the Isles, imprisoned for rebellion

1430   A statute restricts the right to elect shire knights in English
       Parliaments to 40s. freeholders
       The Dublin Parliament authorizes castles for the defence of the
       English enclave
       Adam of Usk dies

1431   Humphrey, duke of Gloucester, suppresses a Lollard rising
       Joan of Arc burned as a heretic at Rouen
       Henry VI crowned king of France in Paris

1435   English, French, and Burgundian envoys attend the Congress
       of Arras
       John, duke of Bedford, dies
       By the Treaty of Arras, Burgundy deserts the English and allies
       with Charles VII

1436   Charles VII recovers Paris
       Henry VI begins his personal rule

1437   James I is murdered and is succeeded by the infant James II

1438   Archbishop Chichele founds All Souls College, Oxford

1439   The English conclude a truce with Burgundy

1440   Henry VI founds King's College, Cambridge

1441   The French recover the Île-de-France from the English
       Henry VI founds Eton College

1444   England and France conclude the Truce of Tours

1445   Henry VI marries Margaret of Anjou

1447   Humphrey, duke of Gloucester, dies
       Margaret of Anjou founds Queens' College, Cambridge

1448   The English surrender Le Mans to the French
       Hostilities between England and Scotland break out
       Bishop Waynflete founds Magdalen College, Oxford

1449   The English sacks Fougères and precipitate hostilities with
       France
       Walter Bower, Scots chronicler, dies

James II marries Mary of Gueldres
The French enter Rouen
Richard, duke of York, arrives in Ireland

1450 Impeachment of William de la Pole, duke of Suffolk, in Parliament
French victory at Formigny, leading to the expulsion of the English from Normandy
The duke of Suffolk is murdered
Jack Cade's rebellion in south-east England
Richard, duke of York, returns from Ireland
Bishop Kennedy founds St Salvator's College, St Andrews

1451 Glasgow University founded
Bordeaux and Bayonne surrender to Charles VII

1452 James II murders the earl of Douglas
Richard, duke of York, confronts Henry VI at Dartford but capitulates
The English recover Bordeaux

1453 French victory at Castillon, where the earl of Shrewsbury is killed, heralds the final loss of Gascony
Henry VI becomes incapacitated
Henry VI's son, Edward, is born
John Dunstable, composer, dies

1454 Richard, duke of York, appointed protector and chief councillor in Parliament, until Henry VI recovers

1455 Richard, duke of York, and his allies defeat Henry VI and the Lancastrians at St Albans
Richard, duke of York, reappointed protector and chief councillor

1456 Richard, duke of York, dismissed as protector and chief councillor

1457 Bishop Pecock tried for heresy

1458 Henry VI attends a reconciliation between Yorkists and royalist supporters

1459 The Yorkists successful at Blore Heath but routed at Ludford Bridge
Sir John Fastolf dies
The Yorkists attainted at the Coventry Parliament

1460 Parliament at Drogheda asserts the authority of Irish Parliaments; an Irish currency is devised

The earl of Warwick captures Henry VI at Northampton
James II is killed at the siege of Roxburgh and is succeeded by the infant James III
Richard, duke of York, recognized as Henry VI's heir
The Lancastrians defeat the Yorkists at Wakefield and Richard, duke of York, is killed

1461 Edward, duke of York, defeats the Lancastrians at Mortimer's Cross and is proclaimed Edward IV
Margaret of Anjou defeats the earl of Warwick at St Albans and rescues Henry VI
Edward IV defeats the Lancastrians at Towton
Henry VI and Margaret of Anjou flee to Scotland
Henry VI cedes Berwick to Scotland

1462 The earl of Desmond defeats the Butler family at Pilltown

1464 The Yorkists defeat Lancastrian forces at Hedgeley Moor and Hexham
Edward IV marries Elizabeth Woodville

1465 Henry VI captured and imprisoned in the Tower of London

1466 James III kidnapped

1467 Edward IV and Richard, earl of Warwick, quarrel

1468 James III marries Margaret of Denmark; the Orkneys are pledged for her dowry
A statute restricts the giving of livery and maintenance in England
The earl of Desmond executed

1469 The earl of Warwick and George, duke of Clarence, plot against Edward IV
Warwick defeats the king's forces, led by the earl of Pembroke, at Edgecote
The Scots annex the Orkneys and Shetlands

1470 Edward IV defeats a Lancastrian rising at Lose-Cote Field; Warwick and Clarence flee to France
Warwick reconciled with Margaret of Anjou; he invades England to restore Henry VI and Edward IV flees abroad

1471 Edward IV returns and defeats and kills Warwick at Barnet; he defeats Margaret of Anjou at Tewkesbury, where Prince Edward of Lancaster is killed
Henry VI murdered in the Tower of London

1472 Archbishopric of St Andrews is created

1473   Edward IV enhances the authority of his son's council in Wales and the March

1474   At Bruges, William Caxton prints his first book in English, *Recuyell of the Histories of Troy*

1475   Edward IV campaigns in France; he concludes the Treaty of Picquigny with Louis XI

1476   William Caxton opens his printing press at Westminster
John, Lord of the Isles, surrenders to James III

1477   Caxton prints his first book in England, *The Dictes or Sayengis of the Philosophres*

1478   George, duke of Clarence, executed

1479   Gerald, earl of Kildare, becomes lord deputy of Ireland
James III arrests his brothers, the duke of Albany and the earl of Mar

1480   A Bristol ship sails in search of the 'Isle of Brasil'

1481   William Caxton translates and prints *Reynard the Fox*

1482   Treaty of Fotheringhay between England and the duke of Albany against James III
The English under Richard, duke of Gloucester, capture Berwick
William Caxton prints John Trevisa's translation of Ranulf Higden's *Polychronicon*

1483   Edward IV dies and is succeeded by his young son, Edward V
Richard, duke of Gloucester, usurps the throne as Richard III
Edward V and his brother, Richard, probably murdered in the Tower of London
Henry, duke of Buckingham, rebels and is executed

1484   James III suppresses the duke of Albany's rebellion
The Treaty of Nottingham arranges a truce between England and Scotland
Henry VI's body reburied at Windsor
Richard III incorporates the College of Arms

1485   Henry Tudor invades Wales; he defeats and kills Richard III at Bosworth
Henry Tudor takes the crown as Henry VII
William Caxton prints Sir Thomas Malory's *Mort D'Arthur*

1486   Henry VII marries Elizabeth of York

1487   The Statute *Pro Camera Stellata* extends the powers of the king's council in England

Lambert Simnel is crowned king of England, in Dublin; he is defeated at Stoke and imprisoned

Pope Innocent VIII issues an indult for the Scottish Church

1488 James III is killed at Sauchieburn and is succeeded by James IV

1489 Henry VII negotiates the Treaty of Redon with Brittany and the Treaty of Medina del Campo with Spain

Henry VII's son Arthur proclaimed prince of Wales

A statute tackles clerical abuses in England

1491 Perkin Warbeck claims to be king of England and seeks support in Ireland

1492 Margaret of York, duchess of Burgundy, and French and Scottish kings recognize Perkin Warbeck as king of England

Treaty of Étaples between England and France

1493 Scotland annexes the Lordship of the Isles

1494 Sir Edward Poynings's 'law' limits the independence of Irish Parliaments

1495 Aberdeen University founded

Perkin Warbeck received in Scotland

1496 The earl of Kildare returns to Ireland as lord deputy

The *Intercursus Magnus* treaty is agreed between England and Flanders

Henry VII licenses the Cabots to explore at sea

Henry VII begins his lady chapel in Westminster Abbey

1497 Cornish rebels crushed at Blackheath

The Treaty of Ayton concluded between England and Scotland

Henry VII captures Perkin Warbeck

1498 Henry VII founds Observant Franciscan monasteries

1499 Erasmus visits England

Perkin Warbeck hanged

1500 Building of Richmond Palace begins

1501 Prince Arthur and Catherine of Aragon married

1502 A Treaty of 'Perpetual Peace' between England and Scotland

Prince Arthur dies

1503 Prince Henry betrothed to Catherine of Aragon

James IV marries Margaret Tudor

1504 Prince Henry declared prince of Wales

1506 Treaty between England and Burgundy

1507 The first printing press established in Scotland, at Edinburgh

1509 Henry VII dies and is succeeded by Henry VIII; he marries Catherine of Aragon

Glossary

appellate jurisdiction: authority of the king's Chancery to make equitable legal decisions to supplement the Common Law

armiger: esquire

ayres: judicial circuits or courts held in Scotland on the king's behalf

betagh: Irish *biatach*, an unfree tenant on an Irish manor, usually of Gaelic origin

bonheddwr: a gentleman or man of lineage in Welsh society

bonnet laird: a minor landed proprietor in Scotland

brehon: Irish *breitheamh*, *brithem*, a local or regional judge in Ireland

brieves: royal orders or writs to justices, in Scotland

caterans: militarized clansmen in Scotland

Chancery: central royal writing office or secretariat, with custody of seals

clerical proctors: representatives of the clergy, below bishops and abbots, in Parliament

coarb: Irish family descended from the original patron saint of a church

commendam: holding a monastery by papal grant, by someone not necessarily in religious orders

coyne and livery: Irish *coinnmheadh*, Scots *conveth*, illegal exactions in kind or money to support soldiers quartered on the countryside and requesting supplies

court of session: a civil court in Scotland

cuddies: Irish *cuid oidhche*, hospitality which an Irish lord exacted for himself and his retinue from his tenants

erenagh: Irish hereditary tenant of church lands, possibly with quasi-legal status

Exchequer: central royal financial office receiving and auditing crown revenues

franklin: free landholder, below the gentry

Gaels: native Irish-speaking population

Gaeltacht: land of the Gaels

galloglass: Irish *gallóglach*, usually a hired soldier from the Western Isles or Highland Scotland

Galls: Anglo-Irish settlers in Ireland

glebe: endowment of a parish in land or other property

impeachment: accusation by the Commons for trial by the Lords, with the king's assent, first used in 1376

justices of the peace: usually local gentlefolk appointed by the crown in each shire with a growing list of regulatory and peace-keeping duties

justiciar: the king's deputy or lieutenant in regions such as north and south Wales, Ireland, or in Scottish regions

kernety: household military servants in Ireland

liberties: *see* regalities

manrent bond: written contract between Scottish lords and their followers for service and obligation

manumission: formal release from unfree status

maor: a lord's collector of customary dues in Ireland; cf. *maer* in Wales

marshal, marasgal: officer in Ireland responsible for billeting and exacting costs for soldiers; elsewhere an official in a lord's household

mensa, bishop's: bishop's household or table

mercat cross: a cross in a marketplace, usually in a Scottish context

neyf: an unfree person, in Scotland

poll tax: taxation imposed on individuals at a fixed rate

Privy Seal office: English royal secretarial office, usually serving the king's council

purveyance: right to exact provisions, especially for the king's household, often at arbitrary cost

receiver: officer charged with accounting to a king or lord for estate income and expenditure

receiver-general: officer charged with accounting to a king or lord for income and expenditure from more than one receiver

regalities: semi-independent jurisdictions with autonomous powers of administration and justice; sometimes called palatinates or franchises

resumption, Act of: Acts of Parliament enabling a king to cancel earlier grants and re-acquire lands and offices

royal demesne: parts of the king's estate remaining under his direct control

scutifer: shield-bearer of a lord or squire

sept: a clan, in Irish usage

serf: man or woman of unfree status on a manor, though sometimes a landholder

sergeant-at-law: trained lawyer available to plead in courts at Westminster

shieling: pasture for grazing cattle

slainte: protection or personal guarantee afforded by a lord to lesser persons

Speaker: spokesman of the Commons in Parliament, elected for the first time in 1376

steward: official of a king or lord who administered estates and other affairs

sumptuary laws: laws to restrict the wearing of clothes to appropriate classes

taeog: an unfree person, in Wales

tanistry: designating the male successor of an Irish lord

taoiseach: ruler in Ireland

tenant-in-chief: landowner holding an estate directly from the king, usually heritable in return for obligations

uchelwyr: free landowners in Wales

valettus: a manservant or attendant discharging personal duties

vill: one or more associated settlements or townships in England, Scotland (*toun*), and Wales (*tref*)

villein: unfree peasant bound to a lord or estate

Map and table section

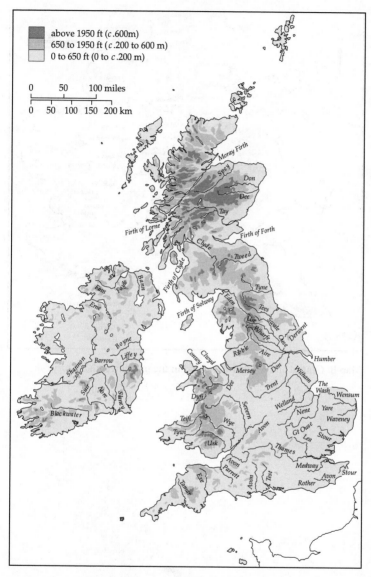

Map A Physical features and main rivers of the British Isles.
Source: *Barbara Harvey ed., The Twelfth and Thirteenth Centuries*
(Oxford, 2001).

Map B Central and southern England in the mid-fifteenth century.

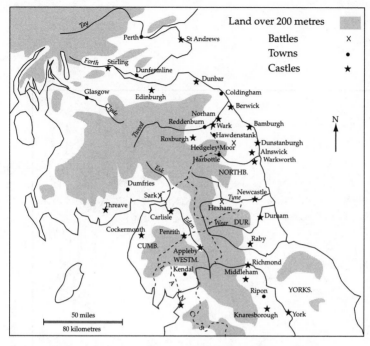

Map C The Anglo-Scottish borderland in the mid-fifteenth century.

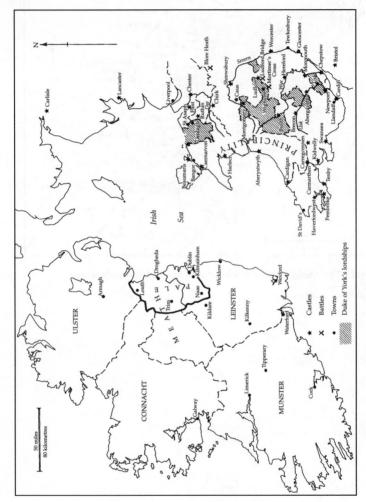

Map D The Irish Sea region in the mid-fifteenth century.

Map E English counties.
Source: University of Southampton Cartographic Unit.

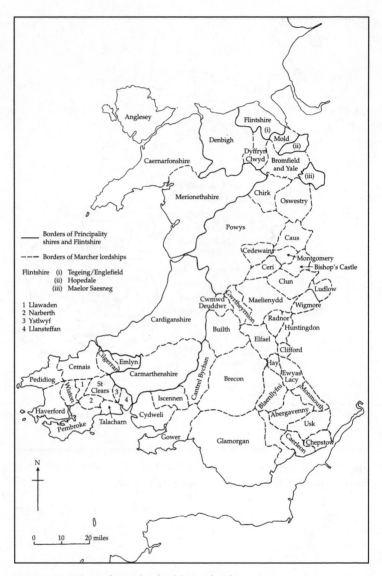

Map F Counties and Marcher lordships of Wales.
Source: R. R. Davies, *Conquest, Coexistence, and Change: Wales 1063–1415*
(Oxford, 1987).

Map G Counties and liberties of Ireland.
Source: R. Foster, Oxford Illustrated History of Ireland (Oxford, 1989).

Map H Earldoms and lordships of Scotland.
Source: A. D. M. Barrell, *Medieval Scotland* (Cambridge, 2000).

Map I Major towns and ports of England and Scotland.

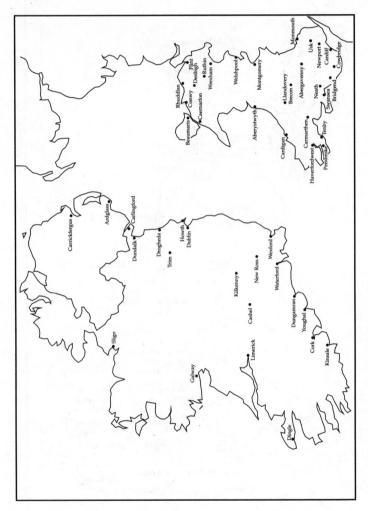

Map J Major towns and ports of Wales and Ireland.

ARCHBISHOPS OF CANTERBURY

John Pecham	1279–92
Robert Winchelsey	1293–1313
Walter Reynolds	1313–27
Simon Meopham	1327–33
John Stratford	1333–48
Thomas Bradwardine	1348–49
Simon Islip	1349–66
Simon Langham	1366–68
William Whittlesey	1368–74
Simon Sudbury	1375–81
William Courtenay	1381–96
Thomas Arundel	1396–97
Roger Walden	1397–99
Thomas Arundel	1399–1414
Henry Chichele	1414–43
John Stafford	1443–52
John Kempe	1452–54
Thomas Bourgchier	1454–86
John Morton	1486–1500

ARCHBISHOPS OF YORK

John le Romeyn	1285–96
Henry Newark	1296–99
Thomas Corbridge	1299–1304
William Greenfield	1304–15
William Melton	1316–40
William Zouche	1340–52
John Thoresby	1352–73
Alexander Neville	1373–88
Thomas Arundel	1388–96
Robert Waldby	1396–98
Richard le Scrope	1398–1405
Henry Bowet	1407–23
John Kempe	1425–52
William Booth	1452–64
George Neville	1465–76
Lawrence Booth	1476–80
Thomas Rotherham	1480–1500

ARCHBISHOPS OF ST ANDREWS

Patrick Graham	1472–78
(bishop since 1465)	
William Scheves	1478–97
James Stewart	1497–1504

ARCHBISHOPS OF GLASGOW

Robert Blackadder	1492–1508
(bishop since 1483)	

Table A Archbishops of Canterbury, York, St Andrews, and Glasgow.

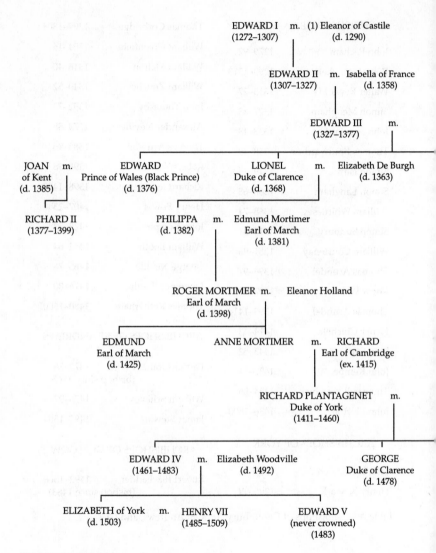

Table B English kings and queens

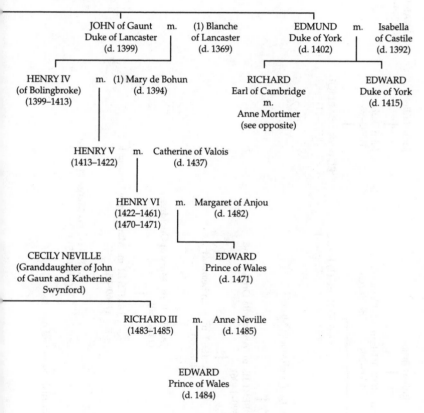

Philippa of Hainault
(d. 1369)

JOHN of Gaunt   m.   (1) Blanche   EDMUND   m.   Isabella
Duke of Lancaster   of Lancaster   Duke of York   of Castile
(d. 1399)   (d. 1369)   (d. 1402)   (d. 1392)

HENRY IV   m.   (1) Mary de Bohun   RICHARD   EDWARD
(of Bolingbroke)   (d. 1394)   Earl of Cambridge   Duke of York
(1399–1413)   m.   (d. 1415)
                                        Anne Mortimer
                                        (see opposite)

HENRY V   m.   Catherine of Valois
(1413–1422)   (d. 1437)

HENRY VI   m.   Margaret of Anjou
(1422–1461)   (d. 1482)
(1470–1471)

CECILY NEVILLE   EDWARD
(Granddaughter of John   Prince of Wales
of Gaunt and Katherine   (d. 1471)
Swynford)

RICHARD III   m.   Anne Neville
(1483–1485)   (d. 1485)

EDWARD
Prince of Wales
(d. 1484)

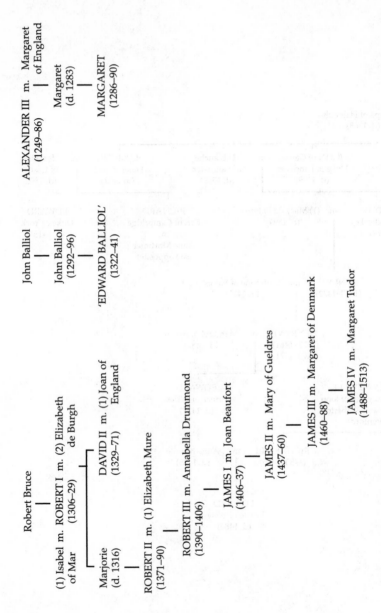

ALEXANDER III m. Margaret
(1249–86) of England
|
Margaret
(d. 1283)
|
MARGARET
(1286–90)

John Balliol
|
John Balliol
(1292–96)
|
'EDWARD BALLIOL'
(1322–41)

Robert Bruce
|
(1) Isabel m. ROBERT I m. (2) Elizabeth
of Mar (1306–29) de Burgh
| |
Marjorie   DAVID II m. (1) Joan of
(d. 1316)   (1329–71)   England
|
ROBERT II m. (1) Elizabeth Mure
(1371–90)
|
ROBERT III m. Annabella Drummond
(1390–1406)
|
JAMES I m. Joan Beaufort
(1406–37)
|
JAMES II m. Mary of Gueldres
(1437–60)
|
JAMES III m. Margaret of Denmark
(1460–88)
|
JAMES IV m. Margaret Tudor
(1488–1513)

Table C Scottish kings and queens.

Index